MAYA ARCHAEOLOGIST

MAYA

ARCHAEOLOGIST

By J. Eric S. Thompson

Foreword by Norman Hammond

UNIVERSITY OF OKLAHOMA PRESS : NORMAN

To Ralph L. Roys
Halach uinic of Maya scholarship,
mentor and friend

BY J. ERIC S. THOMPSON

Ethnology of the Mayas of Southern and Central British Honduras
(Chicago, 1930)
*Archaeological Investigations in the Southern Cayo District,
British Honduras* (Chicago, 1931)
Mexico before Cortez (New York, 1933)
Excavations at San José, British Honduras (Washington, *1939*)
The Rise and Fall of Maya Civilization
(Norman, 1954; revised, 1966)
Thomas Gage's Travels in the New World (ed.) (Norman, 1958)
Maya Hieroglyphic Writing: An Introduction (Norman, 1960)
A Catalog of Maya Hieroglyphs (Norman, 1962)
Maya Archaeologist (Norman, 1963)
Maya History and Religion (Norman, 1970)

Library of Congress Cataloging-in-Publication Data

Thompson, John Eric Sidney, Sir, 1898–1975.
    Maya archaeologist / by J. Eric S. Thompson ; foreword by Norman
Hammond.
        p. cm.
    Includes index.
    ISBN 0–8061–1206–9
    1. Thompson, John Eric Sidney, Sir, 1898–1975. 2. Archaeologists—
Mexico—Biography. 3. Archaeologists—Central America—Biography.
4. Mayas—Antiquities. 5. Mexico—Description and travel. 6. Central
America—Description and travel. I. Title.
F1435.T495 1994
972.81'016—dc20   94-11738
                                                                                    CIP

5   6   7   8   9   10   11   12   13

Contents

Plates

Figures

Acknowledgments

My MOST GRATEFUL THANKS to my roommate at Chichen Itza in 1926 for the designs on Coba stelae and for his charming drawings of Maya types. I am indebted to Mrs. John Christianson and S. R. Richardson for drawing most of the remaining figures and to J. P. Elsden for preparing the maps.

J. Eric S. Thompson

HARVARD, ASHDON
ESSEX, ENGLAND

Foreword

A DOMINANT FIGURE IN MAYA SCHOLARSHIP for half a century, between his first journal article in 1925 and his death in September 1975, John Eric Sidney Thompson was born on New Year's Eve, 1898, in London, the son of a surgeon. He was educated at Winchester College, one of England's greatest and most ancient schools, but left to join the army (underage and under an assumed name) when World War I broke out. After the war he went to Argentina and worked on a family *estancia* as a *gaucho;* an adventure that led to his first publication: "A Cowboy's Experience: Cattle Branding in the Argentine" in the *Southwark Diocesan Gazette.* He considered both a medical and a political career before going to Cambridge University to study anthropology under A. C. Haddon in 1925. He taught himself Maya hieroglyphics and then wrote to Sylvanus G. Morley, who was at that time directing the Carnegie Institution of Washington's new program of investigations at Chichén Itzá in Yucatán, and asked him for a job.

As Thompson tells it in this charming autobiography of the years from 1926 to 1936—one of the few first-hand documents we have describing the glory days of Maya exploration between the two World Wars—Morley "was not anxious to take on any man sight unseen. . . . He arranged that two members of his staff, Oliver and Mrs. Ricketson, who were about to visit London, should give me the once-over. I persuaded my father, who was a connoisseur of wine and good food, to invite the Ricketsons to dinner. . . . On the strength of Father's excellent entertainment, the Ricketsons reported favorably, and I got the job."

Thus, in January 1926, Thompson landed in Yucatán, "a land to which I was to give my heart," and began work under Morley on reconstructing three friezes in the Temple of the Warriors at Chichén Itzá. "It was a sort of giant jigsaw puzzle made worse by the fact that the stones had been carved before being placed in position [so the edges did not necessarily line up]. . . . I labored for weeks in the incandescent sun of Yucatan fitting the stones together, moving them sometimes nearly forty yards to see if I could make a fit. . . . In my memory it seems that I personally shifted every blessed stone."

Thompson was already sure of his abilities: at Chichén Itzá he and George Vaillant, also to become a noted Mesoamericanist, founded "the Young Men's Maya Association to debunk the views of our elders and betters." When he was sent off to investigate the ruins of Cobá to the east of Chichén Itzá, he came back with a set of readings on the Macanxoc stelae dated so early that Morley, then the preeminent force in Maya epigraphy, could not believe them. Morley went back to Cobá with Thompson, and was persuaded.

The following year, having taken up a post with the Field Museum in Chicago, Thompson was seconded to a British Museum expedition working at Lubaantun, in the south of British Honduras (now Belize), under the direction of Thomas Joyce. In 1926, Joyce had identified "megalithic" architecture, which he believed to be early, and an unusual local style of masonry, with overhanging upper courses that he dubbed "in-and-out." Thompson refuted Joyce's conclusions in both cases: the "in-and-out" masonry was the result of root action, and the "megalithic terraces" were not the earliest construction at Lubaantun. (In fact, my own later excavations there showed that they were of Late Classic date.)

The youngest and fittest of the British Museum crew, Thompson was sent off to investigate another reported site some twenty miles to the southwest, Pusilhà. It proved to have more than twenty stelae, the earliest dating to A.D. 593, and the abutments of an impressive bridge linking the two parts of the city across the Moho River. By this time, Thompson was already noted for his correlation of the Maya and Christian calendars—a refinement of Joseph Goodman's 1905 breakthrough that placed the Classic Period between approximately A.D. 300 and 900—and he followed this up with a paper on the Pusilhà dates and another on Glyph G of the Lunar Series, which forms a part of all Maya Long Count inscriptions.

The Pusilhà journey launched him into yet another area of path-breaking research with Faustino Bol, a Mopan Maya from the village of San Antonio near Lubaantun, as his guide. Their long talks on the trail convinced Thompson that "these modern descendants of the ancient Maya still preserved many ancient customs and religious ideas . . . [and] archaeological excavations were not the only means of learning about the ancient ways. Indeed, pick and shovel would never reveal the many customs that had survived in San Antonio from an earlier age." A visit to San Antonio resulted in a compilation of data on agriculture, social structure, folklore, and religion, complemented by similar material on the village of Socotz, in the Belize Valley, collected from his workmen during the 1929 excavations at Tzimin Kax and Camp 6. Published as a Field Museum monograph in 1930, *Ethnology of the Mayas of Southern and Central British Honduras* was the first of a succession of publications in which Thompson brought ethnographic and ethnohistoric data to bear on problems of Maya archaeology and epigraphy.

The companion volume, *Archaeological Investigations in the Southern Cayo District, British Honduras,* was similarly the first of a number of important archaeological studies carried out initially under the aegis of the Field Museum, and then from 1936 under that of the Carnegie Institution, where Thompson remained on the staff until his official retirement in 1958. His next major project, and the first to be published by the Carnegie Institution, was at San José in northwestern Belize. It was conceived of as a study of a small and perhaps "average" Maya center, one in which his grasp of architectural stratigraphy allowed the construction of yet another ceramic sequence to help interpret the development and decline of Maya civilization. The Tzimin Kax, San José, and Benque Viejo (Xunantunich) sequences together formed the chronological framework for the southeastern Maya lowlands for several decades, allowing sites without inscribed monuments to be dated within the pattern of cultural development being documented in the Petén region of Guatemala, at Uaxactun and other centers with abundant historical dates. In 1938, Thompson also added another important site in Belize, La Milpa, to the roster of those with hieroglyphic inscriptions, recording a dozen stelae in one of the largest plazas yet discovered. It was almost his last field expedition, although he did not know it, and a brief mention of La Milpa closes *Maya Archaeologist.*

The remainder of Thompson's life, not chronicled in this book, was one of scholarship, professional fame, and an increasing intellectual dominance over the Maya field. In the 1940s his principal concern was the attempted decipherment of non-calendric hieroglyphs: of the eight papers he published in 1943, for example, four were on epigraphic topics. Together with Morley, who published *The Inscriptions of Peten* in five volumes in 1937–38, he concluded that the content of the stela texts was esoteric and astronomical, and that the accompanying images were those of priests celebrating arcane rituals devoted to the worship of deified Time. He believed passionately that the Maya would not have besmirched their superb carvings with sublunary matters or human subjects, and the possibility of any historical content in the inscriptions was, to Thompson, "well-nigh inconceivable." He also believed that the writing system itself was a hybrid one, in which most of the glyphs represented ideas and phonetic signs played a very minor part. *Maya Hieroglyphic Writing: Introduction* (1950) was the most magisterial summary of epigraphic evidence ever assembled, and it remains a potent source of ideas nearly half a century later, even though its central premises were first challenged, and later controverted.

Thompson's expertise and powers of argument were such that when Yuri V. Knorosov, a young Russian linguist, suggested in 1952 that Maya writing was in fact essentially phonetic, Thompson's scorn (and prompt identification of the weak points in Knorosov's thesis) was sufficient to discourage all but a few scholars from taking the Russian seriously for another two decades. The current flood of decipherments, which has made it possible to name Maya rulers and describe their achievements in their own words, began only after Thompson's death. Well before then, however, he knew that the inscriptions recorded secular history: the demonstration by Tatiana Proskouriakoff in 1960 that the pattern of dates on the Piedras Negras stelae was explicable in terms of successive reigns was something that he immediately recognized as having the ring of truth. Thompson's mind was never closed to rational argument, and by 1971 he admitted that his own long-held convictions had been "completely mistaken." He continued to work on epigraphic and ethnohistoric problems to the end of his life, however, producing *Maya History and Religion* in 1970 and *A Commentary on the Dresden Codex* in 1972, both works of major importance. His eminence was recognized by the conferment of four honorary doctorates by universities in the United States, Yucatán, and in England (from his alma mater at Cambridge), and he was awarded the Orders of Isabel la Católica by

Spain, the Aztec Eagle by Mexico, and the Quetzal by Guatemala. His final honor came in 1975 when he was knighted by Queen Elizabeth II, becoming the first New World archaeologist to receive the accolade. Nine months later he died in Cambridge, and was buried beside his parish church at Ashdon, in Essex.

Maya archaeology has changed dramatically in the decades since *Maya Archaeologist* was first published. Many of Eric Thompson's most cherished theories, persuasively outlined in *The Rise and Fall of Maya Civilization* (1954, revised 1966) have been overthrown, and his entire vision of the Maya as a peaceful, priest-led civilization without cities is now known to be fundamentally wrong. Yet the field data that he gathered, his ethnohistoric research, and many of his contributions towards the decipherment of Maya hieroglyphic writing, are still of enormous value today. *Maya Archaeologist* itself remains what it always has been: a fascinating and charming glimpse into the formative years of the discipline, written by one of its most influential exponents.

Norman Hammond
Department of Archaeology, Boston University
Peabody Museum, Harvard University
November 1993

Glossary and Key to Pronunciation

Acropolis: cluster of buildings and courts on a high platform.

Agouti: cat-sized rodent with short legs. The meat is delicious.

Aguardiente: "fiery water," commonly rum.

Alcalde: mayor; village head man.

Bacardier: collecting point on river bank for mahogany logs.

Baktun: period of 400 "years" of 360 days.

Balche: a fermented drink of honey and the bark of a tree (*Loncha-carpus longistylus*).

Banderilla: a small dart thrust into the nape of the bull in bullfighting.

Breadnut tree (*Brosimum alicastrum*): the leaves are fed to mules; the fruit is edible. Not to be confused with the breadfruit tree.

Cabbage palm: see *guano* palm.

Cabildo: town hall; official hut in a village.

Casa principal: main building. Used with reference to haciendas.

Cay: small island. Pronounced "key." Spanish form, *cayo.*

Cenote: natural well caused by caving in of limestone crust.

Ceremonial center: term used for Maya "cities."

Chachalaca (*Ortalis vetula pallidiventris*): a bird. Always in flocks and noisy as jays. Good eating. In Belize has the onomatopeic name *Cockericot.*

Chacs: the Maya rain gods. They are four, set at the points of the compass.

Chicleros: gatherers of chicle, the raw product utilized for chewing gum.

Chultun: see page 164 in text.

Cohune palm (*Attalea cohune*): the graceful leaves are used for thatching.

Copal *(Protium copal)*: a tree which yields resin used as incense.

Copita: a small liquer glass.

Cura: village priest (Roman Catholic).

Goma: hangover.

Gringo: a north European or North American (U.S.); *gringa* is female.

Guano palm *(Sabal japa)*: used for thatching. When very tall, called *botan*. In British Honduras, the cabbage palm.

Hacienda: a ranch; the owner is a *hacendado*.

Henequen: plant of the agave family which yields sisal fiber.

Jarana: literally, a revelry. Dance in which partners do not touch each other.

Katun: the Maya period of 20 "years" of 360 days each.

Kin: sun; day.

Machete: a long knife carried in a scabbard. Used for slashing vegetation.

Marimbista: player (usually there are four) of a marimba, a sort of xylophone with gourd resonators.

Mestizo: half-caste.

Metate: a curved stone quern, usually with three feet. Maize is ground on it.

Milpa: a cultivated field, i.e., a corn field.

Pich *(Enterolobium cyclocarpum)*: a tree up to 100 feet high, very showy, with small white flowers.

Pimiento: the allspice tree common in the forest; sweet smelling.

Pinole: a drink made of parched maize.

Posole: a drink of maize dough mixed with cold water.

Querida: "loved one," a euphemism for mistress.

Roof-comb, roof crest: see page 48 in text.

Santo: saint; the statue of a saint; archaeological piece thought to be holy.

Stela: stone shaft, usually about twelve feet high, carved with personages and hieroglyphic texts on one or more sides. Sometimes unsculptured. Plural, *stelae*.

Taco: highly spiced meat wrapped in a tortilla, which may be fried.

Tamale: meat enveloped in maize dough and wrapped in maize husk, boiled or steamed.

Tepeu: the latter half of the Maya Classic period in the Peten and British Honduras.

Tortilla: a very thin disk of maize dough, about six inches in diameter, lightly baked on a stone or griddle. Tortillas take the place of a spoon in eating.

Totoposte: large double-toasted tortilla. *Totopostes* are used in traveling as they keep for a long time.

Truck pass: road cut in the forest for extracting mahogany logs.

Tun: the Maya period of 360 days. See also *baktun* and *katun*.

Tzakol: the early half of the Maya Classic period in Peten and British Honduras.

Uinal: Maya month of 20 days.

Zapateado: a dance with much beating of the feet to music.

All accents are omitted in this book except on Spanish Christian names and surnames. Maya pronunciation of vowels follows Spanish: *a*, between that of *cat* and of *father; e*, between that in *bet* and in *grey*, but clipped; *i* as the *ee* in *need; o* as in *pomp; u* like our *oo*, but as *w* before other vowels. Consonants are pronounced as in English except *x* is *sh; c* is always hard. *Qu* has *k* sound before *e* and *i*. The consonants *d, f, j, r,* and *v* are absent in Yucatec and most lowland Maya languages. *K* and consonants followed by an apostrophe are pronounced with a quick closing of the glottis, somewhat as in military commands such as *shun* for *attention*. Final *e* in all Spanish and Maya words is pronounced.

Examples:

Uxmal	OOsh'mal	Uaxactun	Wash-ac-toon'
Yaxchilan	Yash'chee-lan'	Ahau	A-how'
Pusilha	Poo-seel-ha'	Pinole	Pee-nol'e

xvii

MAYA ARCHAEOLOGIST

1

Digging at Chichen Itza

In *Twelfth Night,* Shakespeare puts into the mouth of Sebastian lines pleasing to the ear of antiquarians and archaeologists alike:

> *Shall we go see the reliques of this town . . . .*
> *I pray you let us satisfy our eyes*
> *With the memorials and the things of fame*
> *That do renown this city.*

The reliques and the things of fame in this book are not in Illyria, but in southern Mexico and the adjacent lands of Guatemala and British Honduras. They are the memorials of the ancient Maya civilization which flourished from about the time of Christ until it was extinguished by the coming of the Spaniards, and I like to think that they are of more interest than anything that Sebastian saw in that unspecified city of Albania.

This is not a history of Maya civilization, but an account of incidents of excavation of the Mayas' ancient cities and of contacts with their descendants who, ignorant of their past, still live there. The scenes are as I saw them one-third of a century ago.

Our manner of counting time by years, months, weeks, and days has its advantages; at least by it we know when to plant daffodil bulbs, when strawberries will ripen, and when to start drawing our pensions. Yet, time is also inconstant, for its speed grows with age, whether it be the age of one man or of all mankind. In terms of culture the rate of invention has so accelerated that a year in the second and third quarters of the twentieth century is equivalent to perhaps a decade at the opening of this century and to far longer periods in the two or three preceding centuries.

Attitudes and the pattern of daily life in the Central America of thirty-five years ago were perhaps closer to those which obtained when Maya civilization was collapsing under the impact of Spanish conquest than to those of the 1960's. In this book I have tried to show that life as I saw it in the years before there were planes or buses or radio in most of Central America, and when there were practically no roads fit for automobiles, which were largely prisoners of the cities and large towns. There was no organized tourist trade then; the remote parts of the country were still remote, and the Maya in their villages lived in practically the same way as their forefathers had lived for the past three centuries. Life essentially was not too far removed from what it had been when John Lloyd Stephens wrote in 1841 and 1843 those classics of leisurely travel *Incidents of travel in Central America, Chiapas, and Yucatan,* and *Incidents of travel in Yucatan.* The old haciendas had gone since Stephens' time and the traveler could no longer depend on the hospitality of the *cura* in remote parts, for the revolutions of Júarez and of Madero and his successors had impoverished the church and persecuted the clergy. Railways connected most important towns to Merida, the capital of Yucatan, but the ferment of change had not essentially changed life in the less accessible parts of Yucatan or, for that matter, of nearly all Central America.

In the field of Maya studies the passing years have brought a great change. I had the fortune to belong—although only by the skin of my teeth—to the last generation of archaeologists who were able to have extended interests. Now, with the enormous increase of knowledge, fields of specialization are so narrow that archaeologists are in mortal danger of becoming technicians. One man will know all about pottery and precious little else; another will be in the same position as regards the study of Indian languages. Some years ago a respected young linguist established, by many erudite rules laid down by his fraternity, a most formidable pedigree for the words the Aztec now use for "cat" and "money," reconstructing the original Uto-Aztecan forms of thousands of years ago. In fact, there were neither cats nor money in Mexico until the Spaniards brought them. The ancient Aztec words were pure Spanish and their Uto-Aztecan pedigree of value only as a sad warning of the evils of overspecialization.

In earlier days, it was still possible to have a fair knowledge of every aspect of Maya civilization, past and present, and that made for a richer life because one could relate what was excavated to what one saw among the Maya in their villages. Also, many of the past ways and old beliefs have been lost with the opening of the country to "progress."

Alfred Tozzer, for very many years teacher and counsellor of many students who have entered the Maya field, lived among the Lacandon, an isolated group of Maya in Chiapas who still retain their paganism and pre-Conquest way of life, but he also excavated in the Valley of Mexico and studied Maya ruins and wrote a grammar of Yucatecan Maya. All these studies gave him a broad outlook and an ability to interpret work in one field with information gathered in others. Such scholarship based on wide interests has given way to a system in which some individuals know more and more about less and less.

Thirty to forty years ago it was far easier to enter the Maya field than it is today. Although I had studied anthropology at Cambridge under that great teacher Alfred Haddon, my knowledge of Maya was self-taught. In 1925 I wrote Sylvanus G. Morley, head of the Chichen Itza archaeological project of the Carnegie Institution of Washington, asking him for a job. My chief asset, the ability to read and compute Maya hieroglyphic dates, was one I knew would appeal to Morley, whose whole life had been devoted to that subject; students of Maya glyphs were as scarce as hen's teeth.

Morley, naturally, was not anxious to take on any man sight unseen, particularly with a long field season of nearly six months in the tropics, where uncongenial relations and frayed nerves can cause explosions. He arranged that two members of his staff, Oliver and Mrs. Ricketson, who were about to visit London, should give me the once-over. I persuaded my father, who was a connoisseur of wine and good food, to invite the Ricketsons to dinner. Father put on one of his best dinners. The wine, specially chosen for the occasion, was duly brought to the right temperature by an elaborate ritual which called for the bottle to be set in line between window and fire, the amount the window was open being measured to the nearest inch and the distance from the fire exactly fixed. The dinner went off very well, and subsequently we were invited to dinner with the Ricketsons. On the strength of Father's excellent entertainment, the Ricketsons reported favorably, and I got the job.

About a dozen years later I happened to ask my father whether he remembered Ricketson. He gave a snort of indignation. "I most certainly do," he said. "He took my superb 1911 Chambertin and drank the full glass in one gulp as though it were water. Not only that, when he asked us to dinner he put on the table a bottle of wine [Algerian red it must have been] he had bought at the grocer's shop." I tried to explain that Rick's adult life had been spent under prohibition, and that with bathtub gin or homemade wine, the only thing was to shut your eyes and get it down quick. My explanation didn't make much impression. A gentleman, Father felt, should know how to appreciate the bouquet of the wine and how to savor each sip, prohibition or no prohibition. My father got his wine from good wine merchants; bootleggers and hip flasks were too outrageous to be comprehensible. He had not forgotten that treatment of what should be savored with reverence and quiet joy. Those fine points didn't worry me one bit; I had got the job.

In January, 1926, the old Ward liner from New York came to anchor far off the shores of Yucatan, and crossing the shallow water in a small tender, we landed at the port of Progreso. The dull landscape of low scrub gave no indication that this was a land to which I was to give my heart.

A short train journey brought us to Merida, capital of the Mexican state of Yucatan, founded in 1542 on the ruins of the old Maya site of Ichcanzihoo. The Spanish *conquistadores* so named their city because the Maya ruins reminded them of the Roman remains of Merida in Spain; they were the first of a long line of people to see connections between the civilizations of the Old World and the New, but the resemblance between a Roman arch and Maya corbeled vaulting is tenuous. Merida, like every city in Latin America, is laid out in a grid pattern with a large plaza in the center, the focus of social life for generation after generation of Meridanos. On the east side of the plaza stands the cathedral, a huge fortress-like structure of the sixteenth century with two unmatching towers (Fig. 1); to the south is the home of the Montejos, the *conquistadores* of Yucatan. The other two sides are flanked with colonnaded buildings. In those days the plaza was filled with trees with a dense and very dark foliage locally known as laurel. These may not have been true laurel, but they had a monumental grandeur it would be hard to equal.

I liked to sit on the far side of the plaza just before sunset, when the rays of the setting sun turned the clay-colored stone of the cathedral façade a soft rose. Then alone did the great building lose that severity which perhaps expressed the dourness of those first Spaniards who from grim Extremadura and Leon had come in search of quick wealth and found it not in Yucatan.

7

The building of the cathedral left a lasting impress on the newly converted Maya. With their supreme ability to amalgamate Christianity with their old paganism, they linked its erection

FIG. 1.—Merida Cathedral.

with, of all things, their calendar, and in their sacred writings, the books of Chilam Balam, occurs this passage, as translated by Ralph Roys:

13 Etz'nab was the day when the land was established. 13 Cheneb was when they measured off by paces the cathedral, the dark house of instruction, the cathedral in heaven. Thus it was measured off by paces here. Thirteen katuns was the total count, [that is] thirteen feet in heaven. Four feet, and from there nine feet, the total count of its extent in heaven. Then it is again measured off by feet from the face of the earth. Four feet separate it from the face of the earth.

8

The measuring off by footsteps is an incident in a Maya myth of the creation of time before there was light in the world; the katun is the Maya period of twenty years (of 360 days); and the sacred number thirteen, with its components of nine and four, both of good fortune, is brought into the picture. The passage doesn't imply opposition to Christianity; it is merely a matter of bringing Christianity into the context of the past, just as the present-day Maya invokes the Chacs, his ancient gods of rain, in a prayer which terminates with the words "God the Father, God the Son, and God the Holy Ghost."

Inside, the cathedral is now equally austere; there used to be magnificent seventeenth-century reredoses, but in 1915 soldiers of the revolution destroyed them.

A block away stands the equally austere church of the Franciscan third order flanking a charming little plaza, on one side of which stands the Gran Hotel, at that time the only hotel in Merida. It was largely filled with bored Americans awaiting divorce decrees, for at that time a divorce was more easily obtained in Yucatan than even in Reno. All one needed was a couple of weeks' residence—it wasn't even necessary to inform the defendant, and one could continue to cohabit until the decree came through. A story circulated of one wealthy woman who brought her unsuspecting husband to Merida. The first thing he knew of the matter was when she came back to the Gran Hotel with the papers in her hand, and handing him one hundred dollars, remarked, "That's for your fare back to New York. Now git!"

My companion was the photographer of the Carnegie Institution, who was not, however, a very good choice for the job, as his chief interests were photographing cloud formations and young girls "in the altogether." The archaeological pictures were picturesque, but often failed to bring out the archaeological evidence, and as Maya maidens are extremely modest and drop their eyes in the presence of a man, the surreptitious efforts of our photographer to get them to pose without a stitch of clothing caused a major scandal.

In those days there was no road to Chichen Itza. The daily train to Dzitas left at 5:30 A.M., and one had to be at the station half an hour before starting time. No coffee and rolls were obtainable at the hotel, and at the station it was usually impossible to get near the coffee counter.

However, at Motul flocks of Maya women and girls passed along the platform with fruit and all sorts of pastries, tortillas, and *tacos* of turkey and venison, delicious once your mouth was indurated to the incredible fieriness of the half-ounce of chile peppers with which each one was endowed. It was at the friary of Motul that that remarkable Franciscan, Fr. Antonio de Ciudad Real, composed about A.D. 1580 his *Gran calepino de la lengua maya de Yucatán*, commonly called the Motul dictionary, a Maya-Spanish vocabulary (the Spanish-Maya part is by a later writer). This is a mine of information on the Yucatan-Maya language and on the customs and practices of the Maya, and all students of the Maya bless the composer's name. My copy is in constant use as I try to match hieroglyphs with Maya words.

Its preservation is little short of a miracle. The Maya antiquary, the Abbé Brasseur de Bourbourg, came upon it by chance on a secondhand bookstall in the City of Mexico in the 1860's. It had almost certainly been stolen from a Franciscan friary. Its fate had not the Abbé chanced upon it is to be inferred from the disappearance a few years later of the only known copy of the still earlier Maya-Spanish vocabulary of another Franciscan, Luis de Villapando, who died in 1551. The great loss by deliberate destruction or neglect of priceless manuscripts and rare printed books (Villapando's book had been printed) following Juárez' suppression of the religious orders was appalling.

The most obscure and ephemeral politician in Mexico is commemorated by statue, plaque, or named street, but men such as

Ciudad Real go unremembered. I like to picture him refreshing himself with the good venison *tacos* of Motul when he worked on his *calepino* the best part of four centuries ago. They would have been made by the forebears of the girls who sold to us.

For the first hour or so the train passed between fields of henequen, the source of Yucatan's wealth. This large agave plant produces sisal fiber used in making cord (it takes its name from the port of Sisal in northern Yucatan through which it was first exported). The endless rows of equidistant plants, with their gray-green bayonet leaves rising like *chevaux-de-frise*, interrupted only by little piles of stones to measure each Maya peon's "task," are as typical of the landscape as cotton fields once were of the South. Gradually the fields give place to woods, scrubby because of the low rainfall of northwest Yucatan. Occasional clearings with limestone bedrock more evident than the scant soil mark the Maya's ceaseless preoccupation with his maize crop.

The Yucatecan railway system was largely financed with British capital, but as capitalists and gringos were not too popular at the time of which I write, it seemed almost unpatriotic for the railways to earn money to pay off the foreign loans. Consequently, almost all passengers in first class traveled on free passes; only the uninfluential occupants of the second- and third-class coaches bought tickets. The line was narrow gauge and the wood-burning locomotives, with cowcatchers and smoke stacks which terminated in huge spark-catching funnels, were of about 1870 vintage. At every few miles were stacked cords of wood cut in the woods through which the line ran. Here the train stopped, and while the wood was tossed by Maya woodsmen into the tender, the passengers descended from the coaches to stretch their legs or chat. What with station stops and wood-loading stops it took us four and a quarter hours to cover the ninety miles eastward to Dzitas.

From Dzitas, a pleasant town of Yucatecans and Maya, the station wagon of the Carnegie Institution took us the seventeen miles to Chichen Itza. The road, of dazzling white limestone, cuts through the woods, less scrublike than in the drier western part of the peninsula. It was like passing down an endless trough between green waves ready to break, and one wondered somewhat as the Egyptians must have speculated on whether the banked Red Sea would overwhelm them. After digging began, one or two of us junior archaeologists would be sent every second Friday to Dzitas as an armed escort to fetch the pay roll—an enormous load of silver pesos. I sometimes speculated on how we would fare in the event of a holdup, for attackers could have placed a tree trunk on the road beyond any bend and from the cover of the flanking woods picked us off with ease. Luckily, the Yucatecans and the Maya are little given to violence, and they are usually honest. Nothing untoward happened in all the years the Carnegie worked in Yucatan.

About a mile from our destination the road bends suddenly to reveal a stupendous sight. At the end of the frame of long wooded corridor lies the great pyramid of Kukulcan, its white limestone blocks now weathered gray. Atop it stands the vaulted temple with feathered serpent columns, still well preserved (Plate 1a).

The headquarters of the Carnegie Institution were in the eighteenth-century cattle hacienda building, which was purchased about the end of the last century by some archaeological fans in Massachusetts to be the headquarters of my namesake, Eduardo Thompson, for his archaeological work in the ruins. On a hillside behind the hacienda house stood the little chapel of San Isidro which once served the religious needs of the hacienda workers and their families. In its sacristy John L. Stephens wrote his notes for a chapter of his *Incidents of travel in Yucatan* over a century ago, and here Morley, head of the field work at Chichen Itza, also lived. Its façade, of typical Yucatan construction with three windows for the bells, made a charming picture as a background to the bright foliage of the *pich* trees around the entrance to the

The Maya Area

⊙ Progreso

YUCATAN

Merida ⊙   • Izamal
    • Oxkintok   ⊙ Dzitas
                    ⊙ Chichen Itza
        ⊥ Jaina   • Mayapan   ⊥ Valladolid
    Uxmal ⊥ • Ticul ⊥ Yaxuna ⊥   ⊥ Coba
Xcalumkin ⊥ Sayil ⊥ Kabah   Maya Road
            ⊥ Labna

    • Campeche   Tulum ⊥

        ⊥ Etzna   ⊥ S.Rosa Xlabpak
                    ⊥ Dzibilnocac   QUINTANA ROO

    Champoton •
    • Canasayab

    La Gloria ⊙   CAMPECHE

            R.Desempeño ⊙
                    S.Lorenzo ⊥ ⊙ Rio Bec   Payo Obispo (Chetumal)
                    ⊥ No Te Metas   ⊙ Corozal
    ⊥ Tonita   Oxpemul ⊥ Placeres
                    Calakmul ⊥
                        El Palmar ⊥   Botes ⊙ Orange Walk
                            Icaiche ⊥
        Tortuguero ⊥ TABASCO   Naachtun ⊥ Indian Church
                            Chochkitam ⊥ Hill Bank ⊙
    Palenque ⊥   Tenosique ⊥ La Honradez ⊥ Kaxiluinic ⊙   St. George's Cay
    Tila ⊥   Chinikiha   Uaxactun ⊥   ⊙ San Jose
                    ⊥ La Florida Tikal ⊙   ⊙ El Cayo
    Tonina ⊥   ⊥ Piedras Negras   ⊙ Benque Viejo
    LaMar ⊥ ⊙ El Cayo   Naranjo
                ⊥ Yaxchilan   Socotz   ⊥ Camp Six
    Pocouinic ⊥   Bonampak ⊥ ⊥ Polol   ⊥ Mountain Cow
    CHIAPAS   Altar de Sacrificios ⊥
    Comitan ⊥   S.Antonio   BRITISH HONDURAS
    Chinkultic ⊥   ⊥ Seibal   ⊙ Lubaantun
                            S.Luis • • Pusilha
                        Cancuen ⊥ Aguacate •   • Punta Gorda

                                ⊙ Puerto Barrios

                        Quirigua ⊥

                                ⊙ Zacapa
                        Jocotan ⊙ ⊙ Coban   REPUBLIC OF HONDURAS
    Lake Atitlan ◯ GUATEMALA
            Kaminaljuyu ⊙ Guatemala City

⊙ Places Visited
.... International Boundaries.
--- State Boundaries.
⊥ Archaeological Ruins.
• Towns.

0 10   50
|__|_____|
    Miles

casa principal. In front of the hacienda two stone houses with palm thatch had been built for members of the staff, and at the side two graceful royal palms were framed in the verandah arch. The paths to the staff huts were lined with orange trees which produced a sour but delectably thirst-quenching fruit. A remarkable feature was a stone bird bath erected the previous year. This consisted of an ancient Maya quern or metate for grinding maize which was supported by one of the Atlantean figures which the Toltec-Maya used for supporting their altars (Plate IIa).

It was not yet time for lunch when we reached the *casa principal*, and one of the staff offered to take me to meet Morley, who had gone to visit the outlying group of ruins we called Old Chichen. The narrow trail twisted through the bush, so that one could only see a few yards ahead. Long before I saw him, I heard his unforgettable high-pitched nasal voice and queer accent, which was said to have been Pennsylvanian, but which I've never heard from the nose of any other Pennsylvanian or, for that matter, of anyone else in the world. The voice grew nearer and more piercing, causing the chachalaca birds to scream in alarm, and then round a bend came a very short, slender man with a very high and voluminous Mexican straw hat. A line halfway between the peak of the hat and the ground would have passed through the wide hat brim (Plate VIe). We shook hands, the start of a close friendship, which only his death, twenty-two years later brought to an end.

Morley was filled with an energetic enthusiasm for all things Maya. A. V. Kidder summed him up in words no one could improve: "That small near-sighted dynamic bundle of energy; of warm outgiving friendship, of love for beautiful things, and above all else . . . determination to forward the study of the ancient Maya." He was a most lovable man, but how exasperating at times.

Vay, short for Sylvanus, as he was called by his friends, had spent years in the forests of the Peten district of Guatemala seeking hieroglyphic inscriptions. He hated every minute of those trips, often of months at a time, jogging hour after hour, day after day, along the monotonous trails, camping each night often sweaty, unwashed, tick-bitten and flea-ridden. Something always went wrong: mules would get loose, the old shelter would collapse, the mosquito net would be torn, or, most likely of all, rain would drench his bedding. He kept on because only by so doing could he "bring home the epigraphic bacon," as he used to say. His reward was finding some new site with epigraphic bacon in the shape of those tall stone shafts called stelae with unrecorded texts. I can still see him squatting before a new-found stela to draw the glyphs, often with handkerchiefs around each wrist to keep the sweat from running down his arms on the paper and, at hand, a ruler to scale the glyphs and to drive off mosquitos. Vay had a remarkable ability to get the feel of the most eroded hieroglyph—and how those limestone stelae can suffer erosion. He would probe the pitted stone with his fingers somewhat as a doctor probes an infected area. The trips were worth the effort, for the discovery of a stela unseen except by wandering Indians since a Maya priest set an incense burner before it for the last time a millenium ago brings a surge of exultation not easily forgotten.

Vay's Spanish was atrocious. He had a quite extensive vocabulary, but his genders, tenses, and moods were deuces wild in a poker game. The story goes that on one of his earliest visits to Mexico—and that was long before tourists had brought English to Mexico—he wanted to order a steak for dinner. Not knowing the Spanish term, he drew a bull and placed an arrow pointing to the part he wanted. The waiter nodded in comprehension, and after some delay returned not with the steak but with a ticket for that Sunday's bull fight. The arrow, which he had interpreted as a *banderilla,* made him doubly certain he was correctly carrying out the commission.

On the occasion of some archaeological meetings, papers were read in Spanish and English. Morley gave his in "Spanish." At the end of the meeting, Alfonso Caso, the great Mexican archaeologist, remarked with a twinkle in his eye that it had been a most memorable occasion with speeches in English, in Spanish, and in Morley.

On one occasion at Chichen Itza, Morley told Tarcisio, his Korean *mayordomo*, who was off to Merida for the weekend to bring back additional help of his nationality (Koreans are called *chinos* in Central America just as all Syrians and Lebanese are *turcos*), as he was expecting an influx of guests. On Monday, Tarcisio marched triumphantly into the *casa principal* at the head of eight *chinos* complete with kit bags, very pleased with his success in rounding up all eight at short notice.

"What on earth do these *ocho* [eight] *chinos* want? Tarcisio," cried Morley. "Well, Doctor, you told me to bring *ocho chinos* and here they are," replied Tarcisio.

"*No, hombre*," bellowed Vay, " I said *otro* [another] *chino*." They argued, Vay getting more and more excited, about whether he had said *ocho chinos* or *otro chino*, but Vay was the boss. Seven bewildered *chinos* were bundled on the station wagon to catch the next train back to Merida.

To explain what the Carnegie Institution of Washington hoped to do at Chichen Itza, I must first give a brief outline of the Maya area and its history.

The Maya occupied, and for the most part still do, the whole peninsula of Yucatan and a broader belt of territory south of it almost to the Pacific Ocean, so that the area is roughly in the shape of an inverted T with slightly compressed crosspiece. Below the state of Yucatan and adjacent territory of Quintana Roo, both part of Mexico, lies the Guatemalan Department of Peten, with British Honduras to the east. South of them at the start of the cross-arm of the inverted T the Usumacinta river flows northwestward to the Gulf of Campeche and smaller rivers flow eastward into the Bay of Honduras. The tip of the eastern arm reaches into the Republic of Honduras. In the Peten and the drainage of the Usumacinta, as well as in the extension to Honduras, are found most of the great ceremonial centers for which the Maya are renowned.

In the Guatemalan highlands between the Usumacinta and the Pacific were the highland Maya, who in sculpture, architecture, and hieroglyphic writing were far behind the lowlanders. Their place in history was an important one, but in this book they receive only passing notice.

Maya history, as we now know it, falls into four broad periods. The Formative or Pre-Classic period was one during which the Maya were developing their cultural identity. It was in no sense a primitive epoch, for the Maya and their neighbors were already far past a still earlier period marked by the beginnings of agriculture, and the large pyramids they erected and the richly furnished tombs of their leaders indicate a well-organized society. The period may have started before 1500 B.C. and ended about A.D. 200. The following Classic period witnessed the flowering of the great ceremonial centers, misnamed cities, and the peak of Maya sculpture, architecture, art, hieroglyphic inscriptions, and painting of murals and pottery (approximately A.D. 200 to shortly after A.D. 900). Then came the first Mexican or Post-Classic period, so named because of the influx of Mexican influences in both Yucatan and Guatemala (about A.D. 950 to about A.D. 1200), and, finally, the second Mexican or Post-Classic period which ended with the Spanish conquest of the area in 1541—a few years earlier in Guatemala. (The Itza of Tayasal remained free until 1697.)

When Morley started the program of the Carnegie Institution of Washington at Chichen Itza in 1924, the picture was very different. Nothing was known of a Formative period, and it was believed that Yucatan was not occupied until late in the Classic period, whereas now such evidence of Formative occupation of Yucatan as pyramids and large deposits of its pottery has been uncovered, and the great mass of non-Mexican buildings there are assigned to the Classic period. At Chichen the Classic period is represented by many buildings, notably, the Iglesia (Plate III*b*), the Monjas (Plate III*c*), the Akabtzib, and the Temple of the Three Lintels, although there are certain local differences from the Classic period buildings of the Peten and Usumacinta drainage. The old theory that these buildings were built by immigrants from the south who moved there when they abandoned their cities in the south at the close of the Classic period has gone by the board.

Buildings of the first Mexican period at Chichen clearly drew their inspiration from distant Tula, north of Mexico City, as the French archaeologist, Charnay, established nearly a century ago and as subsequent excavations at both sites have more than proved. Carnegie digging at Chichen established beyond doubt that it was the later style, for Tula-inspired structures had been built on to Maya ones, as one might—God forbid—add a modernistic wing to a Georgian mansion. Indeed, Chichen with its two intermingled styles is something like many a town in England or the eastern seaboard of the United States where modern buildings of glass, girder, and concrete are cheek by jowl with Georgian.

There is information on the conquest of Chichen by Mexicans in Diego de Landa's *Relación de las cosas de Yucatán*, "Account of things in Yucatan," which is the bible of Maya students, but when he collected his data, those events were about six centuries in the past, and, not unnaturally, his picture is not clear.

Diego de Landa gets frequent mention in this book, and so a word about him is in order. He was a Franciscan friar and later bishop of Yucatan who knew more about the Maya than anyone else partly because he was on the spot only a few years after the Spanish conquest, but chiefly because he was interested in the country and its past. He collected much material on Maya life and religious customs and gave us a fair amount of information on the Maya hieroglyphs and calendar. He probably could have given much more, but there was very little interest among his fellow-countrymen in such matters, and authors catered to their readers' interests in the sixteenth century, as now. Poor Landa has been execrated as a bigoted priest because he burned Maya hieroglyphic books—thousands of them according to some popular writers— but one cannot judge the values of one age by those of another. Landa certainly burned books, but the only figure ever given, admittedly in a late account which doesn't cite the source, is twenty-seven. He had just come face to face with overwhelming evidence that supposedly Christian Maya were still practicing the barbarity of sacrificing children, and even performed these rites in churches. He knew that these books were one of the mainstays of the old paganism which had to be eradicated if these ghastly sacrifices of children were to cease. With a choice between saving the books, in which there was no interest at that time, or the children, he elected to save the children.

A main objective of our work was to check and amplify the information Landa and others had left us, and in that we succeeded. Work at Chichen and the subsequent excavations at Mayapan, south of Merida, which replaced Chichen as leader of Yucatan, established that there were two Mexican periods. In the earlier one, the great buildings in Mexican style at Chichen, such as the Warriors, the High Priest's Grave, and the ball court, were built; in the later one, Mayapan was dominant. At the end of the first Mexican period, Chichen was sacked and many of the abandoned buildings fell into ruins. During the second Mexican period it was visited by numbers of pilgrims to its sacred well or *cenote*, as it is called. They and proletarian settlers strewed their pottery of Mayapan types over the ruins and the latter camped in some of the old buildings in a makeshift way, robbing stone from one building to prop up another, but they clearly were a group without civic or religious coherence. The pilgrimages continued even after the arrival of the Spaniards, and the bodies of sacrificed children are known to have been thrown into the sacred cenote as offerings to the rain gods as late as 1560.

Little definite can be said of the people who lived at Chichen Itza during the Classic period. Their costumes and ornaments are not closely related to those of the Maya of the Central area (Peten and the band of cities from Tabasco to western Honduras), but from their use of the Maya calendar and a Maya style of architecture we can be almost certain that they were, indeed, Maya. Yet in even these two features there are differences from the Maya of the central area. The system of linking dates by addition and subtraction, ubiquitous in the cities of the south, was quite unknown at Chichen Itza, which used its own variations in glyphs and its own system of recording dates; architecturally the Classic period buildings of Chichen have their local idiosyncrasies, but essentially they are in the classic Maya tradition. How important are those differences?

Consider the English stockbroker who sets forth from his home beside the mediaeval Gothic church, clad in bowler hat and striped trousers, to catch the 8:57 to London. In the train he reads the four leaders of the London *Times*. Five thousand miles away the Westerner, with ten-gallon hat and Hawaiian beach shirt, gets behind the wheel of his station wagon, about half the length of the British Isles, and swings past the clapboard Southern Baptist church on his way downtown. Beside him lies the *Denver Post* open at the double page of comics. Two different cultures? Not a bit of it—just regional divergence. And that I think is the answer so far as Chichen is concerned; a remote city which reshaped foreign ideas and its cultural heritage to its own way of thinking.

In architecture, too, Chichen Itza followed its own inclination during the Classic period, employing a type of block masonry long after the rest of the northwestern Yucatan had swung to the finely cut veneer masonry of the Puuc style. This type of masonry is so named because instead of cleaving to the old style of façade of stone blocks well anchored into the lime and mortar core of the building, it used very thin and beautifully cut blocks of stone which were laid like a skin, or veneer, on the core of the building. The effect was far more striking, but the lack of good bonding of veneer to core was a weakness which probably the Maya and certainly the archaeologist have rued. Yet there is one building of Classic Chichen, the Temple of the Three Lintels, in the Puuc veneer style. One would like very much to know what were the circumstances which gave rise to this aberration.

There is a Puritan stolidity about those thick-walled Maya buildings of Classic Chichen. The façades are broken by no windows; only by rare doorways with enormous stone lintels, usually one to a room and seldom more than four to five feet wide and just high enough to admit a man without stooping (Plate III*b*). As a consequence, rooms were never well lit, and an inner room, lit only by the light passing through from the outer room, was not far from being completely dark. I think this lack of light was not regarded as a drawback, but was a desideratum for the secret rites of the old Maya priesthood, who seem to have wished to break contact with the outer world when performing their mysteries, for they were much given to worshiping in the recesses of dark caves. Had they so desired, they could have converted the outer room into a light portico by piercing the wall with several doorways separated only by short piers, a type of construction common enough in other Maya cities, although probably used for a different purpose. Maya rites, to judge by the scant information of Spanish writers and observations of students of present-day Maya, did not call for the participation at one time of a group of priests. Some inner rooms were probably used for the storage of the masks, costumes, and utensils used in the diverse ceremonial ritual.

The number of rooms in a building of the Classic period at Chichen vary from one (La Iglesia, Plate III*b*) to eighteen (Akabtzib). The last, which means "writing in the dark," is so named because of a stone lintel carved with a seated figure and a hieroglyphic text which bridges an inner doorway. Lack of light prevents one making out any details of figure or text. If the lintel has not been re-used in its present position, its perfect uselessness from our point of view is probably another element in the secret hide-away attitude of Maya priests in the Classic period.

Occasionally there are small vent holes in buildings of the Classic period and—an extraordinary innovation—a building at Dzibilchaltun has square windows (one almost suspects a European sailor somehow got there—for the site is not far from the sea—and suggested the idea; no other windowed building is known in ancient Central America). Rooms of Maya buildings which still have roofs are cold and damp, and, naturally, the inner rooms are far damper. Luckily the Maya worshipers did not have to risk rheumatism by kneeling; they prayed squatting on their haunches or standing.

I think there can be no doubt that these stone buildings were never permanently inhabited. It is true that some of them show smoke marks on the walls, but in most cases, when the soil and refuse on the floors have been removed—and there are often deep accumulations—the smoke stains are found not to continue below, clear evidence that the fires had been made by campers—wandering Indians or chicle hunters—long after the buildings had been abandoned. On the other hand, some buildings were probably used as temporary residences by priests and novices before some great feast, for it is known that on such occasions they retired to special buildings for periods of up to one hundred days of fasting and preparation. The sooty smoke of copal incense also accounts for many stains.

Soon after the end of the Classic period, Chichen Itza was oc-

cupied by Mexicans or Mexican-influenced people who introduced Mexican religious and architectural ideas. According to
Maya trádition these invaders were under the leadership of Kukulcan, quetzal-bird snake, whose name is a direct translation of
Quetzalcoatl, the name of the great leader of the Toltec whose
chief city was Tula, about fifty miles northeast of Mexico City
in the state of Hidalgo.

We know a great deal about Quetzalcoatl, part myth and part
authentic history. His rule of Tula, despite his hatred of violence,
was turbulent, and he was driven out of that city. After a number
of adventures he reached Yucatan, probably in A.D. 999, and set
up his government at Chichen Itza. Rulers don't sally forth into
terra incognita; they go to places already known and preferably
where their followers have already established themselves. Accordingly, it is reasonable to assume that Quetzalcoatl, on being
driven from Tula, went to Chichen Itza because he knew that
fellow-countrymen or, more probably, coreligionists sympathetic
to him were already established there. It is for that reason I suggested earlier in this chapter a date of about A.D. 950 for the start
of the Mexican period.

If that was, indeed, the case, it supplies an explanation of why
the earliest building with markedly non-Maya influences (the
inner temple of Kukulcan) shows little evidence of the cult of
Quetzalcoatl. Probably the matter will never be definitely settled: it was an open question four centuries ago. Bishop Landa,
that Greek chorus of Maya history, wrote:

It is the judgment of the Indians that with the Itzas who settled
Chichen Itza there reigned a great lord named Kukulcan, and the
principal building shows this to be the truth as it is called Kukulcan,
and they say he entered from the west, but they differ as to whether
he entered before or after the Itzas or with them, and they say
that he was well disposed and that he had neither wife nor children.
[They say] that after his return he was regarded in Mexico as one

of their gods and called Quetzalcoatl, and that in Yucatan they also held him to be a god because of what he did for the commonweal.

Elsewhere we read of his chaste living. This may be a case of once bitten, twice shy, for Quetzalcoatl had lived chastely at Tula until his enemy, the later deified Tezcatlipoca, tricked him into getting drunk on pulque (fermented juice of the maguey). The obscure wording implies that in drink Quetzalcoatl slept with his elder sister, and shame of this was the chief reason for his departure for Yucatan. The date of his setting forth was the Mexican year I Acatl, but this repeats every fifty-two years. The repetition which best fits the evidence is that which fell in A.D. 999, if one assumes that Quetzalcoatl's arrival in Yucatan did not mark the first influx of Mexican influences there.

Controversy about the identity of the Itza who gave their name to Chichen Itza, "the mouth of the well of the Itza" (its original name appears to have been Uucyabnal), and who have a definite association with Quetzalcoatl-Kukulcan's rule at Chichen, has kept archaeological typewriters chattering for many a long year. They were called foreigners and they spoke broken Yucatec Maya; they were abhorred for having introduced oppression, strife, and erotic practices among the Maya. Yet they were also called the Holy Itza—and the Maya don't go in for sarcasm.

I myself feel that the evidence points to the Itza's having already settled at Chichen when those features which stem from Tula were introduced, but there are non-Maya elements at Chichen—phallic rites, for instance—which they probably brought with them. Perhaps they were Maya of the Chontal group from western Tabasco, almost on the borders of Veracruz, but I suspect that shortly after their arrival at Chichen they came under the rule of immigrants from Tula under the leadership of Kukulcan who introduced Toltec architecture and the worship of the feathered serpent and other Toltec gods. Those features will be discussed below.

When the Carnegie Institution's program of work started, the

Temple of the Warriors, now one of the most imposing buildings at the site (Plate 1*b*), was a tree-clad hill covering about two-thirds of an acre and a trifle over fifty feet high. This was picked for excavation, and the first task was to remove the vegetation. Once the hill was exposed, the surface was seen to be covered with rubble from the collapsed building. Earl Morris, who was in charge of the excavation from its inception in 1925 to its completion at the end of the 1928 season, has aptly compared the appearance of the slopes to rock slides on a mountain peak. Of the face of the pyramid and the long colonnades on its west, northwest, and north flanks nothing was visible. Of the temple walls only a small section of the lower part of one wall was exposed. The square or round tops of some columns, rising above the ground or flush with it like scattered flagstones, were the only indication that one was walking over where the huge colonnades lay buried.

In Egypt and Mesopotamia sand drifts have buried ancient buildings, but the hills that were Maya temple-capped pyramids originate in a different way. The Maya never learned the principle of the true arch, but used instead corbeled vaults, such as are found in ancient tombs of Greece and Italy, and survived in other parts of the Old World until superseded by the superior keystone construction of the true arch.

In corbeled vaulting the two sides of the arch sloped gently inward by laying each course to overlap the one below it until the space between them can be spanned by a line of capstones. This produces a strong outward thrust best overcome by carrying the outer walls upward vertically. Thereby an enormous quantity of masonry is used. The Mexicans at Chichen Itza carried these vaults largely on wooden beams strung between columns, thus achieving large airy halls in contrast to the cell-like rooms of the Maya Classic period, but the wood rotted and the roofs caved in. The amount of stone and rubble and mortar in the vaulting is so great that on collapsing it fills completely the room itself to about level with the spring of the vault, and more spills outside the walls, so that a building becomes a solid mass of stone and rubble. That is what happened to the Temple of the Warriors.

An archaeologist, if he is going for stratification, usually works downward (although sometimes a trash dump which has grown in area rather than depth needs tackling laterally). In excavating a building, he likes to pick up a floor at ground level and follow it in. That is, naturally, because the base of a wall is often still in position; by going in at a higher level, he could miss it. In the case of the Warriors that was not the best tactics. Morris started on the temple on top, for had he first excavated the base of the pyramid, falling rocks from later excavation of the temple on top might have seriously damaged the excavated areas.

He drove in at temple floor level with the one exposed section to guide him and soon picked up the entrance. This was divided into three parts by two rectangular columns shaped as giant feathered serpents. The bodies of these formed the shafts. The heads rested on the ground in front of them, and the L-shaped tails were at the top, their bases acting as a sort of capital, on which rested the ends of the wooden lintels; the tips of the tails, carved with the rattles of rattlesnakes, which were the long arms of the L, projected in front of the lintels as though to prevent them from falling forward (Plate 11c). These feathered serpents represent the god Kukulcan, and are one of the many features imported from Tula, where such columns also exist. The wooden lintels, of course, have gone, but were undoubtedly of *zapote* (sapodilla), the tree which yields the chicle latex from which chewing gum is made. Sometimes the tails of the feathered serpents are carved with little Atlantean figures, with upraised arms representing the Bacabs who held up the sky (Fig. 2).

The entrance gave on a spacious room, which turned out to have twelve rectangular columns sculptured on all four sides with persons, for the most part warriors. These columns had supported wooden beams, and on these and the walls rested three lines of corbeled vaulting at right angles to the entrance. A doorway in the wall led into a second room with the same number and arrangement of columns. Low stone-faced benches were built against the side walls, and a large altar with carvings of feathered serpents stood against the back wall. It was supported by nineteen little

Fig. 2.—Atlantean Figures, Chichen Itza. Two of the four Bacabs who stood at the four sides of the world to hold up the sky. One has a conch shell as his attribute; the other, a spider's web.

Atlantean figures, similar to the one which held up the bird bath (Plate IIa). The walls of the temple had been painted with scenes of daily life, battles and human sacrifice, but these had been badly damaged on their collapse.

The outer walls were sculptured with masks of the Maya rain god and a Mexican feathered serpent with human heads set in their open jaws—a nice spirit of cultural compromise (Plate IIIa). In front of the temple stood a reclining statue of the kind called Chac Mool, another concept imported from Tula. These figures, lying on their backs in a most awkward position, hold on their stomachs a small basin or plaque which must have been a receptacle for offerings or for the burning of copal incense. The figure received its fanciful name from Le Plongeon, a queer character who excavated one at Chichen Itza over eighty years ago. Casts of this fine sculpture were distributed to various museums. Some years ago, in the Museum of Natural History in New York, a mother was observed to hold her small daughter over the receptacle in the cast to answer nature's call, a somewhat startling offertory.

The pyramid itself was built in three tiers with a wide staircase with feathered serpent balustrades (Plate 1*b*). Not only the

Fig. 3.—Frieze, Temple of the Warriors, Chichen Itza. I had the job of reassembling the greater part of the 825 feet of this frieze in three tiers. Warriors disguised as animals offer human hearts to the rising sun.

decoration, such as the sculptured warriors on the columns and the serpent columns, but the whole plan of the temple with its flanking colonnades is a replica of the great temple at distant Tula, and one can be reasonably certain that the architect of the Warriors had once followed his profession at Tula. The sculptural detail is in the local style; there are no masks of the Maya rain gods at Tula, and at Chichen local limestone replaces the volcanic rock of Tula; but those are minor factors. The one major difference is that corbeled vaulting, unknown at Tula, was used here.

When I reached Chichen Itza in January, 1926, the temple had been cleared and the collapsed terraces of the pyramid laid bare. As work proceeded on the colonnades, I was given the job of fitting together the three friezes which decorated the tiers of the pyramid. The repetitive motif, also an importation from Tula, comprised large jaguars, eagles, and a stub-tailed wooly-haired animal, which looks something like a bear. The animals, in pairs, back to back, and with hearts in their paws, face half-sitting, half-reclining, gods. These also are in pairs feet to feet, but with heads and shoulders twisted around to face each an animal, at whose feet they point elaborate spears (Fig. 3).

The gods, which have features of the Mexican rain gods, the Tlalocs, are without much doubt representations of a Mexican

Fig. 4.—An Itza Warrior and Scenes of Sacrifice. Typical warrior of the Mexican period at Chichen Itza. The sacrificial victims are drawn from scenes on stelae at Piedras Negras. The quetzal feathers, signifying precious, represent the blood from the heart.

deity with the formidable name of Tlalchitonatiuh, the manifestation of the sun god at the moment of rising. In Mexican belief the sun god at sunset entered the underworld, the land of the dead, to return to the eastern horizon, but as during his passage through the underworld he took on the skeletal nature of its inhabitants, it was necessary to reclothe him in flesh to restore his strength for his diurnal journey. That was accomplished by offering him human hearts and blood, for which a constant stream of sacrificial victims was needed. To keep up the supply, the Mexicans instituted military orders of knighthood, known as the Jaguars and the Eagles, who went forth to battle not to kill but to capture the enemy. This cult was brought to Yucatan from Tula. The eagles and jaguars offering hearts to the rising sun on these sculptured bands were the representations of the warriors.

Parts of the friezes were still in position, giving the key to the design, but for the most part the stones forming them had fallen and lay buried higgledy-piggledy in the debris below. To make matters worse, the Maya boys, in excavating the base of the pyramid, had moved numbers of them to other places. It was a sort of giant jigsaw puzzle made worse by the fact that the stones had been carved before being placed in position, and sometimes an element in one stone was out of line with its continuation on the next, and there were also gaps which the Maya had filled with stucco. Some stones were double length, weighing about fifty pounds apiece.

I labored for weeks in the incandescent sun of Yucatan fitting the stones together, moving them sometimes nearly forty yards to see if I could make a fit. Part of the time I had a Maya assistant to do the carrying, but in my memory it seems that I personally shifted every blessed stone. A few just would not fit well, but I doubt that anyone has noticed those bad fits. The Maya, too, made errors. In one place two pairs of animals were in sequence, probably a miscalculation of the space to be filled, and in another two animals face each other, a sculptor's error. After the friezes were reassembled, Maya masons set them back in their positions.

For this and other work at Chichen we had a force of about sixty Maya laborers, many of whom came from the nearby village of Piste. They were a cheerful, lovable lot. Although the lime dust caked on their sweaty bodies, they appeared each morning in immaculately clean clothes—white vest, trousers rolled to the knees, a kiltlike apron of striped material like pillow ticking, straw sombreros, and leather sandals. The Maya is frugal—he has to be—but nowhere else in the world have I seen such patched clothes, with one neat patch on another until, without exaggeration, it was almost impossible to identify more than the smallest areas of the original garment.

These Maya boys worked with a will, chattering away in Maya, although nearly all of them also spoke Spanish with varying success. They loved a practical joke. For the removal of the hundreds of tons of detritus, Morris had fixed up a huge hopper

FIG. 5.—Restoring the Temple of the Warriors, Chichen Itza. Maya laborer climbs the stairs with snout of long-nosed rain god to be reset in the façade from which it had fallen. Drawing by Jean Charlot, staff artist at the time.

under which the truck was run. The men ran their wheelbarrow-loads up a plank, dumped the load in the hopper, and came down by another plank. When the hopper was full, a lever opened it, allowing the rubble to fall into the truck, which then carried it to a dump on the outskirts of the site. On one occasion the hopper was accidentally opened just as a worker was turning his wheelbarrow over into it. The ton or more of soil, rock and mortar poured into the truck followed by the scared but unharmed boy and his wheelbarrow. The howls of laughter from all the Maya workers disrupted work for the rest of the morning, and for weeks the victim was twitted about it on every occasion to more laughter. I haven't much doubt that the story is still told "with advantages" in Piste.

Scorpions were common around the ruins, and the Maya were adept at catching one with a trick hold which would not allow it to use its sting. As a joke, the holder would make to put it down somebody's neck, and then the rhythm of work would be interrupted by a wild scattering of the gang in all directions with one Maya, scorpion in hand, left in possession of the field.

The stone casing of the pyramid was in bad shape. Parts were standing, but insecure; large sections were fallen. The masons, who were resetting this, cleared debris behind to have a secure backing for their work. In the course of this clearing, two sculptured columns imbedded in the fill of the pyramid were exposed, confirming the suspicion that inside the pyramid there was an earlier structure.

The peoples of Middle America constantly enlarged their buildings in this way, and there are cases of half a dozen enlargements with one pyramid nesting inside another. Preliminary explorations disclosed that this inner building was a gem, but its excavation was a problem if the Warriors above it was not to come tumbling down. Finally Morris drove a tunnel in from the side and, using iron girders to support the Warriors, made it possible to excavate the lower building, named the Temple of the Chac Mool from the discovery of one of those statues inside it. This had undoubtedly stood outside the entrance, but had been dumped inside by the Maya when they built the Warriors.

The ancient builders removed the corbeled roof of the Temple of the Chac Mool, as they planned to lay the floor of the Warriors about level with the spring of the vault, and partly dismantled the feathered serpent columns of the entrance, but the rest of the building was in almost mint condition, the murals and the paint on the columns being as bright as when first painted. The figures on these last were largely Maya priests in contrast to the Mexican warriors which predominated in the later building.

My late colleague, Alfred Tozzer, held that this contrast indicates a period of Maya dominance followed by one of Mexican control, and he formulated a long sequence extending the occupation of Chichen Itza until about A.D. 1480 in which first one group and then the other is on top according to the decorative matter of the many buildings. However, it is much simpler and does not violate archaeological evidence to place all those buildings in the period A.D. 1000 to A.D. 1250 and to assume that the figures vary according to the rite to which each building was devoted. The Temple of the Chac Mool was apparently dedicated to the Chacs, the Maya rain gods, and therefore Maya priests were depicted; the Warriors and its colonnades were for the rites of the military orders of Jaguars and Eagles, so, not surprisingly, sculptured Mexican warriors and scenes of warfare and sacrifice decorate it.

The approximate date of the Warriors—it was probably built around A.D. 1100—will one day be known for certain, thanks to the discovery under the floor of one of its colonnades of a fine tobacco pipe of pottery. This, it is now known, is of a type manufactured in northern Michoacan in northwestern Mexico. It had been brought a distance of over nine hundred miles in a direct overland line, considerably farther by winding tracks and coastal waters. That type of pipe will some day be securely dated and give us the date of the building of the Warriors. Gold found in the sacred cenote at Chichen had been brought from Panama, a

FIG. 6.—A Find in the Temple of the Warriors, Chichen Itza. Tall pottery tubes of the Mayapan period were leaning against a column. They had been deposited when the column was three-quarters buried in debris from the collapsed roof, clear evidence that the Mayapan period flourished after the fall of Chichen Itza.

distance in direct land line of some twelve hundred miles, somewhat more by coastal waters. A pretty competent organization was needed for such a network of trade.

Chichen Itza was sacked and its inhabitants driven out by about A.D. 1200. This date can be calculated from Maya chronicles and is confirmed by the types of pottery found on the floor of a

34

sacked and destroyed building. The conquerors were led by a certain Hunac Ceel Cauich. After its conquest the city was abandoned except for a few campers-out in the ruins, and Mayapan became the dominant city in Yucatan.

The Temple of the Warriors probably was sacked at the time of the invasion, for large banner supports in human shape were deliberately thrown down to the base of the pyramid from their positions in front of the temple. Also, many pieces of large pottery incense burners with figures of gods on their fronts and sherds of special types of red-slipped bowls were strewn over the collapsed structure, and these are the products of the Mayapan period which followed the fall of Chichen. Jars of Mayapan red ware left against a column already half-buried in debris show that the roof collapsed early in that period, nice archaeological evidence (Fig. 6).

Often after work some of us, junior archaeologists and Maya laborers, cooled off with a swim in the nearby cenote of Xtoloc, the chief source of water for the ancient inhabitants. These cenotes, a corruption of the Maya *dz'onot*, are huge natural wells. Surface water in Yucatan passes rapidly through the porous limestone to form underground streams and lakes. In places the covering crust of limestone has caved in, leaving large holes with small lakes at the bottom. A path wound down the side of the cenote Xtoloc, and one pictured lines of Maya girls in times past passing up and down it with water jars on their heads.

To the north lies the more famous cenote of sacrifice. Steep, unclimbable limestone walls form a well seventy yards in diameter and sixty feet deep, at the bottom of which is the lake as deep again as the well. Into this the Maya threw sacrifices to the rain gods, the Chacs. Occasionally, people were hurled into the water at daybreak, and, if still alive at midday, were hauled out to deliver the oracle of the Chacs. Hunac Ceel Cauich, the conqueror of Chichen Itza, cast himself into the cenote to get the Chacs' prophecy, apparently because none of the messengers thrown in had survived, and the people were terrified that the Chacs were angry and would send no message. Gazing into the lake far below, one is filled with admiration of his deed. As Ralph Roys, the translator of the passage, has remarked, "Hunac Ceel was evidently of the stuff of which leaders are made, with sufficient courage and force of character to shape his own destiny."

Nearly fifty years ago, Edward Thompson, former owner of the hacienda, dredged from the mud at the bottom of the cenote many objects, as well as bones of sacrificial victims, which had been cast into the water. The former comprised large quantities of jade pieces, copper bells, many bowls containing balls of copal incense studded with jade beads, pieces of cloth and carved wood, and quite a few gold objects, most or all of which had come from Panama or neighboring Costa Rica. There were also a few gold disks embossed with scenes of warfare and sacrifice in the Toltec-Maya style. The gold for these probably came as pieces from Panama, for there is no gold in Yucatan, and was later melted down and embossed at Chichen Itza.

Because of the damp climate practically no examples of Maya textiles and woodwork have survived except for these pieces in the cenote, which, paradoxically, were preserved by the mud. Such material is so rare that I was much excited when many years later, at Mayapan, I excavated a piece of cloth about thumbnail size. This was in the grave of an infant, not six months old. The fragment owed its preservation to being permeated with verdigris from copper bells. These had formed tiny anklets which, one can suppose, the child had worn in its brief life and which the sorrowing parents had not the heart to remove. The beautiful garments shown in Maya sculpture and painting and the exquisite workmanship of the few wooden lintels that have survived show what treasures would be found in the Maya area had it the climate of Egypt or coastal Peru.

Tradition has it that the victims cast into the cenote were beautiful virgins, but in fact, the bones recovered are mostly of children, the victims usually offered the rain gods; the bones of adults are either of men or women no longer in the first flush of youth. Edward Thompson, temperamentally a romantic, claimed that the bones he had dredged from the mud were those of virgins, a claim difficult to prove.

I liked to laze on the edge of the sacred cenote, sharing the sun with large crested iguanas and the curious motmot birds busy about their business, the quiet disturbed only by cicadas and the plaintive call of doves—"*cuc tuzen*," "the squirrel lies to me," which refers to a Maya folk-tale of how the squirrel robbed her eggs. In that peace I found it impossible to conjure up in my mind those scenes of violence of long ago.

Later in the season, the friezes finally assembled, I was given charge of the excavations of the Caracol, that queer ugly round building which, tradition has it, was built by Quetzalcoatl–Kukulcan (Plate 1c). Tradition is certainly wrong, for the architecture is of the Classic period, although later embellishments, such as a feathered serpent balustrade, were added during the Mexican period. I didn't particularly enjoy this work. Elsewhere I have compared the building and the rectangular platform on which it is set to a two-decker wedding cake standing on the square carton in which it came, and the work of clearing debris and restoring fallen walls was not sufficiently interesting to let me get over my dislike for that aberration in Maya taste. A pottery jaguar which I found in one doorway evidently resented my low opinion of his home. (Fig. 16).

Inside, a narrow spiral staircase (hence the Spanish name *caracol*) leads up to a now much-ruined room, originally it seems, a little less than nine by five feet. From this, according to the reconstruction made by Karl Ruppert, radiated six squints or narrow shafts about eight inches wide which terminated in larger windows. The squints fanned out at roughly similar intervals from northwest to southeast, and it has been thought that they may have served astronomical purposes. The direction from the right inner jamb to the left outer jamb of one squint is due west, and a diagonal line along another squint points due south. The Maya were interested in world directions, but if such was the purpose of these squints, why were they not made far narrower to obviate a diagonal sighting?

As is nearly always the case with Maya buildings, the more you dig, the more complex you find them to be. Ruppert, who continued the work on the Caracol in subsequent years, uncovered earlier structures beneath, and later structures adjoining, the Caracol, so that as it now stands, it is a most elaborate structure. One of the adjoining buildings was a sweat house, of which others occur in the Maya area.

Present-day Maya and other Indians of Mexico take steam baths in small specially constructed buildings for therapeutic reasons, but the habit no longer obtains in Yucatan. Of the Maya of Guatemala the English Dominican, Thomas Gage, observed over three centuries ago, "There is scarce any house which hath not also in the yard a stew, wherein they bathe themselves with hot water, which is their chief physick, when they feel themselves distempered." However, it is steam, produced from pouring water on hot stones or potsherds which they use. The stone sweat houses at Chichen Itza and at the great site of Piedras Negras were large buildings obviously used communally and, one may suppose, for ceremonial bathing, perhaps, for instance, before or after a ball-game contest. Those at Chichen have in front colonnades in which one pictures the bathers lounging after the bath.

In our bachelor hut I shared a room with the French artist Jean Charlot, who was busy copying the sculptured columns and murals of the Warriors. The other room was occupied by Karl Ruppert and George Vaillant, who later became the authority on the archaeology of the Valley of Mexico. Life was very pleasant except after dinner, when Morley's passion for hot music and bridge resulted in his playing for the five hundredth time the raucous *Tiger Rag* on a gramophone much the worse for wear

Fig. 7.—The *Jarana*. Drawing by Jean Charlot, who was present at the dance described below.

or prowling in search of someone to make a fourth at bridge. Jean had the best defense against that. He invented fantastic rules as he went along, claiming that that was how the game was played in France. My bridge was so bad that I was called upon only as a last resort, but when Vay approached after dinner for music or bridge, it was well to act on the call, "To your tents, O Israel."

Sometimes we junior archaeologists slipped off to a dance in Piste or Dzitas, which had the added attraction of beer on tap, for camp was bone dry. I got in bad the first time I danced the *jarana* with a Maya girl, for, at the urging of some of the Maya boys there, I put my hat on the girl's head. At the end of the dance I took it from her and put it back on my own head, thereby unwittingly bringing shame on my pretty partner. As I quickly learned, placing your hat on your partner's head is a sign of admiration, and one must redeem it with money, the size of the payment showing the love the girl kindled in her partner. By taking the hat back without any payment, I had indicated that I wasn't the slightest bit interested in her. When I learned of my *faux pas*, I tried to remedy things by an overpayment. That wasn't too good, either, for though to us gringos it was a small sum, to the Maya it indicated a passion that had swept me off my feet.

Sometimes we had an evening concert in the old Maya ball court, which has extraordinarily fine acoustic properties. The gramophone was in the north temple and we sat in the south temple at the far end of the vast ball court, slightly over five hundred feet away, listening in the soft moonlight of a tropical night to classical music—for Morley conceded that the *Tiger Rag* was not appropriate to that magnificent setting. As the records ended, the chorus of frogs continued the music, and it was not difficult to people the court with players intent on putting the rubber ball through the great rings set high in each of the two great walls which enclosed its length.

A minor activity at Chichen was the founding by George Vaillant and myself (we were the only members) of the Young Men's Maya Association to debunk the views of our elders and betters. Change was in the air, and it was fun while it lasted; but, naturally, with the passing years there has emerged a sort of junior Y.M.M.A to debunk our ideas—"Big fleas have small fleas upon their backs to bite 'em. And small fleas have smaller fleas, and so *ad infinitum*."

Tourists were almost unknown, for the Americans in Merida thought only of their divorces and their next spouses. In any case there was then no hotel at Chichen. It was very peaceful.

Addendum (Spring 1971)

If this chapter were rewritten, the historical outline would be presented somewhat differently. I am now convinced the Itza were, indeed, Chontal Maya (now called Putun, their ancient name, for Chontal is a confusing name applied to several groups). The home of the Putun extended from the Usumacinta delta near Potonchan, "Putun Snake" (the Spaniards often confused *o* with *u*), to near Champoton (anciently Chanputun, which is Potonchan reversed) and included the Chakanputun (Putun province) area in southwestern Campeche, from which the Itza are said to have moved to Chichen Itza and to which they later returned. Furthermore, a song recounting the Itza conquest of Chichen refers to them as the Putun.

The first place on the Itza invasion itinerary according to the Maya historical sources was Pole, on the northeast coast of Yucatan. As this was the port for crossing from Cozumel, it is a fair assumption that Cozumel was the point of departure. Now the Itza were the seamen of Middle America, and at one time they controlled Cozumel. This, then, is confirmatory evidence that Itza was another name for a Putun group. Maya sources indicate A.D. 918 as the date of that Itza-Putun conquest of Chichen Itza.

As the Putun had intermarried with Mexicans and were strongly under Mexican influence (many bore Mexican names), it is understandable that when Quetzalcoatl sought refuge in Yucatan in A.D. 987 (the date A.D. 999 on page 24 for this event is reconstructed from an alternative calendar), he should have been well received by the Putun, who partly shared his background.

The matter is fully discussed in my *Maya History and Religion* (University of Oklahoma Press, 1970).

2

Coba, Uxmal, and Other Ruins

DURING THE 1926 SEASON Thomas Gann, an old hand at Maya exploration, visited the ruins of Coba, deep in the uninhabited forest of Quintana Roo and some sixty miles east of Chichen Itza. Visiting Chichen, he told of finding many buildings and several carved but badly weathered stelae there, and his account of the great stone road leading to the site excited our interest.

It was decided to send some of us on a second visit, for there were important outlying ruins Gann had not examined, and there stelae with legible inscriptions might be found.

Our party of A. V. Kidder, later chairman of the archaeological work of the Carnegie Institution, two friends of his, and myself took train to Valladolid, terminus of the railroad. This sleepy town of Maya and Yucatecans has been named in an outburst of Latin hyperbole the "Sultana of the East." It didn't seem very appropriate, for *sultana* means to most persons of English speech either a rather blowzy chief lady of the harem or something which goes into the Christmas pudding.

A great rugged church, built to serve also as a place of refuge for the early Spanish colonists in the event of a Maya rising, dominates the low municipal buildings and shops on the other three sides of the plaza. Luther must have had such a church in mind when he composed "A mighty fortress is our God." The center of the plaza, laid out in typical Latin-American fashion as a small park, was adorned with monstrous cement fountains in the form of realistic frogs and pairs of seats of the same material in the shape of an S, so that a person seated in one loop of the S faced his companion in the other, like the last two players in musical chairs. I use the past tense in the hope that the Sultana has had a face-lift since then.

A hundred yards away, in the open market, Maya from the surrounding villages squatted beside their tropical fruits and vegetables or offered for your inspection wild turkeys, agoutis, deer, and peccary, skinned, but liberally coated with flies. Now, I make no doubt, stringent sanitary laws to safeguard the buyer have taken away the carefree beauty of the unregulated scene. Fruits and vegetables revealed the blending of Maya and European cultures. Avocado pears, papayas, mamey apples, chile peppers, black beans, squashes, and maize, grown by the Maya for thousands of years, were mingled with oranges, onions, loaves of brown sugar, and bananas, brought by the Spaniards but now completely naturalized.

In another quarter of the market, beautifully made hammocks of henequen (sisal) fiber, straw hats of the low-crowned types used by the Maya or the huge high-peaked kinds brought from Central Mexico, baskets, and sisal cordage were for sale. Native textiles were no more. In their stead Syrian merchants displayed bolts of cotton stamped with the names of Mexican, Lancashire, or New England factories.

At the edge of town is a most beautiful cenote where Maya maidens drew water when Valladolid was known as Saci and Christian Spain reached little south of the Pyrenees.

The man from whom we hired the mules allowed us the use of an empty house on the outskirts of the town. This, comprising one large room with kitchen behind, was not completely unfurnished. In addition to the hammock hooks set in the walls of the front room, a feature of every Yucatecan house in those days, there was an ancient stove in the kitchen; but what really caught the eye was an enamel chamber-pot reposing in lone majesty in the exact center of the living room. We were not sure whether it had been left accidentally or, as was more probable, it had been placed there as a pleasant gesture of welcome.

Thirty years ago the chamber-pot was a conspicuous cultural element in Yucatan. A Yucatecan family from any small town or village in the interior was not completely equipped for travel without one. As it isn't easily packed in a suitcase, it was usually carried in the hand or strapped to the outside of the luggage. Passing down a second-class coach on any train, one's eye was attracted by a series of these enameled articles dangling from the luggage racks.

It had other uses, for should it develop a hole or the children have grown up, it was frequently employed as a flower pot, and it was not unusual to encounter a handsome pair of chambers, gay with *noche buena* or petunias, tastefully placed, one on each side of the front door. Indeed, in a way it symbolized wealth and rank, for the average villager had neither the money to buy, nor opportunities of travel to display, one.

On more recent trips to Yucatan I find this colorful custom is no more. In poking a little fun at it, I trust that no Yucatecan reader will take umbrage, for nowhere is there a more courteous, friendly, and in every way lovable people. Years later I told the story of the room furniture to Robert Redfield, who long worked as an ethnologist in Yucatan. He capped it with the description of the contents of the main room of a local politician with whom he had spent the night: one chair, an ornate table, a heavy gilt mirror, and a machinegun.

We slung our hammocks from the pairs of hooks set opposite each other along the wall. We were up at daybreak, but there are always delays in getting a pack train off. Three hours' riding along a wide rock-strewn road brought us to Kanxoc, a large,

attractive Maya village with a huge ruined church, relic of the
Franciscans, beside the grass-covered plaza on which cows and
horses grazed. Beyond, we followed a track which threaded its
way through forest interrupted by occasional milpas, the Maya
maize fields.

Early in the year the Maya makes a clearing of about ten acres
with axe and machete. Burning off the felled trees as soon as they
are dry, he plants the seeds in holes dug with a pointed pole in
the ash-covered soil just before the rains in early May (Fig. 12).
Milpas are allowed to revert to forest usually after two seasons
(the Maya say that they get too weed-ridden after that to work
again and the yield also drops), and a new section of forest is
cleared. This primitive system of agriculture derives from ancient
times, but it is suited to local conditions, for the soil is thin—often
in small pockets in the living limestone rock, which is either exposed or has only a very shallow covering; plows could not be
used. We passed these milpas in March when the land had been
cleared but not yet burned. Elsewhere were abandoned weed-
choked milpas and other parts where the young trees were beginning to dominate the secondary growth.

After riding eight hours, we reached Bolmai, a settlement of
two families. Here we recruited as guide an elderly Maya, Tomás
Cupul, on his claiming in very broken Spanish to know well all
the forest region around Coba, where he used to hunt. With his
striking figure and pure Maya features, he looked as though he
might have stepped out of a sculptured column at Chichen. He
might, in any case, have been a descendant of one of those carved
figures, for the Cupuls were the ruling family around Valladolid
at the coming of the Spaniards. His clothes reminded me of St.
John the Baptist rather than the ancient Maya, for he wore nothing
but sandals, short white drawers rolled to his knees, and a sack
"girt about his loins"; when he drew out some tortillas, I was
almost shocked they weren't locusts and honey. Like many elderly

45

Maya, he had about a dozen long hairs on his chin, for the American Indian is singularly lacking in body hair. In Maya art, gods or personages sometimes have a sort of sparse goatee, which probably represents a form of flattery (Fig. 2); old Cupul's dozen hairs were above hirsute average.

About two miles beyond Bolmai—from there to the east coast there isn't a permanent settlement—we struck the great Maya stone road which runs west from Coba to Yaxuna, a small site about twelve miles southwest of Chichen.

This great monument to Maya engineering is thirty feet across, wider than most English roads. There isn't a curve and only four changes of direction (none of more than nine degrees) in the whole of its sixty-three miles, a veritable speed fan's paradise, but the jaguars which moved along it had four legs, not four wheels. It averages about three feet above ground level, but across swamps it may be up to eight feet high.

The bed is of great boulders over which is a layer of rocks and stones set in mortar with a surface, now disintegrated, of the rotted limestone called *sascab* or of stucco such as the Maya used for floors. Its construction must have called for an army of laborers, yet it served no utilitarian purpose.

The Maya had no wheeled vehicles and no beasts of burden, so the road was used only by travelers on foot or in litters, and for them a road six feet wide would have been ample; it must have been for ceremonial pageantry. A procession of priests decked in jade and all their splendor with their panaches of quetzal feathers waving in the breeze would have presented an overwhelmingly impressive spectacle of barbaric pomp. Strange that the Maya could achieve such a feat of engineering yet fail to discover the true arch, balance scales, or the wheel (they knew of them for toys but never grasped their application).

To us, among the first dozen white men ever to ride along it, the road presented a very different appearance. A heavy growth of forest (more rainfall brings higher forest in the eastern part of Yucatan) covered the surface. Decaying tree trunks across the scarcely perceptible path made by modern Maya hunters introduced an air of melancholic decay which the surrounding dull-hued tree trunks, dingy ferns, and scant undergrowth did nothing to dispel. In many places generations of falling trees had churned the surface with their torn-out roots, so that it was more like the dry bed of a stream.

Sometimes we walked, mule halter in hand, for riding at a mule's pace is tedious. Much conversation is impossible because a rider can't turn his head for long to speak to the rider behind him for fear of a crack on the skull from the low branch of a tree, and a good deal of effort and noise goes in trying to keep mules up to the standard three and one-half miles an hour, for naturally with pack animals one can't proceed at trot or canter!

Having no lanterns, we halted as night fell at the edge of a swamp about two miles short of Coba. We had been twelve hours in the saddle. We tethered the mules, made a fire for supper, and swung our hammocks from pairs of correctly spaced trees. It rained in the night, adding to the discomfort inevitable when one makes camp after dark.

We were up at dawn, and another mile brought us to a large thatched hut, standing at the edge of Lake Coba, which had formerly been used as a chicle store. From it there was an enchanting view of sparkling blue water set amid the varying hues of the encircling forest. At the east end, the tree-clad bulk of the highest pyramid rose high above lower swells and humps of vegetation above lesser pyramids and mounds; at the west end, a brighter green and a low horizon marked the swampy area by which we had camped.

We set forth for the ruins, Tomás Cupul leading the way. We passed many scattered mounds and plunged into a stand of primeval trees with immense buttress—roots which flowed out along the surface in search of soil in imitation of the sinuous lengths of immense boaconstrictors. Crossing a narrow neck of land, we reached another lake, about half a mile long, called Macanxoc, on the north shore of which the pyramids and courts of Coba were massed.

We clambered over collapsed buildings from which grew huge trees, made our way across courts filled with fallen rubble and more trees, peered into rooms with vaults which still stood, and, grabbing trees and bushes, climbed up the fallen remains of a stairway to the little one-room temple at the top of the highest pyramid. The roof had gone, but there was red stucco still on the walls, as well as a plain stela set against the back wall. The thickness of the walls suggested that many of the stones scatttered far below us had once formed a roof-comb. This type of ornament, often set on the roofs of Maya buildings, is like a high wall decorated with niches and masks and figures in stucco. It served no structural purpose, but it added grandeur and a fine field for display of symbols of the chief deities. With such a roof-comb or roof crest the building would have risen to about 140 feet above the lake.

In masonry and in its compact plan of pyramids and multiple-roomed buildings grouped around courts, set at different levels but joined by broad stairways, Coba was quite different from Chichen and other cities of Yucatan; instead, it closely resembled cities of the Classic period in the Peten district of Guatemala far to the south. Indeed, Coba was a typical ceremonial center of the Central area, as the dated stelae subsequently confirmed.

"Ceremonial center" is a better term than "city," because it is clear these places were never urban centers but places to which the people whose homes were scattered over the surrounding country came for important religious festivals, for markets, and to attend courts of justice and to be kept informed of details of local administration. Except on such occasions, the great centers lay empty, unless, perhaps, for a small staff for upkeep. This picture derived from archaeological sources is confirmed by the "empty towns" of some Maya groups of the present day in Chiapas and the highlands of Guatemala. These towns are almost without permanent inhabitants, but on Sundays and other days of civil and ecclesiastical importance the people converge on them from their outlying rural settlements, families of wealth moving into their town houses for the occasion.

The ceremonial center was the symbol of the small group of priests and nobles (the two were often indistinguishable) who ruled the peasants, directing almost every detail of their lives. This was a small theocracy which had its part to play: the peasants produced the food and supplied the labor and materials to build all those temples, pyramids, and palaces, enlarging and extending them at such frequent intervals; the priests, with their divine knowledge, were the intermediaries between the peasant and his gods of the soil. As long as they did this, the peasants seem to have been content to shoulder the physical burdens—and what burdens they must have been. But there came a time when the theocracy appears to have been seduced by new ideas and paid more attention to new-fangled deities than to the old gods of rain and the crops, beloved by the peasants. The result, apparently, was a revolt by the peasants and the massacre or perhaps expulsion of the small ruling class.

A rough comparison might be made with those old ecclesiastic principalities, such as Salzburg, with the archbishop ruler living in pomp surrounded by his cathedral, administrative buildings, nunneries and friaries, on which were lavished all the art of the age, or, from the religious and ecclesiastical sides alone, one can think in terms of an English cathedral close. Perhaps we shall not be too far from reality in regarding the Classic period, *mutatis mutandis* as a sort of exotic background for Maya cousins of Archdeacon Grantly, Mrs. Proudie, and Mr. Harding, not in top hats but in quetzal plumes, and sipping not the 1820 port—"it's too good for a bishop, unless one of the right sort"—but the native *balche*. Indeed, every important Maya ceremonial center might be viewed as a sort of tropical Barchester, and on a mural at Bonampak there is a splendid portrait of Mrs. Proudie watching the bishop at the seat of judgment (Fig. 8). Only as long as the right sort were in control did the Classic period endure.

FIG. 8.—The Bishop and Mrs. Proudie. The lady faces the ruler, both seated on a dais, and minor characters. Mural at Bonampak, about A.D. 800.

In the course of our explorations we came across smallish fragments of two stone rings, like those in the ball court at Chichen. They lay in debris between two parallel mounds with sloping sides. We paid little attention to these odd-shaped stones, for at that time it was not known that the Maya also used ball courts with sloping sides, and in any case the ball game was believed to have been introduced by the Mexicans at a much later date than the obvious occupation of Coba. It was not until three years later when Blom identified a series of ball courts in various cities of the Classic period that the Coba court was recognized as such, a nice lesson in how preconceived notions can blind one to obvious facts.

At the edge of Lake Macanxoc we came upon a small stone dock of which Gann had spoken. Here canoes for fishing or for use in sacrificial ceremonies in the lake must have been moored.

In 1930, when my wife and I and Harry Pollock were at Coba, we found that three Maya roads had actually been built across parts of Lake Macanxoc, presumably to avoid necessary changes of direction had they skirted the water. For most of their lengths the roads or causeways are now under water, but one can pick them up at each shore and follow their submerged courses by reeds growing on them. One pictures processions along the causeway and canoes converging for some sacrifice in the lake, such as we know the Aztec performed. Dredging the lake would quite likely bring up treasure, as at Chichen. Moreover, such finds would probably be largely of the Classic period, a great haul, for at present we have practically no perishables of that early date.

From the top of the highest pyramid two tree-clad masses were visible a mile to the northeast. They were obviously artificial, and one was enormous. We asked Cupul to take us there, but he was full of excuses, saying that the intervening growth was impenetrable; we wondered whether there were traces there of modern pagan rites he didn't wish us to see (we had come across evidence of offerings to the stelae in Coba itself).

Eventually he agreed to try, and on his return we set out. Most of the way led through an abandoned milpa of *chicleros* (chewing-gum gatherers), a low dense mass of two years' growth, and Tomás had not lied. As the hard work of clearing largely fell on him and he wasn't in the slightest bit interested in ruins, I can't say that I blamed him for his reluctance.

On the far side, Tomás led us to a pyramid almost as high as the tallest at Coba, up which we scrambled. On top was a small temple with roof intact and three niches in the façade. One was destroyed, but we gasped at the figures in the others, for each held a semi-human semi-insect being head downwards as though diving through space (Plate IV*a*). Similar diving gods were known from Tulum (Fig. 9) and other cities of the east coast (later, an example was noted at Sayil in western Yucatan), but they were believed to be very late. Coba had given us two jolts—a type of masonry and architecture and a style of decoration, neither of which had a right to be there according to current ideas. There was, too, the delayed jolt of the ball court.

There were weathered stelae at the base of the pyramid and, less than two hundred yards away, although we did not then know it, was the termination of the great road along which we had wearily urged our mules and which we had left when we had camped.

Nearby we found the enormous mass we had seen from Coba. It was a colossal platform 120 yards long, 140 yards deep, and about 55 feet high, but on the flat summit there were only a few low walls, foundations for small houses of perishable materials. A great many stone metates for grinding maize were in and around them, confirming our conclusion that these were the houses of peasant families. Presumably the Maya had intended to use this as a foundation for a series of courts and temples even more impressive than the main group at Coba, but the project was never completed. The site was abandoned, and then, one supposes, peasant families moved in.

Elated with our discoveries, we returned to camp for a bathe in Lake Coba before supper. Two months later we found that we were not the discoverers of the Temple of the Diving God; Teobert Maler, an old-time explorer of Maya ruins, had visited Coba and photographed the diving figures thirty-three years before our "discovery." We christened the group "Nohoch Mul," "great mound," the term old Tomás Cupul had applied to that "ill-weaved ambition."

On a subsequent visit we found a mass of mounds and courts, including a second ball court in the area between Nohoch Mul and the start of the great Yaxuna road. Three-quarters of a mile

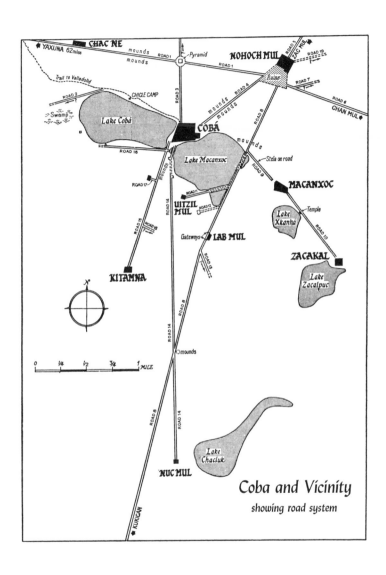

Coba and Vicinity
showing road system

west of that point Road 3 crosses it at right angles (see map). The intersection takes the form of a small octagonal court in the middle of which stands a little pyramid with the remains of a temple on top. The whole was very much like a modern traffic circle. However, instead of easing traffic jams, the Maya arrangement may have had the opposite effect, for litters were probably parked there while their occupants ascended to the little temple to pray and make some offering for a safe journey. There were stairways on all sides of the pyramid, so one may imagine the litter bearers making the half-circle to await their masters on the far side.

We started back for Valladolid, but not in litters; the mules, heading for home, made slightly better time. Soon after nightfall we stopped at Kanxoc for a meal, eating in the road by the flame of a candle which burned without flickering in the windless night. In twos and threes the Maya men gathered round to watch our meal. White cotton vests and drawers caught the candlelight, but the owners were invisible against the curtain of night. With fifty pairs of eyes on us as we ate bread and sardines from the tiny local store, conversation in Maya passed from side to side of the ring. Occasional Spanish words with accentuation shifted to Maya usage indicated that our forks, something the Maya do not use, were one topic of conversation. Three hours' riding through the night brought us to Valladolid. Never did sultan salute his wife so eagerly as we did the Sultana of the East!

Two months later I was again on my way to Coba. Carmen Chai, one of our masons at Chichen, who had once lived near Bolmai, told me of "stone men" he had seen when hunting near Coba. From his account it was clear that the stone men were stelae with carved human figures on them and that they were in a part of Coba we had not visited. As Morley would have cheerfully crossed the peninsula of Yucatan to record a legible hieroglyphic inscription, he readily gave me permission to return to Coba with

Carmen. Jean Charlot, my roommate came, too, to make drawings of the "stone men."

The fourth member of the party was Eugenio Mai, a most *simpático* Maya who had worked with me on the Caracol (Plate vi*b*). He was a native of Valladolid, but had moved a few years before to Piste, where he had lodged with a widow and her young, but decidedly plain, daughter. According to Piste gossip he owed his landlady a few pesos for laundry and, unable to pay, offered to marry the daughter if the debt was canceled. The old lady jumped at the bargain, and Eugenio's laundry bill was remitted on his becoming her son-in-law. Eugenio insists the story isn't true, and in any case domestic efficiency means more to a Maya swain than good looks.

Carmen was that rare bird among the Maya, a bachelor of mature years, undoubtedly because he had lived most of his life in Merida (Plate vi*b*). In a Maya village a wife is essential to make tortillas, cook meals, and draw water, whereas in Merida one can buy cooked meals and water isn't only in a cenote. Even Carmen had found bachelordom impossible when he had lived at remote Chulutan, for there he had had a temporary wife. Nevertheless that spell of illegal uxoriousness hadn't changed him, for he was a regular old maid, withal a nice one, the only Maya old gossip I have known.

Following the same route as before, we reached Chulutan late in the afternoon and stayed the night there in an empty hut in deference to Carmen's many pleas. Perhaps that temporary wife of days gone by still lived there, but, if so, Carmen didn't confide in me. Chulutan was a small collection of huts round the ruins of an old hacienda building destroyed some eighty years earlier in the war of the castes when the Maya almost drove the Yucatecans into the sea. We were up soon after 3:00 A.M., but delays in saddling the mules and a final disappearance of Carmen, perhaps for sad farewells, held us up, so that we didn't get off till 5:30. It had rained in the night and rained on and off all day. We were wet through the whole time, every tree letting fall a shower as we brushed against it.

Next morning, with Carmen and old Cupul, whom we had picked up at Bolmai, we skirted the main ruins to reach yet another Maya road, this one sixty feet wide. After leading us along for a mile or so, Carmen warned us we were close to the stone men. Some pyramids came into view and then a scene which thirty-five years later is still vivid in my memory. There amid the trees a large shaft of grayed limestone stood on a small artificial platform (Plate IVc). We hurried forward to examine it more carefully. The principal personage, with elaborate headdress profusely decorated with quetzal feathers, had his head in profile, but his body faced to the front. His feet, turned out at a wide angle, were planted on two hapless captives, who crouched beneath his weight, their wrists securely bound (Fig. 9). Two other kneeling figures balanced the composition. The back of the stela was carved with a rather similar scene.

I scarcely had eyes for the sculptured figures; they were focused on the heiroglyphic texts, which were unusually long but had suffered much from exposure to the air for over a millenium. It was tantalizing. I ran from back to front of the monument like a dog with two tails, as I recognized on each side badly weathered but undoubted examples of the Initial Series introducing glyph which announces that a date in the involved system of the Maya Initial Series is to follow. Next I made out the Maya glyph for four hundred years and the number nine in front of it. So there were going to be dates of the Classic period, of which only three other examples were then known in the whole of Yucatan. Then I got the glyph for the twenty-year period with the number twelve in front of it. In all the pictures of Initial Series I had read there had never been such a weathered, illegible lump of limestone as this!

Carmen led us to the other stone men. There were eight of them, and several had dates late in the first half of the Classic period. All were a bit weathered, but of the readings there could be no doubt. The style of the carved figures agreed with the dates. Old Carmen had certainly done us proud; a bit of an old maid, perhaps, but, bless him, he had more than delivered the goods. I don't remember whether I gave him an *abrazo*, the embrace with back patting so loved by the Yucatecans; I ought to have. We called the little group Macanxoc as it was close to the lake of that name.

That evening, sitting round the fire in our hut by Lake Coba, we learned from Carmen of another site south of Coba. This was called Kukican by the hunters, he told us, because of a large stucco snake on the façade of the building.

Next morning with Carmen and Tomás we visited them.

Beyond the neck of land separating the two lakes, Carmen brought us to yet another Maya road—he seemed to know them as a taxi driver knows the streets of London. An hour's walk along this with stops to open the trail brought us to an intersection with yet another road, and a ruined building. Its location reminded me of a toll house, but it probably served as a halting point for religious rites; it was too near Coba to be a resting place, such as the *tambos* along Incan roads. Since much of the way was through dense secondary bush (a forest fire had swept the area some years before) where the trail had to be opened with machetes, it took three hours to cover the five miles to Kukican.

Kukican proved to be a small group with two large standing buildings. One had seven rooms, five of which, one behind the other, were enclosed by transverse rooms at each end to form a rectangular block. The front room, with no less than seven doorways, was eighty feet long, and the capstones were sixteen feet above floor level, a most noble building for such a small site. On the exterior were the battered remains of the stucco snake. The second building was of three stories. Usually, the Maya, on adding a fresh story, filled the lower rooms with rubble to carry its weight, but they had not done so here. Indeed, the walls of the third-story rooms rested on the capstones of the second-story vaults, where the support was weakest! Yet this bold experiment had succeeded, for a vault of the second story still stood.

On our return we found a narrow passage with corbeled vault which passed beneath the road, at that point over ten feet high. Probably there was a village nearby, and as the sides of the road were perpendicular, this underpass was a necessity.

Back at Chichen again, I was unable to persuade Morley that I had read the texts correctly; only his own eyes would convince him that such early dates could exist there. Then his enthusiasm flared up, and he proposed that we set out again for Coba that very afternoon. Another two days on muleback through that monotonous forest didn't appeal to me at that moment—I was full of ticks and my backside was tender from contact with what passes for a saddle in the remoter parts of Yucatan. We postponed the trip for a few days.

The mule ride that time was shortened. Morley persuaded the owner of a Model-T Ford in Valladolid to drive us to Kanxoc. The nine miles along that glacier bed of a road took just on two hours; we bounced from side to side and banged our heads against the roof. The driver came out best, for, after we had mounted our mules, he did a bonanza business driving the modern-minded element around Kanxoc plaza at five to ten centavos a ride, for ours was the first car ever to reach the village.

Next morning, on seeing Coba, Vay turned to me and said: "Eric, this can't be a Yucatan site. We must have traveled south for ten days and landed up in the middle of the Peten. I don't doubt your readings of those early dates any longer. They fit right in with this architecture and assemblage and even with the vegetation."

Two days later Vay returned to Chichen; Carmen, Eugenio, and I stayed at Coba a few more days. In later years he used to claim that I had forced his return by the tea I served. I was cook and, as a good Englishman, served tea three times a day. The water could not be drunk untreated, so it was a choice between what I regarded as rather weak tea and chlorinated water. Vay complained that the spoon wouldn't sink in that infernal Limey brew and his stomach lining was being corroded rapidly with tannic acid. Finally, he claimed to have found a pair of my dirty, sweat-impregnated socks in the tea can, charging that I had put them there to add even more strength and flavor to the deadly potion. I never heard the end of that incident.

Vay had a slide made of a sketch map I had prepared of the Macanxoc group. Unfortunately, a couple of fly specks got on it and were reproduced on the slide, which he used in a lecture tour of the season's finds. To my horror, attending his lecture in Chicago, almost the last of a series he had given from one end of the U.S.A. to the other, I noticed that one fly speck had been labeled "Stela 1"; the other, "Stela 4." Vay touched the first with his pointer, and with a dramatic pause, said, "At this spot was found the magnificent stela you have just seen." Moving his pointer to the second, he added, "Here was found the companion monument." The first fly speck was precious close to the location of our temporary latrine.

In 1930 I returned to Coba, on my honeymoon. Coba was a pretty tough spot for a honeymoon, so we delayed our departure until about three weeks after our marriage in Chicago, crossing to Progreso from New Orleans in that old tub, the *Munplace*.

In Merida I had arranged to meet Carmen Chai in the bar of the Gran Hotel—the patched-up romance with the *querida* which I suspected might have resulted from our stop at Chulutan four years before had not eventuated or had not endured, for Carmen was back in bachelor's quarters in Merida. I took my bride to the barroom to await him. I had failed to realize that women never went there, nor did I notice that I had seated her bang in front of the urinal, one of those Latin affairs not overcloaked with modesty. While we were awaiting Carmen, a rather seedy-looking Yucatecan, somewhat the worse for drink, steered a slightly weaving course in its direction. Catching sight of my wife, he stopped, raised his straw hat, bowed to her, and then entered the convenience. On coming out—his head and legs had not been out of sight—he again bowed and raised his hat to my wife. It was for her a strange first instance of the courteous ways of Yucatan which I had previously praised to her.

Morley was also in Merida, and we dined together that night to the music of a couple of troubadours complete with guitars who were entertaining a group at the next table. I rather enjoy their music, but there is a lot to be said for Morley's view: "old blisterers who wail and screech like cats for hours on end about *traición, almas, y amor* [lover's deception, souls, and love]."

After a few days at Chichen (Plate vi), we left for Coba with Harry Pollock, of the Carnegie staff, Eugenio Mai, and Carmen. We again slept the night at Chulutan, in the hut of Carmen's brother. Carmen and two Maya boys had gone ahead to erect palm-leaf shelters, one for my wife and me, the other for Harry Pollock, the hut by the lake having collapsed.

We reached Coba next evening. It had been a long, hard ride for Florence, and she was ready for her hammock. Alas, the marching army ants, making a sweep of the Maya court, began to stream into our shelter, and we had to evacuate it. It was a fascinating sight to watch them pour through in thick, endless columns, and it was half an hour before they had passed through, sending detachments swarming up the posts in a fruitless search of the new palm thatch. Marching army ants well deserve their name. They will encircle an area, such as a hollow in the ground, and close in on the entrapped insects. First two or three ants will cling to some luckless beetle, stinging as hard as they can. As its pace slows, more swarm on its body till life is extinct. Yet the army is welcome if one is in an old hut, for it will quickly rid the place of scorpions and tarantulas. I have seen scorpions thus dislodged fall from the roof with a few ants on them amidst battalions of ants waiting for just that to happen.

Our camp was in a court in the ruins with trees towering high above us, which kept it reasonably cool but sheltered innumerable mosquitoes. Harry and I went off to work each morning, leaving Florence to cook our meal. She is an excellent cook, but the equipment wasn't all it might have been. We had brought a side of bacon thickly protected with tar, to cut through which she had the choice of a penknife or a two-foot-long machete; for cooking she had tin lard pails so thin that anything not completely liquid inevitably burned. Half a morning's struggle cutting bacon went down our throats in two or three minutes. Still, the marriage hasn't yet gone on the rocks.

The days passed rapidly in mapping the various groups, searches for new stelae, and tracing the course of each *zacbe*, "artificial road," as the Maya call the old roads. All together we located fifteen of these in addition to the great Yaxuna-Coba road. No such elaborate network exists anywhere else in the whole New World except in Inca territory.

Shortly before we left, Florence and I climbed the great pyramid at Coba to watch the dawn, which for me has always had a greater attraction than sunsets. Down below in the forest it was still dark, but up where we were, it was getting light. The view to the east as we waited for the sun was a strange one. All kinds of depressions and bumps in the surface of treetops, not visible in full day, showed up clearly. They corresponded to the courts and mounds of the outlying groups. It was like noting how all the

F<small>IG</small>. 9.—Tikal, Tulum, and Coba. Left, top to bottom: head of the god of number 7, Tikal; diving god at Tulum similar to those at Coba; prisoners beneath feet of personage, Stela 1, Coba. Right: design on Stela 20, Coba.

little bumps on a road show up in the headlights of a car. Mist hung in the depressions, further accentuating the unevenness of the treetop roof. Essentially it was the view the high priest of Coba must have seen when he watched for the rising of the morning star and then the sun, save that then the pyramids and courts in the foreground would have been plainly visible in their sharp geometric shapes, not, as we saw them, as gentle swells in the forest. I have sometimes thought that one reason for the great height of Maya pyramids was to get above the mist which often must have hindered astronomical observations at a lower level.

Gradually the eastern sky took to itself a faint red glow. Then a single ray, like a searchlight beam, shot above the low-banked cloud on the horizon, and Lord Kin, the sun, had once more emerged from the land of the dead for his march across the sky.

It was the start of a propitious day. On the way to work we disturbed two ocellated turkeys, which flew off with a great whirring of wings, and a covey of chachalacas (*ortulis vetula*) filled the forest with their shrill calls. The men discovered two new stelae, one of which had fallen face down. When we managed to turn it, we found the sculptured figure in almost perfect condition (Fig. 9). Unfortunately, the top left corner, which would have given the date of the dedication, was missing.

Soon we were jogging along the Yaxuna causeway again—for me the eighth time. We stopped at Chulutan for the night, but the many fleas and a fair number of mosquitoes decided us to get up about 1:30 and continue our journey, as the moon was full. Our muleteer tied a hurricane lamp on the first and last mules of the train, and with our ship's lights for the darker patches of forest which the moon did not penetrate, we rode sleepily on.

Valladolid was sizzling in midday heat. We caught the afternoon train by the skin of our teeth and with a couple of bottles of rum to celebrate our return to civilization. Both Carmen and Eugenio, who had had a few on their own in Valladolid, were pretty happy by the time the train reached Dzitas. That evening we went to a *jarana* dance in Piste, but we weren't sorry to leave early after a day which had started at 1:30 A.M. Next morning Vay told us that after we left the dance he had run into Carmen as drunk as an owl. Vay asked him how much he had had. *"Pues, solamente una copita, Do'tor,"* "Only a liqueur-glass full, doctor." It must have replenished itself as miraculously as the widow's cruse of oil.

My first trip to Uxmal and the chief ruins of the Puuc, the foothills south of Merida, was also in 1926. During Easter week the Maya do not work, although apart from celebrations of the church, formal Christianity sits lightly on them. The party comprised the junior archaeologists—Ruppert, Vaillant, and myself—Jean Charlot, and Herbert Spinden, the great authority on Maya art who was on a busman's holiday in Yucatan.

Now, there is a good road to Uxmal and one makes the comfortable journey in about an hour and a half. Then, it was necessary to take train to Ticul at the foot of the hills and take mules from there next day. However, we persuaded the owners of two dilapidated Model-T Fords to take us, and they were, I rather think, the first cars ever to make the trip. Ticul is a largish Maya town, but it was difficult to find accommodation. I found two trees in a garden between which I fastened my hammock; the others slept in a crowded room.

Ticul is the home of the last of the Xiu "royal family." According to Maya historical writings (the books of Chilam Balam) Uxmal was founded by the Xiu and was ruled by them until the fall of Mayapan. The Xiu were one of the chief ruling families at the time of the Spanish conquest, but they appear to have been of Mexican descent. The trouble is that Uxmal is a Classic period site, whereas, according to the written chronicles, the Xiu founding and occupation fell after the end of the Classic period, and the family did not abandon Uxmal until the fall of Mayapan, a scant eighty years before the arrival of the Spaniards, when they moved to Mani, only some twenty miles from Ticul. I think that the best explanation is to suppose that the Xiu occupied Uxmal after it was abandoned (surface sherds indicate a late ephemeral occupation contemporaneous with the Itza rule at Chichen), and played the fact that it fell in their territory for all the historical kudos they could get out of it. I have never had much sympathy for them; they betrayed their fellow-countrymen and sided with the Spanish invaders.

Morley spent much time in expanding a genealogical tree, made about 1560, of the Xiu family, and, with a long gap, carried it from about A.D. 1000 to the present day, but the gap covers the first four hundred years of their history. In *The Ancient Maya* he writes at length of the decline and fall of the family from rulers to obscure milpa workers at the present time, and tells us of the wedding of the last in line, Dionisio Xiu, at which he and Mrs. Morley stood godparents to the royal scion, the thirty-ninth generation from the founder of the dynasty according to his reconstruction.

I have an appendix to add to the story, a letter, four years after his marriage, to Morley, which in translation (the Spanish is poor and lacks accentuation) reads as follows:

DIONISIO XIU
225 22nd Street
TICUL   October 10, 1944

SR. SILVANUS MORLEY
HACIENDA CHEN KU
MERIDA

ESTEEMED GODFATHER—

In saluting you with my usual affection, I wish to inform you that I have had troubles with the authorities [here] which arose because your goddaughter [i.e., his wife] abandoned our home on September 7th.

The reason for the upset is that she wants us to go and live with my mother-in-law, but that doesn't suit me. As we reached no agreement, the authorities made me hand over her chattels [*trastes*, a rather derogatory term]. Besides, I am paying four pesos a week for the support of the children.

I have thought of divorcing her—and of this I now inform you—because all her relatives are against me [especially] her aunt and her father who has taken the girl into his house and does not wish her to continue with me. Please receive my affectionate wishes [undecipherable word] of my papa and mamma.

Your godson who loves you
DIONISIO XIU

A somewhat pathetic letter. At that time four pesos were worth about thirty-five cents, hardly royal alimony. Poor Dionisio doesn't seem to be of the stuff of his fighting ancestors.

Reverting to our trip, three hours' ride next morning brought us from Ticul to Uxmal, but it was no picnic. At times we had to get out to remove boulders or lift the cars over rock ledges on the road.

Uxmal is one of the most impressive Maya cities. There are not many standing buildings—seven or eight—but those that are in good shape are superb and their loose grouping most picturesque. The site is even more spectacular now than in 1926; Mexican archaeologists have done a wonderful job of restoring damaged buildings, replacing fallen stones, and clearing up the mess inseparable from ruins.

The buildings, of the second half of the Classic period, are constructed in the beautiful Puuc style of veneer masonry, to which I have already referred, the thin slabs fitting together like tiles. The great pyramid of the Dwarf or the "Adivino," as it is also called, rises like a man-made volcano from the plain, and its very steep stairways on either side are best climbed on all fours. How the bodies of victims sacrificed before the temple on top must have hurtled down them to the waiting crowds below! Three hundred yards off, on a high platform stands the "House of the Governor," although there are no grounds for supposing any

governor ever resided there. The upper façade, for the whole
326-foot length of the building, is decorated with an intricate design of undulating lines of masks of the rain gods imposed on
bold *grecques* and lattice work and with writhing rattlesnakes
as an added complication (Plate v). There was little need for the
Spaniards to have come four thousand miles to teach the Maya
baroque.

Inside are twenty rooms. Twenty, the sacred unit in the Maya
vigesimal system—coincidence or symbolism?

With reluctant relief one moves to the nearby House of the
Turtles, a gem of a building with decoration confined to engaged
columns in the upper façade and a line of well-spaced realistic
turtles on the upper cornice. The plan suggests an earlier date than
the "House of the Governor," but what a people capable of such
extremes of exuberance and austerity!

The Monjas, "Nunnery," quadrangle with its four buildings set
around a quadrangle (Plate v) I have described in my *Rise and
Fall of Maya Civilization,* but there was something the significance
of which I and every other Maya archaeologist have overlooked.

Uxmal was abandoned about A.D. 1080, a trifle later than the
close of the Classic period to the south. The Franciscan Alonso
Ponce found the site in ruins and thickly wooded when he visited
it in 1588, the very year of the armada.

In 1951, Mexican archaeologists, completing a magnificent job
of repairing the Monjas, removed debris accumulated over the
nine or ten centuries since the site was abandoned, bringing to
light the dramatic find of which I am writing.

There, in the middle of the quadrangle, stones only one layer
high outlined the plan of a typical Maya domestic residence such
as was being used by persons of no particular consequence in the
centuries immediately before the coming of the Spaniards. It
consisted of a single room just over fifty feet long and twelve
feet wide with a sleeping bench at each end. The walls had once

been of poles, with the spaces between perhaps plastered over; the roof of thatch. The stones outlining the room were dressed and clearly had been robbed from buildings in the vicinity. A few of them, shaped as short balusters, were identical with carved stones in the medial cornice of the east range of the Monjas. One can't say definitely that they came from that particular building, but it is extremely probable that they did; the builder of this unpretentious hut, one can feel reasonably sure, just walked across the court and picked up some stones that had fallen when the building started to decay. He certainly was not impressed by his surroundings, for he made his home face away from the towering mass of the pyramid of the Adivino, hardly more than 120 yards away. It may well be that he was unimpressed because already forest cut off his view of it.

It is not known precisely when this hut was built, but some sherds from the surface of the quadrangle, which must therefore be later than the main occupation, date from the tenth to twelfth centuries. This is not the only case of this sort at Uxmal; another hut had been set down haphazard on the terrace before the House of the Governor, and there are others.

These unspectacular relics of squatters at Uxmal, who, so to speak, thumbed their noses at the greatness of their past, so completely exemplify the decline of Maya culture that one could hardly ask for a better illustration. In terms of our own culture, imagine Rome in ruins and the discovery of a squalid tenement building set in St. Peter's piazza with its back to the fallen basilica of St. Peter and with fragments of Michelangelo's dome incorporated in its walls.

Next morning we left Ticul by another road, as rough as that which we had followed the previous day, to visit Kabah, a large site with one strange building, the whole façade of which is covered with masks of the rain god—originally about 270 of them—a depressing sight a trifle like that occasionally produced by huge pyramids of cans of salmon in a shop window. There is a strange feature inside. From the outer room yet another mask forms a step up to the inner one; the tip of the curled snout is the first step, the root of the snout, the second, and the top of the mask, flush with the inner floor, the third. Somehow the building left me with an impression of evil.

From there we drove to Sayil. The other car broke an axle; ours lost the way, and we followed tracks which petered out in a milpa. Spinden, who was in our car, sang the *cucaracha* song the whole way, but as the only word of it he knew was *cucaracha* and the rest was *tum tum tum*, it was not too good for our nerves.

The whole party reached Sayil shortly before dark. The main feature is an enormous three-story "apartment house" with a broad flight of stairs leading to the top floor. There must be over one hundred rooms, many of which had collapsed. We slung our hammocks in well-preserved ones, tying them to the old wooden poles which traversed the vault space. My room was ideally situated, for there was a fine view through the triple entrance separated by graceful circular columns which supported the stone lintels. The gentle breeze eddied intermittently around my hammock, but romance was banished when one of the chauffeurs, who had put his hammock next to mine, made the night hideous with the loudest snoring it has even been my lot to endure.

Next morning we toured the site, feeling rather dirty as there was no water supply and the little we had brought had to be kept for drinking and the radiators of the cars. After a stop at the ruins of Maler Xlabpak, we drove to Sabacche, a small settlement with a Maya ruin and a famed well. According to a widely held belief, a hat thrown into the well will be immediately blown out again by the strong current of uprushing air. No one volunteered a hat, so the belief couldn't be tested, but the current did not seem strong enough to lift duck's down, let alone a good-sized hat.

Our last stop was Labna, a large city with an imposing corbeled gateway as its chief attraction. There are similar gateways at Kabah, Mayapan, and Uxmal, and I excavated the foundations of another at Chichen Itza. Like the triumphal arches of Rome, they could have served no utilitarian purpose.

That evening, in Ticul, we went to see the Holy Week procession of the Stations of the Cross. The packed church presented a most impressive spectacle. At the front knelt crowds of black-shawled Maya women, whose ancestors had probably worshiped at Uxmal, Kabah, or Labna. Many held candles which threw queer shadows on the white walls. At the back stood the men, their neat white vests and trousers contrasting with the black shawls. Probably among them stood Dionisio Xiu's father, for Xius were no longer at the front of things. Children were everywhere, but unlike European children under somewhat similar conditions, they stood immobile by their mothers, awed perhaps by the solemnity of a great occasion in the cycle of this once alien religion, which had been rewoven into the warp of their old paganism to produce a new cloth which partook of both.

Next day we returned to Merida and thence back to work at Chichen Itza.

3

Lubaantun, British Honduras

EARLY IN 1927 I joined a British Museum party to excavate in British Honduras, that small piece of land bitten out of the peninsula of Yucatan, going first to Belize, the lively seaport capital. (Not long after this was written came news of its almost complete destruction by hurricane.) In its English speech, largely Negro population, and wooden frame houses it differed markedly from any city in the Spanish republics. The place has a stirring past, having originated as a hide-out of buccaneers, for the coast is screened by a fringe of little coral islands and stands of mangrove busily building more land. There the buccaneers could careen their ships and wait their opportunities to pillage. St. George, one of these little cays, as they are called, was once the center of the settlement, but the inhabitants must have spread to the mainland from the beginning, for St. George's Cay is minute.

To this day families on one cay claim descent from Sir Henry Morgan, the greatest of all buccaneers; whether they have Sir Henry's blood in their veins or not, they certainly have none of his treasure in their pockets, although there are perpetual reports of clues to treasure buried on the cays by the pirates—pardon, buccaneers. The name Belize is generally believed to be a corruption of "Wallace," a local buccaneer of some (ill?) repute, but it probably has a Maya origin: like other towns in Central America it probably took its name from the river on which it stood; *beliz* in

Yucatecan Maya means muddy or muddy-watered, a true description of the river during much of the rainy season.

When buccaneering no longer paid, Belize became a little settlement of logwood cutters, for logwood, source of a valuable dye before the advent of synthetic dyes, grows in abundance in the swamps in the interior. Mahogany also became a valuable product, and Honduras mahogany has few rivals. The settlement was a thorn in the Spanish flesh, and forces were sent at one time and another to eject the settlers.

During the years I worked in the country, the "noble experiment" of prohibition was still limping along in the United States, and Belize, relishing a whiff of its buccaneering past, developed as a great rum-running center. At the height of the trade, a dozen or more auxiliary-engined schooners, built on the Bay Islands by descendants of the buccaneers, usually lay at anchor in the bay awaiting orders to sail for the mouth of the Mississippi, where contact was made with high-speed motorboats. It was a heartening sight for those of us who lived under prohibition.

The captains of the rum fleet were a tough but friendly lot. They spent their time ashore around a large circular table, dicing for drinks: I learned not to dice against them unless I wanted to be stuck for round after round. Belize traditionally is built on mahogany chips and rum bottles; the bootleggers certainly added their quota of the latter.

British Honduras seemed to be a magnet for "Explorers," who, after following well-beaten tracks and keeping an ear open in the bars of United Fruit Company steamers, returned to the States or England with tales of astounding adventures. I particularly enjoyed one story of a fierce encounter with an enraged iguana; it had me on tenterhooks, for an enraged iguana equals in the savagery of his onslaught the angriest rabbit. That same explorer had been at Lubaantun, the same site in southern British Honduras for which I was headed that following year. Later, having exhausted the credulity of England, he appeared on one of the national broad-casting systems in the United States. Each Sunday evening he was on the air, introduced amid the throbbing of African tomtoms as "the greatest living authority on ancient Central America."

In the course of his talks he described his life at Lubaantun, where he sat night after night repelling the attacks of prowling jaguars, which invariably bit the dust, and where the climate was so deadly that no white man could survive for more than three weeks. As I had been there on and off for months, I began to rummage around the family tree for my ancestry. He had penetrated the interior of British Honduras to discover this immense mysterious city, which in fact had been known to archaeologists and European residents since the last century and had been described in print many years before. Worst of all from an archaeological point of view, he had workers build a wall on one of the terraces to make a more impressive photograph. Later he and a collaborator wrote a book, *Land of Wonder and Fear;* to me the wonder was how he could write such nonsense and the fear how much taller the next yarn would be.

Another "Explorer" described in a well-known American magazine a terrible encounter with the "fierce" Maya of the east coast of Yucatan and how he survived the showers of deadly arrows they shot at him. Well he might, for no Maya in Yucatan has used a bow and arrow for well over a century. Another gentleman, English by birth but Californian by adoption, burst into print and on to the lecture platform with stories of having explored the impenetrable jungle of Yucatan alone save for two native guides. It turned out that he had visited Uxmal and the other sites in the vicinity, and by the time he came to explore them the roads were considerably better than when we *drove* along them. Yet another, who had visited my camp with a string of mules long enough to cross the Gobi Desert, bravely flew the flag of the Explorers Club of New York a mile from El Cayo, capital of the district of that name in western British Honduras. I could continue with such tales, but enough is enough. The shorter the visit, the taller the yarn.

Joyce of the British Museum and another member of the party had been delayed in leaving England, but Hannay, a young Canadian who had worked with Joyce the previous year, and I had orders to buy supplies, go to Lubaantun, and start work. Despite the friendly hospitality of Belize, it is a relief when all the stores are bought and one can be on the way. The governor of the colony placed his yacht at our disposal. Never before or since have I traveled in such style, and we felt pretty important as the smart *Patricia* with its equally smart crew of Beliceños steamed out of Belize harbor with us, the sole passengers, seated aft. All day we traveled south on a calm sea of deep indigo with scattered coral islands of yellow sand and bow-stemmed coconut palms. Bringing our royal prerogative into play, we bade the captain stop at one cay where we went ashore to visit its sole inhabitant, an old friend, and to have a swim.

We reached Punta Gorda in the extreme south of the country shortly before midnight, but did not go ashore till next morning. Except for two Jesuit missionaries and a couple of English families, it is a Carib town. These "Black" Caribs come from the intermarriage of runaway Negro slaves with the aboriginal Carib Indians of St. Vincent, British West Indies. They were deported by the British in the eighteenth century, following a revolt, to the Bay Islands off the coast of Honduras. From their new homes they spread to the northern coasts of Honduras and Guatemala and as far as southern British Honduras. The Negro element dominates in their physical appearance, but their native language, an absence of marked Negro features in mouth and nose, straighter hair, and their way of living distinguished them from the English-speaking "creoles" of largely Negro blood who live in Belize and the surrounding country. The Black Caribs use some French words, notably those for counting, a reminder that St. Vincent was once a French possession. They are a hard-working, intelligent group, and supply most of the local teachers. In practically every Maya village in the country I have found the schoolmaster to be a Carib, a nice example of the racial patchwork which is slowly making a national quilt. Those Carib schoolmasters—Roman Catholic to a man in contrast to the Protestantism of the Belize Negro—are keen, intelligent men with inquiring minds. From them should come the civil service which from behind its inkwells will rule the Belize moving to independence.

The Caribs, magnificent seamen, spend much of their lives at sea, leaving the cultivation of the land to their wives. They looked down (I don't know how it is today) on the Negroes of Belize as a group economically dominated by the small group of white men engaged in commerce, and owing even their language to the white man. The Belize Negro shows his superiority by fleecing the Carib on a visit to Belize with the three-card trick, fake lotteries, and varieties of the confidence game, so perhaps the two groups finish about all square.

The Toledo District, of which Punta Gorda is the not too imposing capital, has an interesting connection with the American Civil War, for there lives (or lived thirty years ago) a small group of families whose Confederate fathers or grandfathers settled here as a protest against Reconstruction. Although they had sent down representatives to "spy out the land," they can have had little idea of what they would have to face. They settled in virgin forest land in one of the wettest parts of Central America (the annual rainfall at Punta Gorda reaches ten feet). The settlement flourished after a fashion. Most of the rich soil was put under sugar or grazed. An order not unlike the plantation life the settlers had known in their old homes took root in the alien soil. There were environmental variations; Carib or coolie labor replaced the Negro slave and simple frame houses substituted for colonial mansions, but no mint juleps were served in these homes. The Toledo settlement was bone dry, and that was a chief cause of its later decay, for when the price of sugar slumped, the settlers refused to make rum, in which large profits lay.

The settlement was still picturesque when I knew it, but wore the mark of genteel decay: neglected pastures were returning to forest, for the cane was scarcely worth the cost of cutting, and the frame houses, having given up the attempt to appear old plantation homes, were down at heel. Some families had returned to the States; a few stayed, maintaining the name of the South for hospitality and courtesy.

The third element in the Toledo District was the Maya, the ruined temples of whose ancestors it was our purpose to excavate. They lived in the western part and belonged to the Mopan and Kekchi branches of that race. The former speak a dialect which resembles that of the Maya of Yucatan; the latter are descendants of Maya from the Alta Vera Paz district of Guatemala who have expanded greatly in the past century, leaving their mountains to settle in the far different environment of the lowlands of southeastern Peten and this southwestern corner of British Honduras.

We had arranged for dugout canoes from the Kekchi village of San Pedro Colombia, which lies immediately opposite the ruins of Lubaantun, to meet us about five miles above the mouth of the Rio Grande where the small Jacinto Creek enters it; above that point even the shallow-draft *Patricia* could not pass. In fact, she had some trouble crossing the shallow bar of the Rio Grande, a few miles north of Punta Gorda. That negotiated, she slowly nosed her way round the innumerable hairpin bends. The changing views of tropical vegetation unfolded in a world without movement and with that hush which overtakes the forest in the heat of noon. The bow of the *Patricia* cutting the water and the soft throb of her engines were the only movement or sound for much of the way.

Occasional herons, gray or white, skimmed along the surface on our approach, beating the river with their wings before rising above the water. At times the *Patricia's* bow hit a submerged log, the signal for a great outburst of orders, counterorders, and the clanging of bells to disengage by going astern.

At the rendezvous there was no sign of the canoes that were to meet us. I wasn't surprised, for there is usually a hitch with that kind of arrangement made without direct contact with the other party. The *Patricia* was needed in Belize, so in a few minutes we were viewing her stern from the river bank. Around us piled stores and equipment filled most of the available space, for we had been dumped in a small, damp spot, the only part free of under-growth. We were prisoners; on three sides the forest barred our progress as we had no machetes; on the fourth ran the river which we knew had a high population of alligators, and even had we taken a chance on the alligators, there was no point in swimming, for the wall of forest followed the line of the far bank.

After two or three hours in our prison we began to feel a little worried. The clearing was far from an ideal spot to pass the night. The ground was damp, and there was no room to put up mosquito nets (the place was obviously going to be alive with mosquitoes at sunset). Also we had nothing with which to make a fire. However, about two hours before sunset a large dugout, manned by two Indians, appeared. We hailed it, supposing it to be one of those we expected. It was not, but we arranged passage with the brother owners.

We slept at a little landing on the Jacinto Creek where the two Maya, Ramón and Plácido Tesecun, loaded some cargo. The night was intensely cold for the tropics, and a very heavy dew soaked our single blankets, but Ramón and Plácido suffered more since they had only a very thin cotton cloth apiece. The cold was no inducement to lie abed; we made an early start.

All day we traveled along the twisting river. Only a very rare clearing with its hut broke the forest on either side. Ramón knelt in the prow with short paddle, which terminated in a crotchet for his hand; Plácido sat on a low crosspiece in the stern with similar paddle; Hannay and I squatted amidships. Gradually, the river became shallower and small rapids appeared. Over shallows, paddles were exchanged for poles; at rapids, we jumped into the water to lift and haul the heavily overladen dugout over rock and swirling current.

Once in a while an iguana, disturbed at our approach, plunged into the water from the branch on which he had been sunning himself. If the dugout was close, Ramón, sighting the iguana in the clear water, would dive after it, but in the underwater chase it was seldom caught. The Maya regard its fat as a sovereign cure for all sorts of ailments. The meat has been compared to chicken, but I am not competent to pass judgment; the times I have eaten it the taste has been entirely drowned in chile pepper to Maya taste, or the meat had been roasted and smoked to a savorless sort of biltong or jerky.

Even the most beautiful scenery palls in time if there is little variation. The rhythmic splashing of the paddles, combined with the afternoon heat, induced in Hannay and myself an insupportable drowsiness; we could neither keep awake nor, for lack of space, stretch ourselves comfortably in the dugout. Our attempts to paddle were not welcomed by Plácido and Ramón, who indicated that the timing of our strokes was invariably a fraction of a second wrong. Remembering that I had once rowed in a college eight, although a far from good one, I relapsed into dignified inactivity.

Just before sundown we beached the canoe, where we were made welcome by a Honduranian half-caste, the owner of one of the two huts comprising the settlement. On my asking him its name, he replied, "Well, I don't really know; you see I have lived here only two years." This was a surprise to me, fresh from the

PLATE I.—Buildings at Chichen Itza. *a:* The Castillo. *b:* Temple of the Warriors after excavation. *c:* The Caracol after excavation. *(b and c, courtesy Peabody Museum, Harvard University.)*

a

b

c

PLATE II.—Sculptures at Chichen Itza. *a:* Atlantean figures. *(After T. Maler.) b:* Column with Maya warrior. *(After T. Maler.) c:* Entrance to Temple of the Warriors, showing serpent columns. *(Courtesy Peabody Museum, Harvard University.)*

b

c

PLATE III.—Buildings at Chichen Itza. *a:* Corner of façade, Temple of the Warriors. *b:* The Iglesia, a Classic period building. *c:* The Monjas, a three-story building of the Classic period. Note flat landscape. *(Courtesy Peabody Museum, Harvard University.)*

a

b

PLATE IV.—Coba. *a:* Temple of diving god. *(Photograph by T. Maler; courtesy Museo de Arqueología de Yucatan.)* *b:* Half-buried vault of building. Note destructive tree roots. *c:* Stela 1, Macanxoc (Coba). *(b and c, courtesy Peabody Museum, Harvard University.)*

a

b

PLATE V.—Uxmal. *a:* The south half of the Governor's house. *b:* South wing of the Monjas with Governor's house in background. Both circa A.D. 900. (*Courtesy Norman F. Carver, Jr.*)

PLATE VI.—Maya and Their Students. *a:* Dancing the *jarana*. *b:* Carmen Chai and Eugenio Mai. *c:* Jacinto Cunil. *d:* Agustín Hob. *e:* The Morleys (Morley's sombrero smaller than usual) and the honeymooners, Chichen Itza, 1930.

PLATE VII.—San Antonio, British Honduras. *a:* Village. *b, c:* Small fry, one drying cacao beans on bark tray. *d:* Lady in working dress. *e:* Faustino Bol, bride, brother, and mother *(Courtesy Chicago Natural History Museum.)*

PLATE VIII.—Masonry and Hieroglyphs. *a, b:* Masonry, Lubaantun. Dark area at left recently uncovered. Note huge blocks of retaining wall. *c:* Altar, Mountain Cow. *(Courtesy Chicago Natural History Museum.) d:* Date 9.7.0.0.0. (A.D. 573), Pusilha. *(Courtesy British Museum.)*

Middle West, where there would have been signs to indicate the city limits, its name, and when and where the Rotary Club met, with, maybe, an invitation to get in on the ground floor at the new riverside subdivision. In Central America things are different; an expanding settlement means more people after good milpa land and more hunters after deer and agouti.

We put up our cots in the one room, and the Maya boys swung their hammocks on either side of our host and his wife, who occupied an ancient double bed in the center. Both Hannay and I, familiar with the customs of the remoter parts of Central America, felt no embarrassment at undressing and going to bed in the presence of our hostess. In truth, I was pondering how the immense double bed, symbol of civilization, could ever have been transported to this nameless settlement in the jungle. There was no road over which it could have been brought, and even in sections it would have presented a problem in transportation to the most expert paddler of a dugout canoe.

After a hasty breakfast at dawn, we started upstream once more. Our early rising was rewarded by a glimpse of a distant jaguar, who had tarried to drink at the river after his night of hunting. He was far away, and I would not have spotted him except for Plácido's cry of "*tigre!*" Turtles were common; overhead small green parrots screeched to one another. About midday we reached the junction of the Colombia River with the Rio Grande. We took the Colombia fork, and in a few hours reached the village of San Pedro Colombia.

This is a pleasantly situated village of about two hundred Kekchi-Maya, their huts stretched along the high ground on the south bank of the river. Here Plácido and Ramón had their homes, although they had been born in San Antonio, a few miles away and their language was Mopan-Maya, quite different from Kekchi-Maya. In the next few months we were to get to know San Pedro Colombia and its inhabitants very well, for the ruins were situated near the north bank of the river, a couple of hundred yards upstream.

As we passed the village, we were greeted with shy glances from numerous Kekchi ladies, who, naked except for a cotton skirt, were washing clothes on the river bank. A short way beyond the village we tied up in front of the hut of Benito Fajardo, on whose land the ruins of Lubaantun are situated.

Benito, a half-caste from the Republic of Honduras, had acted during the previous season as a kind of foreman of excavations. He was a pleasant man, although it was credibly reported that he had fled from his native country to Guatemala and thence to British Honduras to escape the consequences of a murder which he had committed.

Benito was the John D. Rockefeller of this part of British Honduras, having amassed what was in Indian eyes an immense fortune. By profession a bootmaker, he fashioned one-piece shoes, locally called moccasins, from deerskin, which he himself tanned with cedar bark. The Maya of the surrounding villages, who had recently taken to wearing shoes for special occasions, kept him busy since he had a monopoly of the local bootmaking industry.

The lady who passed as his wife had a similar monopoly in baking bread. Here Benito had showed his business ability by a campaign to break down sales resistance to wheat bread, and had persuaded many Indians to buy his bread, which they could ill afford, as a change from their eternal diet of maize tortillas.

Business genius that he was, Benito had realized the benefits of vertical organization of industry. He had bought a large dugout to fetch flour from Punta Gorda and to hire to others as a side line, while the distribution of the bread was jointly undertaken by himself and his *señora*. Emulating the great corporations he financed his sale of moccasins or bread by means of a loan department, charging extremely high rates of interest to ignorant Indians.

With the arrival of the archaeologists, Benito had extended his business to include the sale of chickens, cooked and ready to eat, eggs, and other produce. On my visit to Lubaantun two years later I found he had branched out into the dairy business. This was doing well, but he complained of being unable to persuade the Indians to wear shoes all the time. They had a bad habit, from his point of view, of carrying their shoes tied around their necks until they approached their destinations. I knew that it would have been useless to have suggested O Henry's scheme of importing cockleburs and strewing them along the paths to increase shoe sales. Benito's fertile brain would have thought of, but instantly discarded, such a scheme long ago, for he well knew that the Maya sole is too tough to suffer even after dancing over a square mile strewn with cockleburs.

With Benito's aid we had soon installed ourselves in an empty hut some twenty yards from the one he and his *señora* occupied. This was the same hut from which our explorer had shot so many jaguars and struggled with so many poisonous snakes; we found the big game confined to fleas, lizards, and Benito's over inquisitive pigs.

A walk of about three-quarters of a mile along a trail through forest and Benito's abandoned milpa brought us to the leveled-off ridge on which Lubaantun stands.

The mounds and walls were hidden under dense vegetation, between seven and eight feet high. This had grown at the almost incredible rate of nearly one foot a month, for the ruins had been free of growth when work had ceased the previous May. Indeed, Benito, like a good businessman exploiting the labor of others, had sown maize on what had once been the floor of the main court of the city. Now the dry maize stalks were smothered by a mass of secondary growth.

Lubaantun differs from the general run of large Maya cities in having no stone buildings on its pyramids and platforms, no stelae, and very little stone sculpture. So far as buildings are concerned,

Lubaantun is the easternmost of a chain of sites extending to the Pasion River which lack stone temples and palaces so far as present knowledge goes (but the newly discovered Machaquila, just north of this belt, has a stone-vaulted building). The answer to this is to regard the Maya area as a patchwork of local cultures, each with its local styles of weaving, pottery, basketry, and other peasant crafts which had probably flourished for many centuries before the imposition of a unifying hierarchic complex, represented by such items as hieroglyphic inscriptions, advanced astronomy, a complex form of vigesimal arithmetic, and a highly developed religious art.

The Mohammedan world supplies an illustrative parallel. From Morocco to Java we find Arabic script, a specialized sacred architecture, best exemplified by the minaret and horseshoe arch, and a nonrepresentational art. Yet local patterns exist. In northern Nigeria, for instance, the mosques are of mud, just as the temples at Lubaantun were undoubtedly of poles and thatch; Iranian miniatures are far from nonrepresentational; dress varies from one Moslem area to another, just as the costumes of the little pottery figurines of Lubaantun are different from those of, say, Uaxactun.

Hieroglyphic writing was known at Lubaantun, for short texts appear on three stone markers and ornamental glyphs occur on some mold-made figurines. As for temples of perishable materials, we found in debris on the summit of one pyramid a piece of plaster with the impress of a pole on the back, and other pieces lay face down, obviously fallen from a temple that once stood there. One is inclined to gauge the cultural standard of a people by what has not perished, but the Maya were not building for posterity; from the point of view of the rulers of Lubaantun, a thatched temple of perishable materials may have seemed just as good as one of stone; it certainly must have been more comfortable.

The day after arriving, Hannay and I crossed to San Pedro Colombia to recruit labor. We managed to get only eight men;

it was a bad time, for everyone was busy felling to make their milpas. Experts, like all Maya, with their cutlas-like machetes, they set to work on the secondary growth. Gradually the green tide withdrew, revealing pyramids, courts, and mound. The felled vegetation was left to dry and eventually was burned.

The main group at Lubaantun is on a low ridge, which the Maya had leveled off and built up so as to form a rough oblong about 300 yards from north to south, with a breadth in the center of about 160 yards, but tapering off at the south end. This artificially modeled hill served to support square courts of varying dimensions, around which were erected the pyramids.

Each pyramid consisted of a core of boulders surmounted by smaller stones set in mortar, and occasional layers of earth and stones. This was faced on all four sides with square or oblong blocks of an exceedingly hard crystalline limestone, little removed in texture from white marble. These blocks were finished so carefully that at a short distance they appeared as straight and even as the concrete blocks of a modern building, while their crystalline qualities caused them to reflect the rays of the tropical sun with dazzling brilliance (Plate VIII).

The pyramids gave the appearance of having staircases on all four sides, for at each double tier of limestone blocks there was a setback of about nine inches. Later in the season thousands of begonias covered the pyramids, their pinkish white flowers contrasting with the dark greens of their broad leaves. They were an enchanting sight, but we had to pull them up, for their carrot-shaped roots, lodging in the interstices between the tiers, were gradually forcing the blocks out of their alignments, and would have done much damage had they been allowed to spread unchecked.

Near the north end of the group a broad flight of steps led down to a large sunken court, about 160 yards wide and 60 yards long. This was once covered with a hard plaster floor, which tree roots had entirely destroyed, but its former existence could be deduced from small pieces of smoothed plaster scattered in the accumulated vegetation mold.

Most Maya cities have at least one such court, enclosed on all sides by pyramids and mounds. Here stelae usually stand; but, as I have already remarked, there were none at Lubaantun. Their presence in the great courts of most Maya cities indicates that here were held important religious rites, but I think, too, that in them stood the people come to witness some great religious ceremony on top of one of the bordering pyramids.

In many Maya cities the ball court (Plate xv*a*) is in or near the main court. This consisted of an alley between two mounds, the walls of which, sloping or vertical, had at their inner bases low terraces or ramps which flanked the central playing alley. At each end there might be an oblong space with its axis at right angles to the passage, giving the ground plan of the whole the appearance of two T's joined base to base. Rings of stone or wood were fixed high in the flanking walls, one on each side of the passage, and the chief object was to pass the ball through the narrow ring, but this was made extremely difficult by a rule that a player could strike the ball only with knee, hip, or buttock. It is possible that the earlier courts were without rings and the rules were different.

Early Spanish writers have left no account of the game among the Maya, but those who witnessed it among the Aztec were astonished at the speed with which it was played, and, to judge by their descriptions, the game was as fast and thrilling as ice hockey. They report that not uncommonly a player collapsed from exhaustion. It was so difficult to drive the ball through the narrow ring fixed high in each wall that a player who did so could claim as his reward the clothing and possessions of all onlookers. The early Spanish writers inform us that on those rare occasions the onlookers scrambled to get away before they were caught and, so to speak, lost their shirts on the game.

Among the Aztec and, presumably, the Maya too, great wealth was gambled on the outcome of an important game, but apart from its sporting aspect, there was an essentially religious side to the play, which was connected by legend with the sky gods. An

Fig. 10.—Ball-Court Marker, Lubaantun. Note rubber ball between players, wall of court, protective knee pads and aprons of jaguar skin. Drawn from a photograph of very weathered stone. Not all detail certain.

Aztec player spent the night before an important game in vigil, praying to the different gods of gaming for victory and invoking the help of the glove and hip pad he would use in the contest, placing them on his family altar and burning copal incense in their honor.

In the great court of Lubaantun there are two parallel mounds, which, with the passage between, may have served as a ball court, but, as pointed out in the chapter on Coba, it was then believed that the game was not played by the earlier Maya of the Classic period. Consequently, we did not think to excavate those mounds.

There is, however, another pair of parallel mounds at the south end of Lubaantun, and down the center of the passage between had been set three circular stones. Their tops, flush with the ground, had been carved with pairs of ball-game players with the large rubber ball between them and the wall of the court as a backdrop. Markers of this type (Fig. 10) have been found in the playing alleys at other sites (Plate IXb); it is possible they marked a line down the center which had something to do with the rules of the game, a kind of offside, for in Mexican paintings of ball courts a line often runs down the center of the court. The puzzling thing about this court at Lubaantun—in view of the markers it is difficult to reject the identification—was that the enclosing walls were neither vertical nor sloping as in other courts, but stepped-back like steep stairways. In such a court play would have been even more difficult with the ball deflected off the steps at every conceivable angle.

However, the same stepped sides characterize the ball court at the great Zapotec site of Monte Alban, in Oaxaca, which, like that of Lubaantun, is steep-sided. At Monte Alban enough of the stucco-covered cement surface remains to show that it was sloped, and the steps probably served as anchorage for the steep slope (though conceivably steps were later converted to a slope). It is likely that the same was true of the Lubaantun court, but roots and weather destroyed all the conjectured slope of small stones in mortar with stuccoed surface, for the Lubaantun court was more exposed.

The court was well situated at the south end of the site, handy for a swim at the close of play. Doubtlessly, too, the ancient Maya, after the grilling labor of pyramid building or at the close of a long day of religious exercises, wandered down to bathe in the river as happily as did their descendants, who, a thousand years later, were engaged by us as laborers.

On the south side of the great court a wide and imposing flight of stairs leads to a narrow passage flanked on each side by pyramids reaching to a height of some forty feet. Work on one of these revealed an earlier pyramid inside it. As I have said, the covering of one pyramid with another was a common Maya practice.

A strange feature of this practice is that the worked stones forming the face of the earlier pyramid were almost always left in position within the core of the superimposed structure. As facing of stone blocks must have involved much labor for the Maya, who had only picks and hammers of stone at their disposal, one would expect that they would have removed the retaining walls of the buried pyramid to face the new one. Reluctance to employ secondhand materials for their temples was not the reason, for carved blocks torn from their original positions were frequently reused in the walls of some later temple. Probably it was thought that removal of the facing of a pyramid would weaken the solidity of the interior core of rock and rubble and so create an unstable base for the new pyramid to be erected over the old.

Earl Morris has shown that the pyramidal cores of the Warriors were erected in cubic units, and he has very plausibly suggested that each of these units, or cubic blocks, of boulders and rubble was the task allotted to a specific gang of laborers. In fact, there is confirmatory evidence from other Maya cities that the pyramids were not built in horizontal layers, constructed one at a time, but by independent vertical blocks, such as Morris describes.

Probably the whole peasant population from the surrounding country was forced to labor four to six months a year in pyramidal construction. It has been calculated that the average Maya today spends about six months a year on his milpa; therefore his predecessor would have had plenty of time for the labor corps.

One pictures a constant stream of men, women, and children carrying rock and rubble to the scene of building operations. No doubt strong men carried, with the aid of tumplines across their foreheads, those huge rocks, weighing up to one hundred pounds apiece, that are common in the heart of a pyramid; to the older men, the women, and perhaps even the children, would have been assigned the smaller rocks.

Lubaantun must have presented a scene of great animation when one of the larger pyramids was being built. Apart from the assembling of the great mass of stone and rubble for the core, limestone blocks, for the facing, had to be quarried and cut to the required shapes. Furthermore, great quantities of lime were required for the preparation of stucco, with which nearly every Maya building or pyramid was once covered, and for making the mortar used to bind the exterior shell of cut stone to the core.

The slaking of this lime, in turn, involved the labor of cutting with stone axes the great quantities of green wood required for the circular open-air lime kilns used by the Maya. Stout beams of the hard sapodilla tree had to be hewn for lintels of buildings and the fan leaves of the *guano* palm had to be collected and bundled ready for thatching the simpler wooden structures; other trees, such as logwood and brazilwood, had to be felled for the extraction of dyes needed for painting stucco surfaces.

After the site had been cleared, we set our Kekchi to constructing a bush hut for our use; the hut by the river, of which we were in temporary possession, was required by Benito for housing his hogs! It had previously served this purpose, as the quantities of vermin clearly attested. Perhaps our visiting pigs had been homesick, not inquisitive.

We might have been watching Maya workmen of a thousand years ago. The Kekchi had abandoned the ancient loincloth for white cotton trousers and a short shirt which they wore with the tails outside the trousers, but the technique of house building was unchanged. As their ancestors had done since time immemorial, our Kekchi boys first planted the corner post, and then, placing the crossbeams in position, erected the roof before building the walls. Every few minutes the workers disappeared into the nearby forest, some to return with loads of palm leaves, others with lianas for tying purposes. Indeed, our hut was built without the use of a single nail, for in every case where we would use a nail, the Maya tied with peeled lengths of liana or strips of pliant bark.

Our new hut was set in the ruins, in a small court a short stone's throw from the main court. Beyond its edge, at the back of our hut, the ground fell steeply to a small stream in a gully flanking the west side of the ruins. On the far side the sharply rising ground was covered with dense, untouched forest, from the margin of which flocks of curious parrots looked down on our camp, discussing in strident accents the curious ways of the intruders.

Like many Maya ruins, Lubaantun had the reputation of being haunted. This had its advantages, since we were quite free of mundane visitors after sunset, for nothing would induce a Maya to prowl around the site by himself after dark. Often I wandered at night through the ruins, rather hoping to meet the ghost of some Maya priest of the past; he might have given me the meanings of some of the many untranslated hieroglyphs, but I was invariably disappointed, and, anyhow, that would be too much like peeping at the solution while doing a cross-word puzzle.

For our Carib cook, Alfredo, we had built a small cook-house alongside our hut, but on the first evening in our new quarters Alfredo appeared in a very nervous condition, explaining that he couldn't sleep alone. He was so scared of the ghosts that he was determined to return to his home next day if he was made to sleep alone. He was lazy and a very indifferent cook, and both Hannay and I would cheerfully have seen him go, except that it would have been extremely difficult to procure a successor in the neighborhood. For this reason we decided to allow him to sleep in our hut until his flimsy cook-house could be shifted closer to our hut.

The days were hot, but at night a cool breeze from the Caribbean blew across the ruins. Then my greatest pleasure was to wander off by myself after dinner and climb to the top of one of the pyramids. The silence was broken only by the unforgetable sound of the soft rustling of the great fronds of the cohune palms in the breeze. A dozen centuries ago some Maya priest-astronomer probably watched from that point of vantage the stars plowing across the dark celestial seas. Perhaps, like his Aztec colleagues, he compared the vault of heaven to an inverted gourd as he noted night by night the erratic approach of a planet to that cluster of stars known to us as the Pleiades, but imagined by him as the rattle of a rattlesnake. Lacking any precise instrument of observation and practically dependent on the naked eye, he must have owed his successes to the exercise of a patience which comes hard to us. On many a night his observations must have been frustrated by the piled-up clouds of the rainy season, while at other times he must have awaited eagerly the rising sun to warm his dew-soaked body or the dawn breezes to drive away the too attentive insects.

Time has constantly inverted his hourglass since that astronomer was gathered to his fathers, and the court where our hut stood now echoed to our gramophone, and a gasoline lamp shone in place of the flickering illumination of a pine torch. The beams of the wooden temples had rotted away, but on cloudy nights the croaking chorus of frogs still chanted for rain or the breezes, that sent the clouds scuttling, harped on the cohune palms the triumph of fair weather.

Romance was nocturnal; by day we had labor troubles. Our Kekchi laborers from San Pedro Colombia did not prove very satisfactory for the hard work of excavation. Gradually we replaced them with Mopan-Maya from the village of San Antonio, about six miles southwest of the ruins. These Mopans, racially and linguistically first cousins of the Maya of Yucatan, were healthier and certainly very much more friendly.

Each Saturday, drawing their week's wages, they went home to San Antonio, returning to the ruins early each Monday with supplies for the whole week. The provisions consisted of an enormous pile of flat, round maize cakes, known as tortillas, or the twice-cooked variety, *totopostes*, a bag of ground maize for making a drink called *posole*, black beans, a large heap of very hot chile peppers, and, occasionally a small piece of pork, venison, or agouti meat. Each package of food was carefully wrapped in large banana-like leaves. These supplies, together with a henequen hammock, a change of clothes, and a small cotton blanket, were carried in a net bag supported on the back by means of a tumpline passed across the forehead.

Each laborer was paid a dollar and a quarter a day and such extras as he might earn by important finds. To encourage careful digging, I paid in my various digs in British Honduras forty cents to one dollar for a pottery vessel reported to me but left untouched in the ground, but if the discoverer broke the vessel or, excavating the vessel himself, broke it while doing so, his reward was halved; if it broke when I dug it out (many were already cracked and held together only by the surrounding earth), the reward was still the full amount. This also insured that information on its position in relation to floors or burials, etc., was not lost, for such are the data the archaeologist needs. The men worked in gangs of two, or sometimes four, one with shovel or spade, while the pick man rested, turn about. Naturally the smaller the number of men working, the better the supervision. Knowing the nature of the area to be excavated, one can use about ten laborers efficiently, but this means that half will be working in areas, such as stairways or the cores of pyramids, where chances of finds are not great and supervision can be reduced to a visit every ten minutes or so, leaving more time for close supervision of important work.

Careful workers, of course, are assigned to the places where prospects of good finds seem best, but things often work the other way, and, much to my disgust, the laziest and most careless workers seem invariably to make the most important finds. Some Maya workers are intelligent and careful in their work; others, if left without constant supervision, blunder through floors and walls or mix up sherd lots with heart-breaking carelessness.

Many of the boys from San Antonio could speak a certain amount of English, while practically all of them spoke Spanish with varying degrees of proficiency, but most of the women could not or, from shyness, would not speak anything but Maya. That the Maya mastery of English was not very good is illustrated by the startling reply to an inquiry about an acquaintance in San Antonio. "We throw him in the mud," was the reply; that is, he had been placed in the ground, indicating that he had died and been buried.

Our workers were reluctant to receive payment in anything larger than a dollar bill, and infinitely preferred payment in silver or nickel. In the villages it was extremely difficult to change even a quarter; consequently, we were forced to provide ourselves with immense quantities of five- and ten-cent pieces. Heavy as these were, one could at least be thankful that the old Maya custom of employing cacao beans as currency had fallen into disuse.

Neither in the Kekchi village of San Pedro Columbia nor in San Antonio were there any shops, although one or two of the more enterprising inhabitants occasionally had small stocks of matches, candy, or contraband rum for sale at exorbitant prices.

From our camp in the ruins we sometimes caught the sound of a conch shell being blown in San Pedro. This was to signal that someone had shot a deer or killed a hog and there was meat for sale. Conch-shell trumpets were used by the ancient Maya for signaling, in dances and in war, and they sometimes turn up in the excavations. The tip of the shell is sawed off and the blower applies the resulting hole to the corner of the mouth, holding the shell sideways. There is quite a knack in blowing a conch trumpet, but once it is acquired, one can make the sound travel over very considerable distances.

After we had been established about a couple of weeks at the ruins, Hannay left for Punta Gorda and thence for Belize to meet Joyce, of the British Museum. Hannay's departure meant that I was forced to depend on the uninteresting Alfredo for social intercourse after working hours, for the Kekchi seemed to resent our presence in their huts.

About ten days later, Joyce arrived by the overland route from Punta Gorda, a much quicker route than by river. He was accompanied by Cooper Clark, a student of Mexican hieroglyphic and picture-writing books. Cooper Clark had spent many years in Italy and spoke Italian to our Maya workers, on the grounds that Italian and Spanish are not very different, but his Italian orders to the men, some of whom were not too good with their Spanish, produced ludicrous scenes of misunderstanding.

With Joyce's arrival we were able to increase the number of workers, for the funds at my disposal had been too limited to hire many men, even had it been possible to supervise them. In fact, I had met the pay roll for the week before Joyce's arrival with I.O.U.'s—probably the first occasion of their use in Maya history. The men were divided into three groups of about nine each. Clark took charge of one gang, Hannay of another, and I of the third; Joyce mapped.

My workers were all Mopan-Maya from San Antonio. One of them, Pedro Tesecun, had been the first San Antonio Maya to apply for work. He stood about five feet, three inches in his bare feet and looked about fifteen; in fact he was twenty-three and father of a son of seven and a daughter of four.

He and his wife arrived one day when Hannay and I were just sitting down to lunch. We exchanged greetings, discussed the chances of rain, and then fell silent. The Indian seldom comes straight to the point, and often you wait half an hour for the object of the visit to be broached. We knew, and he knew that we knew, that he had come to ask for work, but for about twenty minutes the pair of them squatted on their heels with their backs against the side of the hut, watching us eat and later listening to a tune or two played on the gramophone for their benefit.

Occasionally they exchanged comments in Maya on our food or our clothing scattered about the hut, until the moment was judged ripe for raising the question of work.

Pedro was no believer in the equality of the sexes. He admitted quite freely that, although very fond of his wife, he beat her if she was disobedient. He had first beaten her after they had been married about three weeks and had continued to do so about once a month. The week before Easter he told us he would not be coming to work that week. He and a friend had decided to go to Punta Gorda, twenty-five miles away, to buy fifteen half-bottles of rum so that he and a few friends could celebrate the Easter festival. It has always been the Maya custom to get drunk on great religious occasions, and I knew it would be useless to remonstrate with him on the senselessness of throwing away two or three weeks' wages on as many nights of carousal.

"Will your wife also get drunk?" I asked him, for many women join their husbands in these celebrations.

"No!" he replied in broken Spanish, "She earn no money, she drink no rum."

She worked almost without stopping every week end, preparing fresh tortillas to last him through the coming week at the ruins, washing his clothes, and darning the neat patches on his vest and trousers, but there was no cash attached to that work and no rum.

Hannay's gang was composed of Spanish-speaking half-castes. One of them, Nicolás, a barber before he moved to San Pedro, where there was no outlet for his skill, was to cut my hair. When I arrived to keep the appointment, I found he had been celebrating the Easter holiday with the enthusiasm more associated with a New Year's Eve. Nevertheless, he insisted that he was perfectly sober and quite capable of cutting my hair. With some misgivings that he was as capable of cutting my ear, I sat in the chair. He displayed a remarkable steadiness with his scissors and didn't once jab me, as I had more than half expected. It was only when he drew a razor and, with a flourish worthy of some ancestor drawing his Toledo blade, indicated that he was ready to shave me that I decided I could try my luck once too often.

Hannay and I used to call sometimes on another Spanish-speaking family in San Pedro called Requena; the Kekchi were not socially minded and visits to the Spanish-speaking families were a pleasant relaxation. Nicolás, having exhausted other topics of conversation, abruptly asked me what I thought of Dominga, Requena's wife. Incautiously, for there were quite a number of people loafing around, I replied that I thought that she was very good looking. Whereupon Nicolás whispered in a hoarse voice audible to every one of the onlookers: "I was sure you admired her. Pay her a visit this evening. Her husband has gone to Punta Gorda and won't be back till tomorrow."

The Spanish have a saying *"pueblo chico: infierno grande"*; in paraphrase, "the smaller the town, the busier the devil," which often refers to gossip and tale-bearing. Our innocent visits, passing from mouth to mouth, had grown into the intrigues of Don Juans. Some of those who had heard the remark would, I knew, pass it on to Dominga's husband on his return, and he was fiery tempered and quick to draw his machete for a fight. With Requena's sharp machete in my mind's eye, I hastily replied in a voice that would reach everyone that my friendship and respect for him were such that I wouldn't dream of visiting his hut when he was not present.

The next time I met the absentee husband I got a dirty look, but that was infinitely preferable to the prospect of running through the village with an irate half-caste, complete with drawn machete, at my heels. In real adventure books the hero sends the villain's blade spinning into a bush with a flick of his wrist, but that trick was not in the curriculum when I studied archaeology, and, anyhow, the villain's part would have been mine had I followed Nicolás' advice.

Excavations brought to light many little pottery whistles with a mouthpiece and two finger holes. They carried on the front scenes which illustrated the daily life, clothing, and customs of the ancient inhabitants. Some showed chiefs being carried in litters, seated sideways with feet dangling over the side; one had on it a kneeling Maya woman grinding maize on a metate (grinding stone), while another portrayed a hunter giving the *coup de grâce*

FIG. 11.—Drummer. This type of upright drum appears also in Mexican pictures. Mural at Bonampak.

with a stone knife to a wounded deer. An extensive series of headdresses, usually decked with feathers, surmounted most of the heads, while the original molds in which the miniature portraits were cast had been so carefully made that even the patterns on women's skirts were plainly recognizable.

The commonest type showed a man wearing a visor which faintly resembled those worn by knights in armor and usually with one hand in a glove. Occasionally a pair of visored figures faced each other on the same whistle plaque in attitudes that suggested dancing or some game. These figures represented players in the ball game, the visor protecting the player's face from being hit by the ball. The glove on one hand was not for striking the ball, for the rules of the game did not allow that, but served to protect the hand when the player threw himself to the ground or against the side walls to take a difficult shot on the hip.

These figurine whistles, seldom more than four inches high, among other things served as children's toys, for later I found a number in children's graves in the ruins of San Jose, about eighty-five miles north of Lubaantun. However, at Lubaantun they are so plentiful and, in most cases, so well executed that they may have been used in religious dances and kindred ceremonies. We also came upon parts of the pottery molds in which they had been made.

As I have said, the main group of ruins at Lubaantun was situated on the leveled-off top of a hill. Part of the east side of this hill was held in position by a series of terraces, the walls of which were composed of limestone blocks of great size. The largest of these was over five feet long and one foot high, and must have weighed somewhere in the neighborhood of half a ton. Many other blocks were almost as large (Plate viiia).

The moving and placing in position of such heavy and unwieldly blocks must have presented a very serious problem, but these blocks at Lubaantun were mere paperweights in comparison with some of the stelae erected at Quirigua, one of which weighs no less than sixty-five tons.

Peter Martyr, whose account of the New World and its conquest by the Spaniards was written early in the sixteenth century, has a paragraph on the methods employed by the Aztec in transporting the great wooden beams they used in their buildings, and a very similar method was undoubtedly used by the Maya, except that they had no copper tools at the time Quirigua, Lubaantun, and the other great cities of the south were built. In the English edition, published in 1612, the account reads as follows:

> With their Copper Hatchets, and Axes cunnyngly tempered, they fell those trees, and hewe them smooth, taking away the chyppes that they may more easily be drawne. They have also certayne hearbes [agave], with the which, in steed of broome, and hempe, they make ropes, cordes, and cables: and boaring a hole in one of the edges of the beame, they fasten the rope, then sette their slaves unto it, like yoakes of oxen, and lastly in steede of wheele, putting round blocks under the timber, whether it be to be drawne steepe up, or directly downe the hill, the matter is performed by the neckes of the slaves, the Carpenters onely directing the carriage. After the same manner also, they get all kind of matter fitte for building, and other things apt for the use of manne.

This suggests that the Maya used blocks and manpower in moving the stones from the quarries, but their erection was another matter. Since they were unacquainted with the wheel, they could not have blocks, tackle, and pulley wheels, but probably obtained leverage by passing ropes or bark strips over the polished surface of a log raised on a scaffolding above the position to be occupied by the stone that was being moved, for they use that method today.

The excavation of even a small section of these terraces at Lubaantun was a lengthy business, as an enormous mass of debris from the collapsed structures above had buried the terraces completely, but the clearing of a section was well worth the effort, as it gave us an idea of the original appearance of the city. When viewed from some of the scattered mounds to the east, the site must have presented an extremely imposing spectacle with steep terraced sides surmounted by pyramids crowned with wooden temples, the thatched roofs of which must have stood almost 110 feet above the foot of the terraced hillside. The Maya, however, lost one opportunity for dazzling splendor by covering the beautifully cut crystalline stone with dull stucco, but perhaps that is a question of taste. After all, the Greeks thought their statuary improved by painting.

4

A Wild Goose Chase and Pusilha

THE FOUNDERS OF SAN ANTONIO, which supplied most of our labor at Lubaantun, had moved there from San Luis in Guatemala in the nineties of the last century. One of the old men at San Antonio told me that when he was a boy at San Luis, some fifty years before, ruins about ten miles from the town had been discovered by a Maya when clearing forest to plant maize. The village schoolmaster, the only non-Maya in the town, with the aid of himself and other boys had succeeded in turning over a number of very large stones which had fallen with their sculptured faces downwards. My Maya friend said that he remembered having seen carvings of eagles on several of them. Now, many of the Maya stelae carry sculptured figures of men or deities with gorgeously plumed headdresses which might easily be mistaken for eagles by a young boy.

The scent was not particularly fresh after fifty years, but the information suggested a good chance of an archaeological strike, so with Joyce's permission I decided to see whether I could find them. Obviously, the site had reverted to forest, but there was a good chance hunters might know of it, and the Maya have an uncanny knack of locating any such feature in what seems to a gringo a thousand square miles of monotonous forest where the only difference is between high ground and swamp. "Oh, yes," they will tell you, "that is near where I cut down that tree to get a hive of wild bees." It may have been ten years since they were in the vicinity, but with a little casting around, they will find just where they got the honey, and from there lead you to the place; the old needle in the haystack just isn't in it as we see the forest, but we don't have their eyes and their interests.

Faustino Bol, a young San Antoniero in my gang offered to go with me (Plate viie). He knew the trail to San Luis, as his father lived there. Karl Sapper, the German geologist and ethnologist, had made the trip from Punta Gorda to San Luis some thirty years before, but no other European had covered that route before or since to the best of my knowledge, but only because no one had occasion to do so.

To travel as light as possible, I took no bedding except a thin blanket and all the food we had between us were some tortillas, two cans of bully beef, and some sourdough scones. The distance was about fifty miles, two days' fairly strenuous going, but I had managed to get a horse. We decided to go to San Antonio in late afternoon to get an early start next day. I slept that night on the mud floor of the large hut which serves as the village *cabildo* (town hall).

We started just after daybreak after an early meal at Faustino's mother's hut. The trail joined a truck pass a mile or two from San Antonio, and this we followed. These are roads the mahogany contractors cut through the forest to get their logs to the nearest deep river. There they are kept until they can be floated to the sea on the rainy season floods. The heavy loads, drawn by tractor or, often in those days, long teams of yoked oxen, swiftly convert the unpaved roads into seas of mud when the rains start. This is partly remedied by widening to let in more sun, but the width is still too little to let in a breeze from the sides, so that in the tropical heat they are veritable furnaces. It was too much for my horse, for after two hours at a walk he collapsed under me, and from there to San Luis and back we had to lead the wretched useless animal.

From the truck pass we came into the comparatively cool shade of the forest, and, except close to two little settlements, the only ones in the whole distance, we were in virgin forest the whole way. We crossed the Rio Blanco, a raging torrent in the rainy season but then a slow-flowing stream less than five feet deep. That was just as well, for we would have had trouble getting our horse across a deeper river. Like a number of rivers in the limestone country, the Blanco disappears underground to tunnel through a hill.

We spent the night at Mohijon, a little Kekchi-Maya village of eight huts on a small hilltop. Luckily Faustino spoke Kekchi since none of the inhabitants had a good command of Spanish, for Faustino, like quite a few San Antonieros, had a remarkable command of languages, speaking Kekchi, Spanish, and a little English besides his native Mopan. A few San Antonieros were said even to know a little Carib.

Faustino arranged for us to have the inner room of one hut (sometimes a pole partition converts the Maya hut into two rooms). We went to the outskirts of the village to cut some fronds of the cohune palm. Some were for the horse, although this fare is not much relished by horses or mules; they much prefer leaves of the breadnut tree—grass, naturally, is not to be found in the forest. Other fronds Faustino slit down the central stem and arranged with the leaves inward and the split stems on each side to form simple beds. The cohune is one of the most beautiful palms, with fronds very like those of the coconut, but these are set on edge, not horizontally as in the coconut, and that gives an extra grace (Plate xiii*b*). We had stinted the supply of fronds and the stones in the earth floor had no difficulty in making themselves felt. This, as well as the cold, for Mohijon is high, and overweariness gave me a wakeful night.

The family on the other side of the pole partition didn't go to bed at all. Indeed, half the settlement was there, and there were comings and goings all night, and when dawn at last came, they were still there. I wondered whether possibly they could be frightened of us, although we had no weapons but our machetes. Yet there had been no drinking party or celebration to account for the all-night session. It transpired that the owner of our hut had been ill for some time, and as ordinary remedies had not availed, he had spent the night in vigil, a common Maya practice for sickness, before the maize is sown, and at the consecration of a new house. We learned that he was somewhat disappointed that we hadn't shared it with him, but as I explained to him through Faustino, I had, so to speak, been with him in spirit, since I had not slept for more than half an hour at a time. On the return journey we found our host much better; a vigil had clearly been the best treatment.

Faustino and I soon finished our breakfast of tortillas and a little corned beef washed down with a substitute coffee supplied by our host, and before sunrise we were once more in the forest.

The country was hilly, and the dense forest prevented the sun from penetrating through the foliage to the narrow path, with the result that the low parts were ankle deep in mud, and in places there were veritable swamps. Great mahogany trees towered above us, and the rough-barked sapodilla trees, from which chewing gum is obtained, were in such profusion as to make the mouth of any employer of a chewing gum company to water or, perhaps, to cause him to groan in those days of restricted production.

During the day we walked over twenty miles without seeing a single hut except at the tiny settlement of Piton, which we passed shortly after leaving Mohijon. The country was truly a hunter's paradise. We saw the spoor of tapir, deer, and peccary and the tracks of one jaguar; and in the early dawn, as we finished breakfast, we had heard the roars of bands of howler monkeys scattered in the forest that just failed to engulf Mohijon. Their deep, anguished bellows hailing the dawn epitomize for me the virgin forest, a fitting substitute for the cock crow of civilization. The more phlegmatic Maya, well acquainted with their beef-worm-scarred bodies, say that the monkeys bellow because of the pain of those beastly maggots which lodge in one's body.

Parrots screamed and chattered over our heads, and toucans, with their ridiculously large beaks, not then a symbol of Dublin stout, traveled with their slow and awkward flight from tree to tree as though they were having their first lessons in flying. Most beautiful of all were the rare trogons, first cousins of the quetzal, with delicate blue-green plumage and red breasts. An occasional break in the dense forest revealed high overhead the blazing reds, blues, and yellows of macaws against a sky blue as the Madonna's robes, while in the gloomier parts of the forest giant morpheus butterflies glided down the trail.

The elusive odor of tropical rain forest pervaded everything. It is impossible to analyze, perhaps because it is compounded of so many elements, the strengths of which vary at every pace one takes. It seems to be a potpourri of the fragrant scent of the wild pepper tree, the acrid odor of *higuera* (wild fig) leaves, the faint but not unpleasant smell of decaying tree trunks, the steamy hothouse atmosphere of damp plants unable to dry in the sun's rays, and a dozen other scents that defy explanation. The perfumed tropic breeze figures largely in romances set in those climes, but the odor of the rain forest of British Honduras and the Peten District of Guatemala, while not unpleasant, is seldom fragrant; contrary to popular belief, tropical flowers seldom possess the sweet perfumes of those in more temperate climates. For that matter, flowers are not plentiful in the rain forests. Those there are, bloom in the treetops hidden from the view of travelers far below. Bromelias and other aerial plants were everywhere.

About ten miles from Mohijon, Faustino, who was walking in

front, suddenly branched off the main trail along a scarcely visible path with the laconic explanation, "Water here." Descending a steep cliff, we suddenly came on a deep pool of clear water, from the bottom of which a few bubbles were slowly rising. This was another case of an underground river, for here the Pusilha River, after flowing some miles underground in a southerly direction, once more comes to the surface.

It was indeed a beautiful spot. The cliffs rising sharply on three sides were covered with trees shrouded in ceriman, while from the overhanging branches lianas hung down almost to the surface of the pool. A few trees had crashed from their insecure footholds on the sides of the limestone cliffs into the pool below; their waterlogged trunks resting on the clear floor of the pool provided a small shoal of *machaca* with shelter and the means of playing the fishes' equivalent of hide-and-seek.

I was sorely tempted to bathe in the pool, but as we wished to reach San Luis before sunset, we contented ourselves with a few minutes' rest. Leading our useless riding horse made our progress slower, for there were many fallen tree trunks across the trail. On foot one could scramble over them or with a few blows with a machete cut a path around them, but with a horse it was necessary to make the detour sufficiently wide and high for it to pass.

As we approached San Luis in the afternoon, the forest gradually changed. Thick patches of low bush and glades of cohune palms replaced the mahogany and the chicle-producing sapodilla trees. The smooth light-barked breadnut trees became sparse and occasional patches of grass grew beside the trail, indications that the country we were now traversing had been cultivated in recent years and that the permanent rain-forest flora had not had time to become re-established. Occasionally patches where the forest had been recently felled showed that we were now in the area in which the San Luis Indians made their milpa plantations.

Two miles from San Luis a terrific downpour soaked us to the skin. Neither of us had jackets, let alone raincoats, and there was no cabbage *(guano)* palm at hand with which to make the usual Central American substitute for an umbrella by holding over your head two or three of the large fan-shaped leaves.

In San Luis, a Mopan-Maya town of perhaps six hundred, we lodged in Faustino's father's hut, where gourds of hot *posole*, a milk-like gruel of boiled ground maize and a Maya stand-by for the past three thousand years, took a little of the chill out of our bones, for the rain, coming from the north, had caused the temperature to drop some twenty degrees. Faustino managed to borrow some dry clothes from his father, and taking off his own, offered me his wet vest to wear while my own shirt dried by the fire. Faustino was (he died many years ago), like the average Maya, about five feet, four inches tall and of small frame, but with a great effort I managed to get into his undervest; by moving my arms cautiously and taking care not to take a deep breath or throw out my chest, I succeeded in not splitting it.

A night's rest in borrowed hammocks put us in more cheerful mood when we started out next morning to tour the village. At every hut we asked if anyone knew of the ruins with the great stones. Unfortunately many of the men had gone to Punta Gorda, and none of those in the village had ever heard of any large carved stones. All we could learn was that a few miles away there was a cave containing "things of the ancients." We visited it, but found nothing more interesting than a few small pieces of coarse domestic pottery, which might have been made any time between the early Maya period and the present day. This was certainly a disappointing return for the long journey we had made. Moreover, it was almost impossible to buy maize for the horse or tortillas for ourselves, for the San Luis crop had failed and the town was very short of supplies. As we could get no information about the stelae and there was precious little for us or the horse to eat, we decided to start back next day.

San Luis, probably the chief town of the warlike Mopan-Maya until conquered by the Spaniards in 1695, had played a somewhat amusing part in the history of San Antonio, the home of most of our Maya laborers at Lubaantun. In 1883 some of its inhabitants, irked by heavy taxation, military service, and forced labor on the roads, decided to cross the frontier and settle in British Honduras. A hundred or so, including the old man—then a boy—who had told me of the stelae, migrated to British territory, settling at San Antonio.

At first the new community did not prosper; crops were bad and fever rife. A council, called to discuss matters, unanimously decided that these misfortunes were because their old patron saints, of whom the principal was San Luis (St. Louis), were too far away to be able to keep an eye on the new community, for although many of the most important members of the San Luis community had migrated to the new settlement, those who had remained in San Luis had insisted on retaining the village saints in the San Luis church.

San Antonio finally decided to raid their old home town and take the saints by force so that they might be set up in the new church at San Antonio, where they would be able to see with their own eyes all the evils that were besetting the young community and take the necessary steps to restore prosperity. Preparations, which included the purchase in Belize of a barrel of gunpowder to be used in blowing in the door of the San Luis church, if this should prove necessary, were carried out in complete secrecy.

Eventually, on the chosen day, San Antonio to a man set forth on the raid, armed with shotguns, axes, machetes, and the barrel of gunpowder. By the second evening the army had reached the outskirts of San Luis, and was safely hidden in the forest awaiting the dark. When by 9:00 P.M. San Luis in all innocence was safely asleep in its hammock, the San Antonio army advanced. Half the force was left in reserve; the other half crept into the town, and, reaching the church, soon smashed in the door with axes—the gunpowder was not needed. It was the work of a moment to seize the coveted saints and, as good measure, the church bells as well. Before the people of San Luis had thoroughly realized what was happening, the invading army was scurrying back towards San Antonio.

The return was rapid. By the following evening the saints had been installed in the little palm-thatched hut that served as the church of San Antonio, and the stolen bells chimed across the hills, summoning the inhabitants to hear the story of the bloodless rape of their loved saints.

An attempt by the outraged inhabitants of San Luis to recover their stolen saints was to be expected, but the people of San Antonio decided not to be caught sleeping. The head man of the village, officially known as the mayor, composed a letter to the governor of British Honduras to the effect that for some totally unknown reason the inhabitants of San Luis seemed to bear the good and peaceful inhabitants of San Antonio ill-will, and, according to report, were even planning to invade British territory to attack San Antonio. The letter went on to plead that the governor supply the men of San Antonio with arms with which to defend themselves against any unprovoked attack. The government at Belize, completely ignorant of what had happened, replied with the gift of a few old rifles and a consignment of lead to make bullets.

When the counterattack of the San Luiseños materialized, practically the whole male population of San Antonio was absent on a visit to Punta Gorda, but the women held off the invaders until the men could be summoned from Punta Gorda, distant eight hours' walking from San Antonio. On the arrival of the rest of the San Antonio men the San Luiseños were taken prisoners and marched to Punta Gorda, where they were released on promising not to make any further attack on San Antonio.

It was obvious that the saints preferred their new abode. Needless to say, disease abated and the crops improved once the saints were acquainted with the true state of affairs and were able to see with their own eyes the troubles that beset their flock. To this day San Antonio proudly displays to its infrequent visitors the famous saints, and when, some years ago, the visiting padre tried to replace the old and somewhat crude images with some brand new ones imported from the United States, there was almost a riot. The saints have certainly justified the devotion of their followers, for the population of San Antonio has grown from one hundred to over six hundred.

Strangely enough, saints were traveling the trail from San Antonio to San Luis when we were on our way back, for near Mohijon we met the San Luis men who had been absent in Punta Gorda during our stay in San Luis, the only people we met on the trail, going or coming. Four of them were carrying on their shoulders a large litter containing the image of a saint. This *santo* had been purchased in Guatemala City and was now on the last leg of its long journey to San Luis via Puerto Barrios and Punta Gorda. Eight men had made the long journey to the coast to fetch it to San Luis by easy stages, one group of four men bearing the litter, the other group waiting their turn to spell their comrades.

Besides the eight carriers, quite a number of fellow-townsmen had gone to Punta Gorda as a kind of reception committee, but, with an eye to business, each had purchased a case of English soap at Punta Gorda in the certain expectation of being able to sell the bars in San Luis at a handsome profit, since by bringing it via San Antonio they had to pass no customs or frontier posts, for the duty on imported soap in Guatemala was high and freightage, direct from Guatemala City, prohibitive. A photograph of these

Maya on their journey of over 70 miles (about 150 miles round trip) would have made a fine advertisement for the soap manufacturers. The name of the Liverpool company was clearly visible on the large cases which the men carried on their backs, the weight supported in the ancient Maya manner by a tumpline across the forehead.

The trip was an experience still vivid in my memory but disappointing with regard to finding the stelae. Thirty years later oilmen exploring in the Peten, discovered a new site, Xutilha, which, to judge by the very inadequate information, may be the one we sought. San Luis, once at the back of beyond, is now on a bus route from the Sarstoon to Flores.

A few days later Faustino and I were off on another trip. Two brothers from the Toledo settlement had a concession to cut mahogany on the Pusilha River perhaps fifteen miles below the point where it emerges from underground beside the trail to San Luis. James Mason, also from the Toledo settlement, had discovered some ruins, and these included the stone abutments of a bridge, a very rare feature of Maya architecture. First reports attributed the bridge to Cortés, but I felt certain that wasn't true, although the famous march to Honduras must have brought him close to the Pusilha River. His straggling, famished soldiers were in no condition to build a bridge, and a view of the abutments themselves later made it clear that the great labor needed for their construction could not have been available and that the construction was typically Maya.

The journey from San Antonio was strenuous but uneventful, and we reached the mahogany camp soon after nightfall. The Pearce brothers and Mason made us welcome. Spare bunks with palm leaves, thicker than those we had made at Mohijon, were available.

The work of getting the giant mahogany logs to the *bacardier*, where, when the floods came, they would be thrown into the river and floated to the sea, was at its height, but Mason found time to show us the ruins and the remains of the bridge. The former— the main court of the ceremonial center had not then been dis- covered—were not very impressive, for they comprised a scatter- ing of small mounds lacking the carefully faced masonry of Lu- baantun, and a high hill, the sides of which had been terraced by the Mayas. The bridge, however, amply repaid the journey to see it.

The two abutments, one on each side of the river, were clearly of Maya construction. The masonry, similar to that of the core of any typical Maya pyramid, consisted of largish boulders piled up without mortar in a manner frequently described as dry fill. The large stones that formed the faces of the abutments had been laid in the same general style, but with a little more care. Probably these faces were once filled with spalls and had been covered over with coatings of heavy plaster, but of those refinements no evi- dence remained. The space occupied by the river between the inner faces of the two abutments was about thirty feet wide, and presumably was bridged by long logs lashed together with vines or henequen cords.

Except at Palenque, where stone bridges with Maya corbeled vaulting cross narrow streams, and another which I found near El Baul on the Pacific Coast of Guatemala many years later, no aboriginal bridges have ever been reported from Central America.

A liana suspension bridge or a tree cut so that it would bridge the river in falling with a taut liana as handrail would have served perfectly well for ordinary purposes since the Maya had no wheeled traffic or beasts of burden. Indeed, both types of bridge are used by the present-day Maya. This bridge must, one supposes, have been built so that religious processions to the ceremonial center would not lose any of their splendor by having to break ranks to cross a narrow one-log bridge.

A sacrificial procession passing across this bridge would have presented to an onlooker from the Old World an exotic spectacle of strangely mingled beauty and imminent horror, of piety and evil. The nearest European eyes have come to witnessing an analogous display of barbaric splendor and evil was when from afar Cortés' soldiers watched, helpless to intervene, their hapless comrades taken prisoner by the Aztec being led up the steps of the great pyramid of Tenochtitlan, now Mexico City, to have their hearts torn out as offerings to Huitzilopochtli, the Aztec war god. With reason the Spaniards ruthlessly extirpated that religion when they had conquered the country.

Standing by the bridge, I tried to picture a scene of a thousand years ago. I saw the junior priests, clad in long cotton dresses, with their long hair matted with the blood of sacrificial prisoners, leading the procession, their pottery braziers trailing clouds of copal-incense smoke.

Behind the junior priests march the god impersonators, whose features are hidden behind masks representing the deities to be honored in the ceremony to follow. In the front row march abreast four impersonators of the Chacs, the rain gods who bring the needed rains for the crops growing in the milpas. Even the youngest Maya boy watching the procession by his father's side easily recognizes the Chacs by their long noses derived originally from the heads of snakes, but now so elongated as to resemble rather the trunks of elephants. Each Chac carries in one hand a gourd of water; in the other, a zigzag staff, symbol of the lightning. The four Chacs are painted red, white, black, and yellow respectively, the colors indicating the world direction over which each presides, but all four wear similar headdresses of superimposed long-nosed representations of the rain gods. These are surmounted by panaches of quetzal feathers, the iridescent greenness of which recall the leaves of the growing maize crop.

Behind the impersonators comes a litter, decked with maize

leaves, borne on the shoulders of the four junior priests. In it a young man is seated sideways, his legs dangling over one side. From the crown of his head rise maize leaves which sway to the motion of the litter. Necklaces, armlets, and ear-plugs of apple-green jade enhance the illusion that he is the personification of the growing maize crop. Behind the litter come four children who are destined to be sacrificed when the procession halts.

As the children pass on their way to the temple and pyramid of the rain gods, the spectators eagerly crowd forward to scan their faces. They smile as they see the tears in the children's eyes, for these tears indicate that the rains required for the growing crops will be forthcoming. The priests may have beaten the children or rubbed their eyes with chile peppers before the procession started, or the children may be crying from sheer fright. The spectators do not concern themselves about what caused the tears, for the weeping, however caused, is a guarantee to them of rains to produce good crops. It is the age-old magic that like produces like—tears in the children's eyes bring weeping skies.

As I stood watching the procession climb the slope beyond the bridge, the roar of a sixty-horsepower tractor hauling logs on the newly made truck pass hurled me forward once more through the centuries. The thread was broken, and when I looked again, the quetzal feathers of the Chacs had been transmuted into the lazy leaves of cohune palms and the colored masks had merged into varicolored patches of lichen on tree trunks.

Perhaps it is as well that we did not follow the procession to witness the consummation of the sacrifice, for not understanding the Maya outlook on life and not sharing with him a belief in the necessity of bargaining with nature for its gifts, our horror would prevent us from seeing the ceremony as a necessary bribing of those powers in whose hands lies the future of the crops.

My vision of a Maya procession is not based entirely on known facts; it derived from accounts of Maya ceremonies left us by the Spaniards, scenes on Maya pottery vessels and monuments, and known Aztecan rituals.

Pusilha may have been an important point on the great overland trade route which cut across the base of the peninsula of Yucatan. Merchandise from Veracruz on the east coast of Mexico would have been taken up the Usumacinta River (with portage at the bad falls above Tenosique) to the limits of canoe navigation, and then carried the short distance overland to Pusilha, where it could be loaded afresh in canoes for the journey down the Moho River, as it is called below Pusilha, to the coast, and thence to ports on the north coast of the Republic of Honduras, where in Cortés' time there was a trading post.

Our short examination of Pusilha revealed nothing else of importance at that time, so in the afternoon we said good-bye to our hosts of the mahogany camp, and started back for Lubaantun, planning to stop the night at Flour Camp, the Pearces' deserted base camp, about four hours' walk. We got there at sunset, but soaked through, as we had run into a bad storm shortly after starting. We soon had a good fire going to dry our clothes and keep us warm, for although it was May 1, the storm had brought the temperature down with a run. With nothing except the clothes we stood in, we felt the cold during the night. The mosquitoes also disliked the change of weather, for few were about. That was just as well, as we had no mosquito nets.

Work at Lubaantun was ending, and the rainy season was at hand. The ruins looked very different now from what they had when first cleared of vegetation. Excavations at various points had revealed structures and earlier pyramids not previously visible. In some cases these earlier walls were almost perfectly preserved and still retained their original coatings of stucco.

On May 3, we broke camp. The day, although we didn't then realize it, was most appropriate. It is the commemoration of the

Holy Cross, a minor festival of the church, but celebrated with more fervor in Central America than anywhere else in the world, not because the Maya are particularly interested in the story of St. Helena's discovery of the true cross, but because in Maya eyes it marks the start of the rainy season. It is the turning point in the agricultural year—the milpa must be cleared, burned, and sown by that date in time for the arrival of the rains which will make "the grace," the holy maize, germinate.

This association of the cross with the rains is a pleasant illustration of how the Maya wove the weft of Christianity into their old pagan warp. The old Maya rain gods, the Chacs, were believed to live at the four points of the compass, where were also set up four trees, which, in turn, were closely associated with the crops. Illustrative of this is the account of the creation in the great Maya book of Chumayel, associating each tree with its world color and produce of that color. For instance, "In the north is the white tree of abundance ... white-breasted are their turkeys. White lima beans are their lima beans. White corn is their corn." The trees resembled highly ornamented crosses so much that the temple in which one is represented at Palenque was named by early explorers the Temple of the Cross. The Maya were not slow to note that the festival of the Christian cross fell at the very start of the rainy season—thus the cross in both religions had close connection with rain. They amalgamated the two concepts, and soon a great cult had developed. The Christian symbol became a living god, but in the process was largely divorced from the crucifixion. Crosses are worshiped and receive offerings everywhere; they are sentient divinities able to talk to their worshipers. An account of practices in one Maya town well exemplifies this. Some years ago the great cross of Jacaltenango, in a remote corner of northwestern Guatemala, needed replacing. A shaman went to an imposing grove of trees on a high mountain to request a tree to volunteer to be the new cross. One volunteered, and on being asked how high she wished to be, she replied that she would indicate the height by breaking at the appropriate place when she fell. This she did, the smaller part serving as the crosspiece of the cross. The tree was dragged to the distant village to the accompaniment of music and dancing and set up with great pomp.

In the Quintana Roo territory on the east coast of the Yucatan peninsula, the cross is not only able to talk, prophesying and advising the people, but it is the parent of children—little crosses. From one end of the Maya area to the other the family cross set on a table in the innumerable huts wears a *huipil*, the sacklike woman's blouse. The reason for a woman's garment is, I think, because in Spanish *santa cruz*, "holy cross," is feminine.

At the very time we were traveling down the Rio Grande in canoes, a procession of other canoes with pilgrims in hundreds of decorated boats throwing flowers and fruit into the water was making its way across Lake Amatitlan in Guatemala. The festival is ostensibly in honor of *el niño de Antocha*, but a leopard doesn't change its spots; the child of Antocha was probably adopted to hoodwink the church authorities. Flowers and food offered the water on the day of the Holy Cross is a survival of old rites to the rain gods. So on that day we gringos were fleeing from the rains, but our workmen and every Maya far and near was preparing to welcome them, an illustration of the vast gap between our outlook and theirs.

Next day we were steaming north to Belize as the low coast rising to the Cockscomb Mountains behind flowed slowly past.

All things considered, the results of the season's work were valuable. There had been no startling discoveries, but the work had yielded very interesting archaeological information, and the excavation of so many pottery figurine whistles of various types threw new light on the customs of the Maya, particularly on their clothing and ornaments. The bridge at Pusilha was a discovery of prime importance, and, although we did not know it at the time, Pusilha was to prove a very important Maya city. Furthermore, my contacts with our Maya workers from San Antonio and long talks with Faustino on our journeys had indicated that these modern descendants of the ancient Maya still preserved many ancient customs and religious ideas. This seemed to be a mine well worth working, so I decided that at the first opportunity I would stay in San Antonio, living just as the people there do, to learn everything that was possible about such survivals, for it was clear that archaeological excavations were not the only means of learning about the ancient ways. Indeed, pick and shovel would never reveal the many customs that had survived in San Antonio from an earlier age.

5

Maya Ancient and Modern

ONE OF THE CHARMS of Maya research is the rewarding continuity from pagan past to ambivalent present. For the Egyptian fellahin the past is meaningless, and the great gods of Egypt—Ra, Isis, and Apis—survive only in cross-word puzzles. In contrast, the present-day Maya has preserved much of his ancient ways, he remembers the old folk tales of the creation of the world and the doings of the old gods, and in his prayers he still names the old gods mixed with the saints of the Roman Catholic church. Those dark-skinned men, women, and children, so earnest in their devotions whether crowding Catholic church or outdoor rain ceremony, are the physical and, without much question, the spiritual legatees of the pagan past. One cannot forget that, despite their success in welding old gods and new saints into a living whole, they go off the rails occasionally, reintroducing human sacrifice with a Christian apologia, as has happened more than once among the Maya of Chiapas.

Because the Maya are so conservative and so even-keeled, one has good assurance that fundamentally they act today as they acted a millenium ago, and therefore one can infer much of the past from the present. With such thoughts in my mind, I returned to Punta Gorda a few months after we had retreated before the rainy season.

I had chosen a bad moment, for I arrived from Puerto Barrios two days before the anniversary of the battle of St. George's

Cay, which is to British Honduras what the Fourth of July is to Americans. I had intended to start for San Antonio the following morning, but it was impossible to hire a mule and muleteer to return with it until the excitement was over.

The great celebration is not without its comic side. In 1798, Great Britain and Spain were at war. The British settlers were supposed to acknowledge Spanish rights to the territory, but in practice they were quite independent, and more than once summarily expelled Spanish officials who visited the settlement in an attempt to maintain the theoretical sovereignty of Spain or to protest against the continual expansion of the settlement. Spain was resentful of the attitude of those cockney sparrows in a corner of what was once the nest of the Hapsburg eagle.

When war broke out between the two powers, a fairly large Spanish force was collected in Yucatan to capture the settlement and to expel once and for all the British logwood cutters. The expedition set sail under the command of a gentleman with the good Spanish name of O'Neill.

According to the version of the British settlers, the forces under the command of the Ibero-Hibernian made two attacks—"the enemy came down in a very handsome manner, and with a good countenance"—but were totally defeated in the shallow waters between the cays by inferior British forces comprising only a naval sloop, a few local ships, and an army recruited from the Belize settlers and their slaves, with a small stiffening of regular British soldiers. Among the settlers was a certain Mr. Paslow, who, clad in a brocaded court dress once owned by King George II, sailed his raft of Negro slaves to the attack with the cry of "Yarborough or Fingarico" (Yarborough is the local cemetery; the meaning of Fingarico remains a mystery). I would dearly have liked to have seen Mr. Paslow go into action. The British forces suffered no casualties, but claimed to have inflicted great losses on the enemy.

According to the Spanish version, there were no casualties on either side and not even a battle, but the fact remains that the Spanish fleet turned back and the attempt to expel the settlers was abandoned. A ballad is invariably sung during the celebration, the chief verse of which runs:

> *We jooked them and poked them and drove them like fleas*
> *Right into salt water right up to their knees,*
> *And each —— Spaniard to the other did say,*
> "Vamonos compadres de St. George's Cay."
> [*"Let's get away from St. George's Cay, fellows."*]

I finally managed to arrange for a mule for the morning after the close of the festival. I was ready at daybreak, but there was no sign of the muleteer, who for at least a week had been celebrating the festival with liquid patriotism the more commendable in that he was Guatemalan and, therefore, so to speak, on the losing side. Eventually he appeared to announce that the mule was loose and nowhere to be found. We walked to the cemetery at the village edge, but despite the best crop of grass within the village limits, it wasn't there, and a survey of several streets in which the grass was growing with almost equal luxuriance also drew blank. It looked as though I would have yet another day in the dreary place when we had word that the animal had been found straying and had been shut up by the police in the dog pound! On payment of twenty-five cents, an exorbitant charge in view of the per capita wealth of the village, we recovered our mule and were soon on our way. The overland trip to San Pedro was much quicker than by river, and, with the aid of a borrowed dugout to cross the Colombia River, that same afternoon I was shaking hands with Benito, our landlord of the past season, who with the traditional welcome of Central America made room for me to swing my hammock.

Hearing the gossip and listening to the gentle murmur of the Rio Grande, I felt life in England and the United States slipping away as a dream fades on waking. The afternoon sun entered the hut in little rivulets that flowed through the interstices between the wall posts to form a loom pattern on the floor of dried mud. My foot set my henequen hammock gently swaying, and like a giant shuttle its shadow passed to and fro across the warp. In the adjacent hut the *crick, crick, crick* of the muller on the grinding stone murmured that Benito's *señora* was preparing tortillas, and a faint odor, which I had not smelled for four months, told of black beans.

Next morning I walked over to the ruins of Lubaantun. Even in the short space of four months the stone walls had been almost entirely covered with a fresh growth taller than a man. One of the workers' huts had collapsed, and our own hut looked unutterably old and mildewed. Plants were growing on the floor, and the legs of the homemade tables were wreathed with light-bereft creepers with sickly yellow-green leaves.

Later I visited the hut of one of our mestizo workers (not Requena's), where the family welcomed me to a meal and a musical recital, the latter an ordeal I would thankfully have escaped. At the end of the previous season Hannay had presented his gramophone, already in the last stages of collapse, to this family. The machinery had now completely broken down, but that was no reason why the only gramophone within a radius of many miles should not continue to entertain. The difficulty was overcome by a boy twirling the record round with his finger, the speed depending on how tired he felt at the moment. This method produced extraordinary results. A snappy jazz tune was played at a funeral pace, but just previously Madam Jeritza had simply galloped through *"Un bel di vendremo";* her shrieks when the turntable revolved at 150 revolutions a minute would have brought down the Milan opera house in more senses than one.

Moving to San Antonio next day, I received a warm welcome

from Faustino and my other friends, and they arranged for me to rent at two dollars a month a brand-new hut, and for the same amount to eat with a family.

San Antonio then comprised about sixty palm-thatched huts strung along three ridges, so that one had to cross one or more small canyons to go from one part of the village to another. The entire population except for the Carib schoolmaster was Maya, almost all Mopan-speaking, but there were a few Kekchi families (Plate vii). The highest point was occupied by the town hall (*cabildo*) and the church. All lived by the produce of their milpas scattered through the surrounding country. Pigs were raised, chiefly for sale in Punta Gorda, and a fair amount of cacao was harvested. Few visitors from outside ever came to San Antonio in those days—an occasional Carib to buy pigs, the priest from the Jesuit mission in Punta Gorda, and a very, very rare government official. In almost every respect, San Antonio was its own little isolated world.

Government was in the hands of the alcalde and two assistants who were chosen by the village. They also constituted a court for trial of minor cases. Sometimes I would listen to proceedings, although my knowledge of Mopan was extremely limited. Cases were tried with a gentle kindness and an obvious wish to see both points of view which epitomizes Maya character. One case I heard concerned a complaint by one Mopan-Maya, Roberto, that his neighbor's pigs had broken into his milpa and done much damage trampling the maize and eating the ears. Roberto gave his side of the matter to the accompaniment of a running commentary by the alcalde, which was so completely favorable to the complainant that I formed a low opinion of Mopan-Maya justice. It ran something like this: "Yes, of course, you are quite right in what you say. A man works all those months only to have much of his labor destroyed by his neighbor's pigs in as many hours, and that despite the fact that he has taken the trouble to build a fence around the field to keep out the wild animals. Of course, no man can spend all his time watching his crops"—and so on, with nods and little murmurs of encouragement, repeating the complainant's points. Then Juan, the neighbor, began his side of the matter to the same encouraging patter from the alcalde: "You speak truly. A man with a milpa should see that his fences are well made. You have your own work to do; you can't watch the pigs all the time, and no one can be expected to keep his pigs shut up all the time"—and with other comments, he took Juan hand in hand over the bastions and moats of the defensive position.

Finally, after a strong effort to get each man to see the other's case, there came a judgment which left both complainant and defendant reasonably satisfied—surely a better solution than a strict application of the letter of the law. For the Maya, whose attitude was and is akin to the Greek "moderation in all things," a blindfold justice isn't quite the solution—the Maya prefers to see a comprehending light in her eyes and a nod to show that she can see both sides of an argument.

The San Antonieros would journey to Punta Gorda a few times a year to sell their pigs and buy household goods, and sometimes they took their wives with them. They camped out for the night beside the store, and in the morning Carroll sold them soap, kerosene, and lengths of cotton just as though they had walked to his store across his native Yorkshire moors, blue eyes and sandy hair bobbing like a cork across a sea of black eyes and black hair. He also sold them something which was as un-Yorkshire as the machetes he also stocked—bottles of raw rum from the sugar fields of the north of British Honduras. A fair proportion of these were consumed before starting home or along the trail.

Passing down the trail one day, I noticed a little clearing about six feet long and as much deep beside the path. It had been planted with some flowering shrubs and showed evidence of being carefully tended. There was no cross or religious emblem, but it looked like a tiny garden of remembrance, and that, in a manner of speaking, was what it was. When I asked my Maya companions what it signified, they told me, once they could stop laughing, that at that very spot Anselmo Tzul's wife had succumbed first to the effects of the rum and then to the casual advances of a passing Carib. The couple were caught *in delictu* by other San Antonieros, and the garden of remembrance had been made as a witness to the shame she had brought on her husband, her family, and her village. Several times the lady and some close friends had tried to destroy this memorial to her impropriety, but each time others had reconstructed it. To me it seemed to express the Maya attitude of live and let live. The sinful lady may have had a private chastisement from a shamed husband, but the public punishment, as we have seen, took the form of contemptuous ridicule, which one suspects was extremely efficacious, just as were the stocks in past days, for they also relied largely on ridicule as the punishment to fit the crime. The garden of remembrance was, I believe, a spontaneous matter; it had not been a sentence passed on the poor lady by the alcalde, but I make no doubt that a sociologist would explain in a verbless string of polysyllabic words that the garden was a manifestation of some defense mechanism of the mores of the group. Maybe; but after listening to the laughter of my Maya informants, I wonder.

The San Antonieros were extremely honest. I would leave my hut open, but nothing was ever stolen, although I had many things a Maya would covet. Superficially, everyone seemed on good terms with everyone else, but there were a lot of suppressed animosities which drink let loose. At some festival, Jorge, having drunk enough raw rum to make him thoroughly bellicose, would remember some insult he had, or fancied he had, received from

Pedro weeks or months before. He would look for Pedro and start a fight. This usually meant battering your opponent's head against the outcropping rock, but occasionally involved fights with machetes, victory going to the least drunk.

The Maya are not overly generous, but perhaps that it because they usually lack the wherewithal to be charitable. On one occasion I attended mass when my old friend Father Allan Stevenson, S. J., was on one of his visits to San Antonio. I arrived late and stood at the back of the pole-and-thatch church. After the service I made my way to the sacristy, where the good father was counting the collection. He greeted me with the words, "I knew somebody from outside must be in the congregation because of these," and he held up two large coins. Except for them the highest denomination was a five-cent piece.

I made a better contribution to the Jesuit mission. Father Stevenson had to struggle with Kekchi, Mopan, Carib, Spanish, and what was almost another foreign language, creole English. He had translated various prayers and the Nicene creed into Mopan. Now there is no such thing as a relative pronoun in Maya, and, looking at a copy of the creed, I found to my surprise that interrogative pronouns had been used, so that there were a series of startling questions all through the creed: By whom were all things made? Who came down from Heaven? Who proceeds from the Father and the Son? Who is worshiped and glorified? Who spake by the prophets? And so on. Now the Maya, with their philosophy of moderation in all things, would have felt quite at home in that spirit of taking nothing for granted, for they are much addicted to qualifying statements with a dubitative *"quien sabe,"* "who knows," or a *"puede ser que si,"* "it may be so." Nevertheless, it seemed to me that, good Anglican as I am, I ought to help Rome in this matter. The creed was rewritten without that agnostic flavor the interrogative pronouns had produced. With my poor knowledge of Maya

I am thankful I wasn't called on to check a translation of the Athanasian Creed.

Maya is a pleasant language with some charming metaphors. A girl or a boy approaching marriage age is called "maize plant coming into flower"; a meddler is rebuked with the words, "Why are you wearing a loincloth that is not yours?"; a red-hot ember is called a fire flower. Infinity is more than the hairs on a deer; a man will speak of his father's being dead as "my father's bones are piled up." A clever businessman is said to have a snout that sticks out (cf. our expression "a good nose for business"); and in that connection it is interesting that the Maya god of merchants has a sort of nose like Pinocchio's, and one of the names of the chief Aztec god of merchants was "he with the pointed nose." Old men are called mighty rocks; a hard-hearted person is "he with a tree-trunk face"; when a person forgets what he is going to say, he remarks that the bat carried off his story.

With a careful choice of words one can reduce ill effects. If a tiger-ant bites you, say, "A dry leaf bit me," for if you admit it was the bite of a tiger-ant, you will feel it for several days. A similar psychological routing of the odor of skunk is achieved by ignoring the skunk and remarking instead, "How sweet is the scent of the squash seed my grandmother is toasting," a sentence which sounds as though it came out of French for beginners or the Sayings of Confucius. Strange, too, that we discard the seed of squash and marrow, but the Maya consider them extraordinarily tasty. The Maya understand the pangs of love, for the word *yail* means both love and pain.

Sometimes a knowledge of such terms helps in interpretation of Maya art symbols. For instance, axe blades in Maya sculpture sometimes terminate in maizelike vegetation. The explanation of this probably lies in the fact that the word *tzuc* means the beard of an ear of maize, horse's mane, as well as the back of an axe blade.

The present-day Maya retain some of the gestures of their ancestors. I noticed in the village of Socotz that when the children entered a hut to say good morning or, at the hour of the angelus, to say good evening to their parents or other adults, they stood feet together with arms folded across their breasts and tips of fingers under forearms. Exactly similar poses occur in ancient Maya sculpture and on painted vessels, and always, I believe, are those of persons apparently of humble rank. So there in Socotz, almost in the shadow of the old Maya center of Benque Viejo, that ancient pose was still used in the ceremonial greeting of morning and at the moment of sunset.

One season, the wife and sister-in-law of my Maya foreman, Jacinto Cunil, cooked for me in camp, and brought me my meals, but if I addressed any remark to them, they would turn their backs to me before answering in low monosyllables. Similarly, a woman coming along the trail from the opposite direction would turn her back and bow her head till I had passed. I found this treatment disconcerting until I remembered that although I was being given the shoulder, it was not necessarily the cold shoulder; four centuries ago Bishop Landa had written that at the Maya feasts "beautiful women served them [the men] with drink, and after giving the cup these women turned their backs on him who drank until the vessel was empty."

Continuity with the past was what confronted me the deeper I penetrated the Maya pattern of life. Continuity with a subtle inflection. When those children of Socotz stood with folded arms, the thatch above their heads was no different from that of Maya huts of a millenium ago—both had that purple-gray tone of weathered cabbage palm, but the angelus bell had rung in the village church, an occasional truck passed the village, and by the road a soft drink stand reared its monstrous frame of rusted sheets of corrugated iron.

Soon after my arrival at San Antonio, I was invited by the owner of the hut I occupied to join in an all-night ceremony for the cure of his son, a boy of about eleven who had nasty sores on his leg which would not heal. He was in a pretty emaciated condition, probably the effects of hookworm, and a spell in the hospital at Punta Gorda had failed to cure him.

I probably owed my invitation to my possession of a gramophone (not the one with the broken main spring), which would help to while away the long hours. We met at sunset but spent the first hours in conversation and listening to the gramophone. The reason for the all-night vigil is to insure the continence of all participants, for any failure in that respect would invalidate the cure, or any other rite, for that matter.

At midnight the father fetched a candle, water, a small pottery censer, in which embers were aglow, and a hemispheric gourd of water in which some minnow-sized fish were swimming. The sorcerer held lightly for about half a minute the boy's ankles, then his legs below the knees, then above his knees, his wrists, and lastly his temples, praying the whole time in a low voice. Next he touched the same spots lightly making what seemed to be the sign of the cross at each. The prayers I could not follow, but my interest was keenly aroused when, after sprinkling copal incense on the embers, he set the censer on the ground beneath the hammock in which the boy lay, and catching two of the fish in the gourd, held them for some minutes against the patient's leg one above and the other below the sores.

Oily clouds of copal smoke billowed up from the ground and encompassed us with its acrid fragrance as we stood around the hammock. The flame of the candle in the boy's hand made light and shadow cut capers across our faces—the intent group around the net pattern of the hammock, the copal eddy, and my fair hair contrasting with the black of the Indians were a composition which would have delighted many a Renaissance painter.

The sorcerer replaced the fishes in the gourd and, taking copal-impregnated embers from the censer, seemed to press them against the same spots above and below the sores. He probably did not do that for the boy showed no sign of pain and I could see no sign of a burn when they were removed two or three minutes later.

I know of no other case of fish being used in a cure, although it is known that the Maya sacrificed fish. I think that as minnows love to nibble at any sore or tick-bite on a person's body when he remains still in the water, they were supposed to nibble away the evil in the boy's sores while the copal incense acted as a purifier. The explanation of nibbling the evil away is strongly reinforced by what happened next, something which hurled us back through the centuries to the pagan rites of pre-Columbian times.

The sorcerer, gathering up the gourd of water, the gourd of fishes, and the copal censer, carried them to the edge of the village, where he threw away their contents, and then returned to the hut with the empty utensils. Our much cited Bishop Landa describes how the Maya purification ceremonies ended with a man carrying the utensils employed in the ceremony to the outskirts of the village and, by inference, leaving them there, "and by this they said the demon remained cast out." It is the old quasi-magical rite of the scapegoat driven into the wilderness bearing with him the evil of the community.

On the sorcerer's return from casting out the evil, we were served chicken and rice well flavored with chile. This more or less ceremonial dinner well illustrates the Maya's peculiar flair for assimilating alien ideas and practices. Turkey was the old ceremonial meat, but as turkeys were scarce in San Antonio, chicken had taken its place. However, for the Spaniard chicken and rice Andalusian style is a favorite, and this the Maya had borrowed, but they had, so to speak, baptized it as Maya with a more than liberal flavoring of chile, a condiment unknown in ancient Spain.

Even the preparation of the cocoa reflected the blending of the two cultures, for to each gourdful of cocoa were added about two tablespoonfuls of ground maize and a heavy-handed sprinkling of black pepper, a most foul concoction. Typically the Maya flavored their cocoa with chile pepper, but black pepper may have been substituted as a far rarer condiment.

After supper we sat outside the hut on the stone ledges of the barren hillside, telling stories and watching the stars. Pondering on what I had witnessed, I felt that in studying the modern Maya to learn about the old, I was a sort of restorer of old masters. Over-painting had to be carefully removed to reveal the original Maya scene below; the thick varnish of Roman Catholicism had to be dissolved to bring out the paganism beneath; folk-tales had to be treated in the same way to remove European and Negro accretions. Even then features remained which might have either Maya or Old World origins, and quite a few had neither, having evolved from the mingling of the two cultures.

An interesting illustration of how a knowledge of present-day beliefs and customs can be used to interpret archaeological prac-tice came my way some years ago. I had found in a votive cache on the summit of a pyramid at San Jose an incense burner and two bones which turned out to be the ear bones of a manatee. I couldn't imagine why the Maya should have attached value to the ear bones of that queer sea mammal and published the find without comment. Years later, C. M. Barber, director of a mu-seum in Flint, Michigan, told me that sixty years ago he had found that the natives of Maya descent around Lake Izabal, Guate-mala, regard the ear bone of a manatee strung on a cord around the neck as a magical protection for the wearer. He thought that was because the manatee's sharp hearing is its best defense. He had surely hit the nail on the head and from his observations given the correct interpretation of an archaeological find.

A less certain reference to modern practice I advanced as the explanation of another votive cache I found at San Jose, in this case in a refuse deposit. The cache consisted of nine roughly fash-ioned disks, about seven and one-fourth inches in diameter and one-half inch thick, made of lime and mortar. Seven were piled one on top of the other to form a sort of column; the other two were above on edge and leaning against each other so as to form a sort of roof over the others. The disks looked for all the world like tortillas or thin scones. Now the Maya of San Antonio in curing disease do not normally use fish; instead, they pass small tortillas, seven or nine in number, made of maize, copal incense, and the blood of a hen, over and under the body of the sick man. They are said to draw the sickness out of the patient. The sorcerer keeps them for three days and then takes them into the forest and either burns them or throws them away. Could the disks I had found have been used as substitutes for maize scones in a curing ceremony and have been deposited on a trash dump to get rid of the evil drawn from the patient's body? It is a reasonable explanation, but, alas, must remain a conjecture.

John Evelyn said of Pepys that he was a curious person, and all archaeologists must be curious and seek in all sorts of places for odds and ends of information. The dangers of neglecting present-day folklore are well illustrated by the actions of a lady archaeologist who is addicted to ban-the-H-bomb processions. For several years she marched in a bright red hat, and thereby became a source of innocent merriment to her less militant colleagues. She knew her archaeology of East Anglia, but had paid less heed to its folklore. In the lore of the area in which I live, a girl wears a red hat as a signal to the young men of the district that she has left off her drawers.

We have strayed far from our vigil at San Antonio. The autumn night was deliciously cool, apparently too cool for the pigs, for the occasional squeal of a young porker hinted that bundling together for warmth sometimes meant too much weight on the bottom-most member of the huddle. Long before the eastern sky turned to pearl and lemon, lights were twinkling in the huts across the ravine, and the gratings of mullers on metates gave notice that the women of the village were already at work preparing tortillas for their masters' breakfasts. Yearning for the sleep ceremony denied us, we fell silent as we watched the morning star pilot the onrushing dawn. The light of day gained on him, dimming his brilliance. Then wisps of smoke, filtering through the palm thatch of chimneyless roofs showed brown against the lemon sky, and our vigil was ended. And the boy? I'm ashamed to admit that neither my field notes nor my diary say whether he recovered and lived happily ever after. I can only say that he and that night are very much alive in one participant's memory.

Not much later I took part in another all-night vigil, that time for the consecration of the hut in which I was living. Candles were placed on each corner post and one in the center of the crossbeam. After the sorcerer had censed the six main posts and smeared a piece of raw meat on each corner post, he walked round the hut, first outside and then inside, asperging the pole walls and posts with *posole*, the gruel of maize and water of universal use throughout Indian Central America. Later we withdrew from the hut so that the posts of the hut and the gods of the earth might enjoy their meal undisturbed. While they had their food, we mortals had ours in an adjacent hut. Two hours were judged long enough for the divine repast, and at the end of that time we returned to my hut to await the dawn.

The Franciscan López de Cogolludo wrote about the Maya: "Whenever they make new houses, which is every ten or twelve years, they won't enter or live in them until an old sorcerer comes from a distance of one, two, or three leagues to bless them with his silly charms."

Silly charms or not, the ceremony I witnessed was in the direct tradition: the Maya smeared the hearts of sacrificial victims or the flesh or blood of animals on the faces of their idols and made their offerings of *posole* long before the first Spaniards arrived, and charred copal resin was found in large quantity in or around censers during the excavations of the Carnegie Institution of Washington at Mayapan.

The collection, packing, and sale of the immense quantities of copal used in ancient times (one item of tribute to Montezuma was eight thousand balls of copal) must have been a vast business, as it still is. At the time of the Spanish conquest there were plantations of copal trees (*Protium copal*) in Yucatan, but nowadays the Maya are dependent on wild trees. These are not slashed as is a rubber tree or the chicle-yielding sapodilla tree, but the surface of the trunk is gently scraped. It is a slow process, for the yield is small and the gum takes a long time to collect. Moreover, one must gather the gum fasting; only a little *pinole*, parched maize and water, may be taken before setting forth.

Lumps of copal about the size of a small cake of soap are wrapped in maize husks and traded over wide distances. Here again the packaging is surely the same as in pagan times. In a cave in the northwest corner of British Honduras several hundred pannikins of copal were found stored on shelves, but these had been made of palm leaves. Balls of copal retrieved from the sacred cenote at Chichen Itza had been painted blue-green, and in them were set jade beads like fruit and peel in a plum pudding.

Plum pudding brings me to the Christmas I spent in San Antonio. All through December 24 families were arriving from the scattered settlements outside to spend the fiesta with relatives in the village. Drums beat and there was an air of unwonted activity.

After sunset lights appeared one by one inside the huts. Outside, men gathered to pass around their bottles of rum and gossip. The flickering tongues of fire escaped through the wide-spaced poles of the wall to illuminate their high cheek bones and to produce shadows which distorted their features to make them strangely like the artificially deformed heads of their ancestors. Inside, women and girls at their domestic tasks perspired freely in their heavy gala dresses in the fashion of 1880 with layer upon layer of scarlet or pink cotton which cascaded over a dozen flounces to swirl around their bare feet.

The dance was held in a large hut. One end was filled with closely packed wooden benches, on which the women and girls sat; the center was for dancing; and at the far end was a bar and shrine with a corner reserved for the musicians. At the rude counter which was the bar, the sacristan and his helpers dispensed *copitas* of fiery rum at five cents apiece. Behind them, a small shrine decked with palm leaves held a picture of the Virgin Mary and a statuette of St. Joseph. At his feet an offertory plate held the take from the sales of rum, for the dance was ostensibly for the benefit of the church. Two or three candles burned before the shrine.

There were to have been two bands, but very early in the evening all four marimba players succumbed to the rum, leaving all the work to the second band. This comprised a violin and a huge handmade harp, the hollow base of which, beaten by a man squatting at its feet, served as a drum. The violin was no Stradivarius; the strings were of henequen fiber and produced most un-violin-like noises. Even with such handicaps the players were not too bad, but they could play only one tune. This was composed of an almost endless repetition of the same arrangement of fourteen notes. Just as one felt like screaming, there would be a minor variation for a while.

A young man approaching the girl of his choice, waved a neck scarf in front of her saying, "*Cox ti okot,*" "Let's go and dance"; but the girl usually pretended to be shy, so that the youth kept waving his scarf and repeating the set invitation. His eye might stray, and he would find that some Maya wallflower had accepted with alacrity his unintended invitation. So far as I can see from a long experience of Maya dances, it doesn't matter whom one chooses, for partners dance apart, never touch hands, and never even glance at one another. Each dancer continues his or her monotonous shuffle with complete lack of interest in the partner and with gaze firmly fixed on the opposite corner of the hut (Plate vi*a*).

Each dance is an eternity, for the music continues as long as there is anyone on the floor. A couple perhaps does not start until the band has been playing for fifteen minutes, and will then continue as long, with the result that the musicians may play those same fourteen notes for half an hour without rest for themselves or respite for the listeners.

As the night wore on, the shouting and din around the bar almost drowned the unchanging music, and soon practically all of the men and not a few of the women were badly intoxicated. The former staggered about, colliding with the few remaining dancers, maudlinly grasping their friends around the neck and swearing eternal friendship, or in a spirit of bravado shouting, "*Uinicen, xiben! Soy hombre!* I am a man!" to impress the world in three languages of their virile qualities. A few started fights; some lay in drunken stupor on the ground outside the hut, while one was stretched full length immediately in front of the band for two hours, no one troubling to remove him.

I left the dance and undressed, but I could not sleep, so getting out of my hammock, I wrapped a blanket around me and returned to watch the dance. One of the Maya men who had made quite a few five-cent contributions to the offertory plate, now almost afloat in spilled rum, came up to me and, unwrapping the blanket around me, rearranged it so that we shared it, or rather it rested lightly on both our shoulders, the only occasion on which I have attended a dance in pajamas. After a bit I managed to recover my blanket, and, taking a swig from the bottle of a charming old lady who was pleasantly lit up and insisted on thus sealing for all eternity the affection which had so quickly blossomed between us, returned to my hammock. It was 4:00 A.M. and the full moon was shining on men huddled against rocks. Pedro Tesecun, who had worked for me at Lubaantun and who looked like a fifteen-year-old boy, was fighting drunk. His face was covered with blood, and blood, mud, and vomit had soiled his white vest. He wouldn't give in, but after each battering staggered forward for more. A few drunks were aided home by their patient wives.

Early Spanish writers speak of Maya dances and drunkenness before the idols at Tayasal, only some fifty miles from San Antonio; and good old Bishop Landa tells us that the feasts ended in drunken brawls and the wives had a hard job to get their husbands home. Totally uninhibited while affected by the liquor, they fought and killed each other, mistreated their fathers and mothers, and set fire to their own homes. Perhaps the Bishop in his friary at Izamal heard the shouts of *"uinicen, xiben"* and in his Franciscan brown, not unlike my blanket, witnessed those sad brawls. With the Maya things don't change much. Minor changes there were: the statue of St. Joseph had taken the place of the idol of pagan times, and these Maya were nationals of a country whose subjects in Landa's days were barred from the New World or appeared before the Inquisition if they were caught there.

One other thing had changed. Before the white man brought sugar cane and rum to the New World, the Maya drank *balche*, a kind of mead made of honey, water, and the bark of the *balche* tree (*Lonchocarpus longistylus*). I have drunk this concoction, and can only echo the ghost in Hamlet, "O, horrible! O, horrible! most horrible!" I don't know which is the worse, *balche* or Belize rum; the latter is guaranteed in the words of the same royal personage to "Make thy two eyes, like stars, start from their spheres."

San Antonio was very subdued on Christmas morning. The few persons around looked sorry for themselves and complained of *goma*, "hangover." My Christmas dinner was chicken with a superfluity of chile and tortillas. The old woman who had prepared it busied herself around her fire. Nearby were her metate for grinding corn, two or three pottery vessels, gourds, and calabashes, but little more. I ate seated on a low hollowed-out half-section of tree trunk such as the Maya use for stools; a box served as my table, and for Christmas decoration there was the pattern of the fan-leaves of the palm thatch, golden-brown except above the three stones of the hearth, where smoke and heat had blackened and charred them. The simple surroundings gave to my meal a touch of the humble poverty of that first Christmas in a stable, which one may suppose to have been thatched and certainly furnished with equal modesty. Strange, that in all the tens of thousands of nativity paintings the child Jesus is never shown with flies crawling around his eyes and mouth, as they do around the faces of Maya babies and surely must have done in that stable. How better illustrate that He came with great humility?

I spent New Year's Eve in the hut of my old friend Benito, the Rockefeller of Lubaantun. It was my birthday, so we celebrated. After several toasts and a fair amount of rum-swigging, Benito gave a toast which I am never likely to forget. With a slight lurch he raised his glass and called to the company, *"Vivan Dios y meester Tonson."* "Long live God and Mister Thompson!"

From there I•crossed the river in a dugout to take in the dance at San Pedro. This was very much like the one at San Antonio except that the Kekchi have a very pleasant custom of strewing the floor with leaves of the pimiento or allspice tree which give off a delightful odor when crushed. In the highlands of Chiapas and Guatemala the Maya strew pine needles on the floors of churches, and before the white man came, the Maya laid the leaves of the wild fig on the ground for certain of their ceremonies. The source for that statement? You've guessed it. The good bishop.

There was a slight break of half an hour when the harpist, a special constable, was called out to break up a fight and convey the brawlers to what passed as a jail. Pointing to the embowered shrine, I asked one elderly Kekchi why they did not have an image of Tzultacah, the Kekchi mountain-valley god, deity of the soil, in the shrine. He replied that it was not necessary as San Jose, whose figure was in the shrine, was the same as Tzultacah, a pleasant example of how the Maya have succeeded in merging the two religions.

I paddled back to Benito's just before the New Year came in, and was in my hammock not very much later. At 3:00 A.M. I was awakened by a certain Carmen García, to whom I had advanced five dollars against a canoe trip to Punta Gorda. Carmen wanted another couple of dollars. A thirst is not discerning, but even the most pot-inspired optimism would hardly have led him to suppose that awakened at that ghastly hour I would be an easy touch. I wasn't. Carmen passed on to Benito's hut twenty yards away telling him that I had authorized the advance. Benito, having heard all Carmen's pleadings with me and my indignant refusals, gave him short shrift.

Next day brought more fiesta, drunks, and fights, but I have written enough of them. Yet they have their importance; the Maya, like most Indians, is reserved, and he has been in hostile contact with Spaniards or Spanish-speaking people for four hundred years. In drink that reserve turns to enmity or to friendliness; the cups of *aguardiente* I've drunk with the Maya may have done my kidneys no good, but they made friendships easier. For instance, a most important piece of information on pagan agricultural rites came from a man who was maudlin drunk and kept throwing his arms around me. He told me of certain sexual practices before sowing which he would never have spoken of had he been sober. Not even our good Bishop Landa had sniffed that out. The man's Spanish was poor and his inebriated condition did not improve things. He had come to some dance from the back of beyond where old ways survived, but I could never find him again, and I make no doubt that sober he would have denied his statements. The old men in San Antonio wouldn't talk on the matter; the younger ones were willing enough, but their generation knew nothing of such rites. One can be sure that all such ideas are now completely gone.

In the course of my stay at San Antonio and later when I had men from San Antonio as laborers in excavating at the site of Mountain Cow, I collected a number of prayers used in the yearly round of clearing the forest, burning the dry brush, and sowing. Typical are the prayers made before the forest is cut down to make the milpa and addressed to the winds a month or more later when the felled brush is to be burned. Strong wind is essential, for if the dead brush does not burn well, it will be even harder to burn it a second time.

> O God, my father, my mother, Holy Huitz-Hok, lord of the hills and valleys, lord of the forest, be patient. I am doing as always has been done. Now I am making my offering [of copal] to you that you may know that I am aggravating your good will, but perhaps you will suffer it. I am about to damage you, I am about to work you so that I may live, but I pray that no wild animal of the forest follow my footsteps, that no snake perchance, nor scorpion perchance, nor hornet perchance attack me. I pray that no tree perchance fall on me, nor perchance the axe nor perchance the machete cut me. With all my soul I am going to work you.

and

> O God, holy wind, now I desire that you do your work for me. Where are you, you red wind, you white wind, you whirlwind? I do not know where you are—in the remotest end of the heavens, in the midst of the mighty hills, in the midst of the great valleys. Now I desire that you play with all your strength here where I have done my work.

In the first prayer the words "I am about to damage you" bring out the Maya's realization that in cutting down the forest he is doing harm to the surface of the earth, to the face of the earth god, Huitz-Hok, the mountain-valley god, the Mopan equivalent of Tzultacah. Another prayer refers to damaging the god's face. It has been affirmed that no primitive people has an appreciation of the beauty of nature, but I sometimes wonder how true that is. Here one might claim that the milpa-maker is merely apologizing for the physical damage he is about to do to the face of the earth god, but I think that beyond this he is apologizing for the scars he is inflicting on beauty, and that in converting a piece of forest with its trees, its lianas, and its bromelias, almost all of which have a name and a use, into a brown expanse of dead foliage and fallen tree trunks, he is well aware that he is destroying beauty.

FIG. 12.—Scenes from Hieroglyphic Codex Madrid. Left to right: the rain god sowing; rattlesnake biting hunter's foot; the rain god pouring water on the young maize plants; birds attacking the maize god (i.e., eating the seed); cutworms eating the maize god. From divinatory almanacs for farming and hunting.

The fear of snake bites is widespread. It occurs in prayers from Yucatan and among the Lacandon Maya and in another prayer used by the Mopan when poisoning water with noxious herbs to obtain fish. It has its roots in the past, for the illustration for one section of a hunting almanac in the Maya hieroglyphic codex of Madrid is of a hunter being bitten by a rattlesnake (Fig. 12).

In the prayer to the winds, the red and white winds are the winds of the east and the north, but those two colors are sometimes used together to contrast strong with weak, so that they could be translated as boisterous winds and gentle zephyrs.

Inquiry also brought out a large selection of myths and folk-tales, some of which were Maya, but others European and quite a few of the Brer' Rabbit type which were probably brought to

FIG. 13.—The Moon Goddess as Patroness of Disease. She carries the fire sign, *kak*, rhebus for *kak*, skin eruptions.

Central America by African slaves. One of the most interesting cycles of legends recounted the life and adventures of the sun god when he dwelled on earth before there was any sun in the sky. As a young man he courted the girl who later became the moon, and persuaded her to flee with him (he changed into a hummingbird which the girl took to her room when it was wounded by a pellet from her father's blowgun). After various adventures they settled down to married life, but the moon goddess was a fickle wanton. She had an affair with her brother-in-law, the god of the planet Venus, and later eloped with the king vulture.

Sun wanted his wife back, but was faced with the difficulty of getting to the celestial love nest of the king vulture. A resourceful person, if one can thus speak of one of the greatest of Maya gods, he hit on a plan. From his friend the deer he borrowed his skin, and dressed in that, he pretended to be dying. The blowflies were quickly on the spot, and at Sun's request they passed on the news of the tasty meal to the vultures, who, as is their custom, flew down to form a circle around the carcass, which with ungainly hops they contracted until the boldest and greediest came close to peck out the eye of the dead deer. Sun shot out his arm, grabbed the vulture by one leg, and forced it to fly with him astride it to the home of his master, the king vulture. There Sun finally persuaded his wife to leave her lover and his white house—pretty from a distance but not so pleasant inside as it was made of bird droppings—and return to her husband.

They still have their matrimonial differences, for eclipses mark their fights. Some Maya say the moon is less bright because the sun gave her a black eye in one of their fights; others have it that the sun plucked out one of her eyes because people on earth complained that they could never sleep because whenever the moon shone, night was a bright as day.

The long story—I have only summarized two or three incidents—was amusing and threw much light on the beliefs and mentality of the Maya, but as certain incidents in this cycle of legends turn up in the folk-tales of non-Maya peoples of Mexico, there was some doubt whether this was a real Maya story or something they had borrowed from their neighbors, perhaps in quite recent times.

The answer came from the discovery of three different Maya vessels—one from Yalloch, scarcely eighty miles north of San Antonio—which carried pictures (two painted, one carved) of the incident of the sun donning the deer's skin to catch the vulture. There is much variation in detail, but in each case the human arms

inside the deer's forelegs bend in the wrong direction for a deer's
forelegs. In the Yalloch example (Fig. 14), Sun's human hands
stick out beyond the deer's forelegs, the hindlegs show the outline
of the human legs they encase, a blowfly hovers above, a vulture
watches for the moment to descend, and a hummingbird in the

FIG. 14.—Mythological Scene on Vase from Yalloch, Peten. The sun
god clad in skin of deer (note human legs) waits to catch the vulture,
to whom the blowfly will carry news of the carcass. The hummingbird is another disguise of the young sun god.

guise of which Sun originally won Moon's favor is prominent in
the center of the design. Here archaeology has authenticated modern folk-tales as first-class data on Maya religion and psychology
in pre-Spanish times.

The moon goddess, as I have said, was a wanton, and from that
she came to be patroness of sexual relations. She was also goddess
of weaving, of child-birth and of medicine (Fig. 13), and added

to her regular lunar activities that of being a protectress of the maize, a special deity for all women, and mother of all mankind. As such, she was known over almost the whole Maya area as "Our Lady" or "Our Mother."

When the Spaniards introduced the cult of one they also called "Our Lady" and filled the New World with paintings done in the Spanish manner with the Virgin Mary standing on the crescent of the new moon, there was bound to be trouble. The Maya solved the confusion by merging the two.

Thus time passed at San Antonio in indirectly reconstructing the rites, the views, and the reactions of the Maya past from the Maya present, but there was direct contact with archaeology as well. Reports reached me that the Pearce brothers, in the course of making truck passes to get their mahogany logs out, had found stelae close to the old stone bridge at Pusilha which I had examined earlier in the year, so one morning Faustino Bol, who had gone with me on the wild goose chase to San Luis, and I set out for Pusilha. As we were on foot and heavy rains had made the trails bad, we traveled light. I had some tortillas, a pair of socks, and notebooks in an old army pack; Faustino took some balls of corn meal to make *posole* and a shotgun of ancient vintage.

Fate was unpropitious almost from the start. Rain fell on and off all day, and in addition to soaking us, it made the trails slippery and every tree I caught to steady myself seemed to bristle with thorns or to house stinging ants which were shaken out of its branches and down my neck. Streams were badly swollen with the rains. To cross one, I had to swim to a point where I could stand, and there catch the clothes Faustino threw to me and then throw them to the far bank, but I missed Faustino's net-bag, and the balls of corn meal when retrieved were a soggy mess. After six hours' walking, part of it knee-deep in swamp, we reached the Moho River, only to find it flowing like a millrace and nearly fifty yards wide.

Reluctantly we turned back. Nightfall caught us at the Rio Blanco, which we swam for the second time that day. We found some tumbled-down huts at an abandoned camp where mahogany logs had been collected the previous year for dumping into the river, and made ourselves at home as best we could.

We lit a fire, but swarms of mosquitoes denied us the pleasure of stripping off our clothes to dry them, and after a supper of the soggy corn-meal balls, delicately flavored with the muddy water in which they had been soaked, and a few tortillas, we retired to rest in our wet clothes. There were some rough beds—simple forked posts which supported poles tied together with liana—with some palm leaves on top to serve as mattresses. We had to try each one, for most of them were so riddled with termites or rot that they collapsed as we gingerly sat on them.

I didn't sleep much; Faustino's curses, moans, and slaps at the intolerable mosquitoes would have made a decent rest impossible. I mentally patted myself on the back for my fortitude until I realized that I had an unfair advantage, for I was wearing high boots and corded breeches, whereas Faustino wore moccasins and thin trousers through which the most newly hatched mosquito could get his proboscis with ease. We were both soft, for San Antonio was free of mosquitoes.

A week later I started once more for Pusilha, but without Faustino. The evening before we left, Father Stevenson of the Jesuit mission arrived at San Antonio, and Faustino took advantage of his presence to get married. I couldn't persuade him that Maya hieroglyphic texts were more important than marriage. The padre would not be back for another three months, and by something approaching a miracle, Faustino had several dollars to his name, enough for the marriage and a dance. His somewhat stolid bride was about eighteen, quite old by San Antonio standards (Plate viie).

Sebastián Yaxcal and I started off, sorry to miss the dance. We took a different route, passing through the Kekchi-Maya villages of Aguacate and Machaca, and reaching the Moho River higher up at a point where a Kekchi ferried us across in an extremely leaky dugout. The going was better than on the previous occasion, but it was 5:30 P.M. before we got to the Pearces' mahogany camp, and the last few miles had been a sea of mud. We had been eleven hours on foot with only one rest, a half-hour for lunch— "In the days of thy youth when the evil days come not nor the years draw nigh."

Next morning I was taken to see the stelae. They were broken and scattered over an area about twenty yards wide in a small court enclosed by three small and unpretentious mounds. This little ceremonial center was about in the middle of a spit of land formed by the junction of the Pusilha and Hobente rivers, and less than two miles from the bridge I had examined on my previous visit. Some of the stelae had fallen face downward and I did not have the means (poles and heavy lorry jacks) or the time to turn them, but I did turn three and part of a fourth which gave interesting readings in the first half of the Classic period. At that time no legible hieroglyphic texts had been found in that southeastern corner of the Peten, and therefore these texts filled a gap. Later, an expedition from the British Museum worked at the site for three seasons, and the final haul of stelae reached the respectable figure of twenty-one.

The first monument I read, Stela O, proved to be the earliest of the lot with an Initial Series corresponding to December 5, A.D. 573 (Plate VIIId), transcribed as 9.7.0.0.0 7 Ahau (3 Kankin). That is to say it records that 9 baktuns (periods of 400 "years" of 360 days) plus 7 Katuns (periods of 20 "years" of 360 days), no tuns (years of 360 days), no uinals (20-day months), and no kins (days), a total of 3,740 tuns of 360 days (that is, 3,686 of our years), since the mythical starting point of the Maya calendar. That falls on the day 7 Ahau, the old sun god is lord of the night, the moon is 25 days old and this is the sixth moon of the group. The present moon will be a 29-day moon. This is the completion of the 7th Katun.

Strangely, the month and its number—3 Kankin—are not given on the surviving piece, and even were they on the bottom fragment now lost, they would be out of place. Very rarely, indeed, did the Maya make such an omission. The starting point of the Maya calendar, the equivalent of August 11, 3113 B.C., which is transcribed as 13.0.0.0.0. 4 Ahau 8 Cumku, probably represented the last creation of the world, and was a projection far into the past without any historical basis. Maya numbers have an extraordinary attraction for many people, some of whom have expended much effort in showing all the exciting astronomical events that happened on this starting point in the particular correlation each favored, but they forget that they are crediting the Maya with a knowledge of the exact average length of the synodical revolution of difficult planets at the very outset of their career as astronomers, roughly the equivalent of supposing that Catherine the Great ruled a corps of sputnik makers.

The architecture at Pusilha was miserable. In contrast to the finely cut blocks of crystalline limestone of Lubaantun, mounds at Pusilha were made of unfaced blocks of stone. This, I think, was the result of local conditions. Lubaantun limestone is Miocene, whereas Pusilha, like much of the Peten, is on Oligocene beds. The figurines, so typical of Lubaantun, are quite rare at Pusilha, although pottery showed the two sites to have been contemporaries.

It is possible that Pusilha is the ancient name for this site, and if that is so, a very rare case of survival of an original place name. Fray Joseph Delgado, a Dominican friar who penetrated this area in the seventeenth century, mentions a settlement called Pusilha on the Pusilha River. As the Maya often name their towns from the rivers on which they stood, it is quite likely that Pusilha was the old name of the ceremonial center retained through the centuries by the Chol-Maya living in its vicinity. The name probably means "the water of the sweat baths," but might be a corruption of *p'usilha*, "the water of the hunchback." Delgado's settlement was a small Chol village; the ceremonial center had been abandoned nearly a millenium earlier.

Now after its sleep of centuries at the junction of the two rivers, Pusilha re-echoed to the shouts of Negro mahogany cutters, the backfiring of tractors, and the dull sounds of steel biting into wood with a voracity which would have astounded the ancient Maya with their pathetic limestone axes and celts of polished stone.

Early next afternoon Yaxcal and I reached the little Kekchi-Maya village of Aguacate, "alligator pear," where we lodged in the hut of the alcalde (mayor). Not only the alcalde and his wife but several of their children with their own families lived in the same hut, and there were eight or ten "matrimonial" hammocks in the large room. Our host produced for us to sleep on two excellent reed mats of a kind common in the highlands of Guatemala, but never used by the Maya of British Honduras. They had almost certainly been brought by Maya traders from Cajabon and Coban in Guatemala, who occasionally visit the Kekchi villages in the south of British Honduras.

Our host was a little distrait owing to the disappearance of several hogs, but prayers and an offering of copal incense made to the Tzultacah, the mountain-valley gods, were efficacious: before we left next morning the hogs were safely back in the pen.

My usual inquiry as to whether anyone in the village possessed any *pichingos* (playthings, i.e., archaeological objects), brought the information that one man in the village had a beautiful *santo*. As *santos* can mean regular saints of the Catholic church or stone idols or the pottery figurines occasionally dug up in the fields, I went off posthaste to find the owner, who informed me that the saint's head was of stone and that it had come from a cave. This sounded good, as stone figures and other archaeological objects are often found in caves. He had left it in the hut he had used the previous year to store his maize crop. We arranged to go and see the head first thing next morning, for after hearing the owner's enthusiastic description of its beauty, I began to feel that I was really on to something outstanding.

At daybreak we started for the owner's abandoned milpa. There had been a very heavy dew, and long before we had walked the two miles, we were soaked from the waist down. We found that

FIG. 15.—The *Maggie B.* off Punta Gorda. The combined diningroom and saloon is at stern; the projection behind is the lavatory. All passengers seated on one side of the table had to leave their bench to let anyone enter or leave the lavatory.

the hut had collapsed, and it was first necessary to remove the roof of rotting cohune-palm splits. Eagerly we set to work, paying no heed to possible scorpions which like to shelter in the old thatch. At last with a cry of triumph the Kekchi owner pulled out his saint. It was a stalagmite, and look as hard as I could, I failed to see the remotest resemblance to a human head, let alone the features of a beautiful saint.

Wild goose chases are the lot of the archaeologist. One is forced to follow up such clues, for although the chances are decidedly against any important find, one can never tell, and sooner or later a lucky strike makes up for many useless trips. Luckily this one only wasted about two hours.

In the afternoon we were once more in San Antonio, and next morning, again employing Shanks' mare, I left for Punta Gorda, where I caught the *Maggie B.*, a small coastal boat named after a local belle. After several trips on the miserable *Maggie B.*, I can't help thinking that it was a backhanded compliment to the lady in question (Fig. 15). On the other hand, in my many visits to Punta Gorda I don't recollect seeing any lady I would even name a rowboat after.

Almost awash with a cargo of chickens, beans, bananas, coconuts, and all the produce of the tropics, in addition to a full passenger list of Negroes and Caribs, the little boat, which could not have been more than thirty-five feet in length, made good time, and landed me in Belize next day in time to catch a fruit boat to New Orleans.

The wintery weather of Chicago contrasted unfavorably with the climate I had left behind, and I felt little inclined to echo the remarks of one of the southerners sent to British Honduras after the fall of the Confederacy to advise on the prospects of settlement in the Punta Gorda area. He wrote:

> We have every reason to believe that country to be covered with jungle and lagoons, from which the exhalation of phosphuretted and carburetted hydrogen gas, consequent upon decomposition of animal and vegetable matter, must be so great as almost to prevent the possibility of strangers escaping its influence and suffering from a malaria that will produce remittent, intermittent and pernicious fevers.

Phosphuretted gas or anopheles mosquito, I never had malaria in that part of British Honduras, although I had more than my share of it in later years at San Jose.

6

The Cayo District, British Honduras

I RETURNED TO BRITISH HONDURAS at the start of the 1928 dry season in charge of excavations for what is now the Chicago Natural History Museum, but was then known as Field Museum of Natural History. An announcement of the projected work produced letters from various persons who wanted to join the expedition. One which began, "I am nineteen years old, *blonde*, slim, and looking for adventure. . . . let me be your special," conjured up visions of a far from dull field season, but the blonde went on to state that she had worked her passage across the Atlantic on the *Lusitania* (I reckoned that she was only six when the *Lusitania* was sunk) and had served as a stoker on a Lake Erie steamer. She signed the letter "Andrew."

Despite various offers I reached Belize alone, leader of a one-man expedition. A few days passed in buying stores and arranging for a concession to dig in the western part of the colony at Camp 6, which was then the headquarters of the mahogany operations of the Mengel Company of Louisville, Kentucky.

Thomas Gann, who had been doing archaeological work in British Honduras for many years, was going in the same direction, so we shared a flat-bottomed motorboat to take us up the Belize River as far as El Cayo, limit of navigation even for the shallow boats used on the river. Apart from the fact that we both had large amounts of stores to transport, the privacy of a chartered boat was well worth the price, for the small boats which regularly plied between Belize and El Cayo were invariably so loaded to the gunwales with passengers and cargo that there was no room to swing the proverbial cat, let alone a hammock.

Now there is a good road connecting the two towns or one can make the journey by plane in half an hour, but then the only way was by boat, and the time varied from two to four days. The time depended on the height of the river, for there are nasty rapids below El Cayo, and when the river was low, boats had to be winched up them. On the whole, the scenery is dull. The lower part of the river passes through mangrove swamp and then a belt of low-lying land now relinquished by the mangrove.

Travel on the river was never speedy, but as no one except an occasional European was ever in a hurry, that did not matter. At first I was annoyed by the constant and tedious halts at little settlements along the river, at each of which the captain would disappear for an hour or two, mumbling a sentence about having to see about some cargo for the return trip; several trips on the Belize River taught me that these frequent halts were due to the captain's adherence to the sailor's tradition of a wife in every port. After all, it is nowhere specified that the ports have to be seaports. Once I learned the reason for the delays, I was divided between annoyance at the constant delays and admiration of the captain's skill in keeping so many sweethearts in a general atmosphere of tranquility, although they were literally within striking distance of each other. Moreover, he had shown great skill in choosing some of his homes, locating them in great loops of the river, so that he could dally with his lady love and rejoin his vessel at the other end of the loop.

Starting from Belize in the early evening, we ran through the night and the following day, except for the captain's trips ashore. The second evening we tied up to the bank a few miles below El Cayo, reaching the village early in the morning of the third day.

Thirty years ago El Cayo, a town of about six hundred Spanish-speaking mestizos with a sprinkling of Indians, Negroes, and mulattos, was the center of the chicle trade. Chicle, the raw material from which chewing gum is made, was brought by mule from the remote chicle camps deep in the forests of the Peten district of Guatemala to Benque Viejo, the first village on the British Honduras side of the border, where it was loaded on light lorries and transported over nine miles of fairly good road to El Cayo; or it was brought directly by mule to the Belize River, where it was loaded on flat-bottomed boats for shipment to Belize and thence to the United States. All that is now a thing of the past. First Guatemala, following an upset with British Honduras, stopped the transport of chicle through the country, and later the development of small air strips made it far more economical to bring the chicle out by plane. Even little one-engined planes make a trip in half an hour which in the old days took eight days by mule.

The *zapote* or sapodilla tree (*Achras zapote*), which yields the chicle sap, grows wild in the forests of the Yucatan peninsula, and as it requires high ground, it is often found in the vicinity of Maya ruins. The Maya used its very hard wood for lintels and undoubtedly for making many utensils. The tree also produces an edible but rather cloying fruit. *Chicleros*, the gatherers of chicle, go into the forest during the rainy season when the sap is running. They make V-shaped gashes in the trunk so that the sap trickles down into receptacles at the bottom of the tree. The sap is perfectly white with a thick, milky texture, but for shipment the moisture is removed by boiling so that the resulting chicle is shipped in hard bricklike blocks, turned brown by smoke, dirt, and constant handling. *Chicleros* are fond of slipping earth or stones into the blocks before they solidify since they are paid by weight.

Temporary camps are set up near a convenient water supply in an area which is rich in *zapote* trees, and in the past their only link with the outside world was by the narrow trail by which mule trains brought in supplies from outside and took away the collected chicle. The *chiclero* had to buy his necessities, such as coffee, sugar, and flour, from the chicle contractor, for there were, of course, no shops in the forest, and the nearest village might have been anything from four to six days' journey away. The very high prices he paid were partly due to the expense of transporting food to outlying camps, often through great stretches of swamp in which the mules sank sometimes to their knees, partly to the greed of the contractor. There were no doctors in the camps, nor anyone with medical training; anyone seriously ill or injured had to be brought out by mule or in a litter to the nearest doctor, perhaps six days' journey away, a thought which often disturbed me when I was on archaeological trips deep in the forest.

At the start of the rainy season a *chiclero* would receive an advance of $100 or $150 on signing up. This was a huge sum to a *chiclero*, particularly when one recollects how much farther a dollar went thirty years ago, but at the end of three or four days it was usually all gone on what passed for wine, women, and song in El Cayo, Benque Viejo, and a dozen other towns in Tabasco or Campeche on the periphery of the Peten forest. The *chiclero* consequently started the season tied to his contractor by debt. Sometimes *chicleros* received advances from contractors and then skipped out.

Some years ago I met in the little town of Tenosique a most friendly contractor, who, about four months previously, had sent his foreman and another man across the Usumacinta River, where it is the frontier between Mexico and Guatemala, with instructions to make a surprise raid on a chicle camp on the Guatemalan side of the border and make reprisals on some *chicleros* who had skipped across the frontier and signed up with a Guatemalan contractor after receiving his advance. It was quite a lesson. The two men waited till all were asleep and then entered the camp, one with a flashlight, the other with two guns. The flashlight man threw up mosquito nets and flashed his light on the sleeper. If the man was one of the absconders, he was shot where he lay by the gunman. Four *chicleros* were dead before the rest could flee into the forest.

Knowing this story, I was fascinated as we chatted with Don Fulano, the contractor, over a bottle of beer. He promised his aid in our projected trip and agreed to hire us mules in the most affable manner. Like everyone else, he was dressed for the tropics, and his white shirt was open at the neck showing a gold cross against his tan skin. My eyes kept returning to that cross.

Perhaps because of his brief butterfly existence after he has received his advance, the *chiclero* considers himself superior to many jobs offered him in the dry season when, in theatrical parlance he is resting. The real trouble is that the Maya who goes into chicle is uprooted. He ceases to be a member of his community and often has no real home. Because of his absence in the forest, he is unable to make his milpa, and a Maya without a milpa is a fish out of water. In the Maya village of San Jose, north of El Cayo, where I worked for three seasons, practically all the beans and much of the maize were brought in from outside because so many of the men were away chicle bleeding and couldn't make milpa. Such a situation was enough to make any right-minded Maya turn in his grave, which perhaps accounts for the confused state of the bones of some of the burials I excavated at the nearby ruins.

From El Cayo, Gann and I moved to Benque Viejo to recruit labor there and in the nearby Maya village of Socotz. We made our headquarters in the town hall, a small shed with a floor of powdery lime which rose in clouds of acrid dust at every step we took. On one wall hung a large oleograph of King Edward VII, news of whose death some eighteen years earlier had apparently not reached the town.

The village, half-Indian, half-mestizo, picturesquely drowsed away the hot hours in Latin-American resignation. Its streets, which ended a couple of stone throws from the grass-covered plaza at the edge of the forest, were silent except when they echoed to the noisy arrival of a train of chicle-bearing mules and its shouting muleteers. In the evening two or three oil lamps and the lights from the *cantinas*, where the *chicleros* celebrated their return to "civilization," supplied a broken illumination, and an occasional shout or the impatient stamping of a tethered mule rose above the low murmur of small sounds from the surrounding forest. A guitar added its notes or, in the distance, howler monkeys plaintively roared their deep-throated music. Soon the *cantinas* closed, the oil lamps were economically extinguished, and Benque Viejo slept.

Some years later I tried to destroy for a few minutes the village's eternal somnolence. At the head of my gang of eighteen or twenty Maya laborers I marched into Benque at siesta time yelling, "*Viva la revolución*," but we might just as well have saved our breath; not a soul came to the door to see the revolution. Perhaps all the village's energies are spent in holding back the forest which besieges it.

There are scores of such villages in Central America which can scarcely man the ramparts against the attacking vegetation. Passing once through one such village in Yucatan, I descried a large group gathered in the center of the grass-covered plaza, and learned that it was Arbor Day, on which every patriotic Mexican town or village must plant a tree, a custom, like Santa Claus and snow on Christmas cards, more appropriate in the U.S.A., from which they were introduced. My suggestion that the best way to celebrate Arbor Day was to cut down a few trees was met with uncomprehending stares.

From Benque Viejo I walked next morning to Socotz, about a mile away, a village of about two hundred Maya prettily situated on the bank of the Mopan branch of the Belize River, where I was to live when I excavated in 1938 in the nearby ruins known locally as Xunan tunich, "beautiful lady," a name which apparently arose from the wrong identification of a figure on one stela as a woman.

My attempts to recruit labor were not successful. A motley crowd offered to work, but more than half were boys of fourteen or fifteen, little fitted for the hard work of excavation; almost all the remainder were clearly suffering from malaria or hookworm to such an extent as to be equally useless. Many campaigns to rid the village of hookworm had failed because as soon as vigilance was relaxed, the infestation returned because of a complete lack of sanitation. Practically all the children had greatly distended bellies, a symptom of advanced infection, and many had taken to eating earth, which further aggravated their condition.

Among the men asking for work was one of fine physique, whom I promptly engaged. He was Jacinto Cunil, a Maya of twenty-five or twenty-six who proved to be far and away the hardest and most intelligent worker I ever had (Plate vic). For the next ten years he continually worked with me in the excavations, first as laborer and then as foreman, and a strong friendship grew up between us. I am godfather to his children, and by Spanish-Indian custom this makes us as close as brothers. Other archaeologists in British Honduras have employed Jacinto in positions of trust, just as my other find, Eugenio Mai, has been the standby of many archaeologists in Yucatan since I picked him to go to Coba so many years ago (he was foreman of the excavations at Mayapan carried out by Carnegie Institution from 1951 to 1955, and during that time he worked both with me and with my son). I like to claim credit for those two first-rate contributions to Maya archaeology. Of Jacinto I have written at some length in *The Rise and Fall of Maya Civilization*.

With arrangements completed for laborers, albeit in a far from satisfactory manner, I got a dugout canoe from El Cayo to Vaca

Falls, following the Macal branch of the Belize River. The river was extremely beautiful, somewhat more open than the Rio Grande. Occasional backwaters were carpeted with water-lily leaves which folded as the ripples from the paddles reached them, and which served as causeways for small birds.

Little clearings with two or three palm-thatched huts were sparsely scattered on the high ground. Small dugouts of cedar hauled up on the banks, a few chickens and lean hogs, a patch of banana or plantain trees, a little sugar cane and, perhaps, a bread-fruit tree (a native of the Pacific which Bligh of *The Bounty* was commissioned to bring to the New World) suggested a paradise for the lazy, for the corn patch and other evidence of hard work were usually hidden from view.

About five hours' paddling brought us to the pool below Vaca Falls, the limit of navigation even for dugouts. This lies at the foot of a cliff nearly six hundred feet high, down which mahogany logs used to be lowered in cable cars to be dumped into the pool, there to await the rainy season's floods to bear them to the mouth of the Belize River.

Mahogany is scattered through the forest with only about one tree suitable for felling to the acre. When a fair number of trees has been found by cruisers, a road is made to the area with short branches to each tree. Hills have to be graded and swampy sections corduroyed. The axeman stands on a small platform built around the trunk about five feet above the ground so as to avoid the hard work of cutting near the ground where the trunk swells to throw down great buttress-roots. A bed has to be prepared so that the felled trunk will not split when it hits the ground. The fallen tree is trimmed, cut into sections, and hauled (formerly) by oxen to the main truck pass to await the tractors. By early March the roads are normally dry enough for the tractors to get to work, and with luck one can expect about ten weeks to get the logs out. It is a matter of working almost day and night to beat the rains.

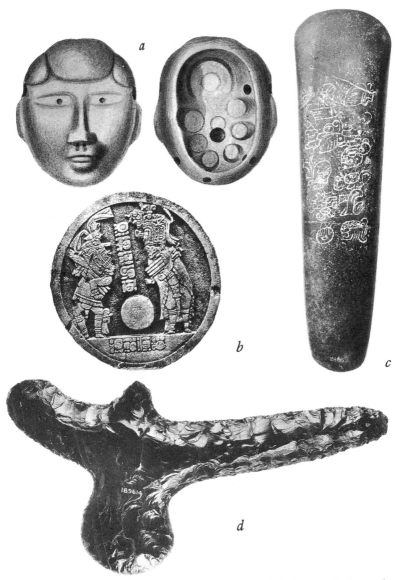

PLATE IX.—Ceremonial Objects and Ball-Court Marker. *a:* Jade mask,
Camp 6. *b:* Ball-court marker, Cancuen. Note players' protection.
c: Incised stone celt, Mountain Cow. *d:* Obsidian axe, San Jose. *(a,c,d,
courtesy Chicago Natural History Museum.)*

a

b

PLATE X.—Uaxactun. *a:* Reconstructionary drawing of two of the eight groups as they looked circa A.D. 800. *(After T. Proskouriakoff.)* *b:* Pyramid E–VII sub, with stela in front, after excavation. *(After Ricketson and Ricketson.)*

PLATE XI.—Camps. *a:* Lean-to shelter of cohune palm leaves, La Honradez. *b:* Permanent camp, San Jose. Tables are for drying sherds. Kinkajou's home is at top of tree in foreground.

a

b

PLATE XII.—Architectural Effort in a Large and a Small Ceremonial Center. *a:* Pyramid and Temple 1, Tikal, after reconstruction. *(Courtesy University of Pennsylvania Museum.) b:* Building at San Jose which contained votive cache with obsidian axe. *(Courtesy Peabody Museum, Harvard University.)*

b

c

PLATE XIII.—Indoors and Outdoors. *a:* Interior of a room, Uaxactun. *(After A. L. Smith.) b:* Cohune palm near San Jose. *c:* Reconstructionary drawing of the Mercado, Chichen Itza. *(After T. Proskouriakoff.)*

PLATE XIV.—Copan Sculpture. Portrait of the youthful maize god, from a façade. *(Courtesy British Museum.)*

a

b

PLATE XV.—Reconstructionary Drawings of Copan. *a:* The ball court with stela in foreground and great court behind. Players usually two or three to a side. Note square markers in floor. *b:* Temple 11 with hieroglyphic step, grotesque torch bearers, niches, and conch ornaments. *(Both after T. Proskouriakoff.)*

a

b

c

PLATE XVI.—Copan. *a:* Stela H. *b:* Stela N. Erected respectively in A.D. 731 and A.D. 761. *c:* Seated figures on part of the step of Temple 11. (*Courtesy British Museum.*)

The Vaca concession, which covered a great tract of land in western British Honduras, produced magnificent mahogany, but the cost of exploiting it was prohibitive. Logs had to be hauled for ten or twelve miles by tractor to the railhead, and thence by railroad about fourteen miles to Vaca, where they were lowered into the pool. The trouble was that every season the haul grew longer. The concession had been held by three brothers named Starkey, who, well aware, like good generals, that lines of communication must not be allowed to get too long, felt the time had come to unload. They sold out to the Mengel Company, whose financial resources were far greater, but even they could not make a go of it. When I returned to Mountain Cow the following year, the concession had been abandoned and the locomotives which had hauled the logs to Vaca had been left behind. Thatched roofs sheltered them from rain, but they couldn't protect them from the vegetation. Lianas, yellow from lack of the sunlight they sought, had wound themselves around the cylinders and, using the rails on each side of the boiler to help them climb, had reached to the funnel. It was a fantastic sight—a kind of cross between Dante and Emmett. The forest was inflicting a vengeful humiliation on those collaborators in its defacement, for I fear that no member of the Mengel Company had thought to ask pardon of the Maya gods of the soil for desecrating their face or had agreed to authorize the purchase of propitiatory copal, and so stockholders had dropped perhaps a million dollars because no efficiency expert in Kentucky knew of the efficacy of a little copal in keeping the friendship of the Central American forest!

On my first visit, in 1928, Camp 6, in a beautiful valley about nine miles south of Vaca, was the headquarters of the mahogany operations. On one side of the railroad the Negro laborers and their families occupied about sixty thatched huts; on the other were the wooden houses occupied by Stuart Williams, the Kentuckian manager, and his wife, the American engineer, and two mechanics. Mr. Williams assigned me a pleasant house and huts across the tracks for my laborers.

As soon as possible, I visited the ruins which lie less than a mile south of the camp. They form a small ceremonial center comprising three largish pyramidal structures, each thirty to forty feet high, a long low mound of unknown use, two rather small parallel mounds which may have formed a ball court, and two other smallish mounds. These were grouped on and around an oblong raised court situated at the foot of the range of hills on the east side of the valley. In addition, a few other mounds were scattered over the valley west and southwest of the main group. As Maya ruins go, this was no great shakes, but I was attracted by the problems posed by a quite small site such as this. Until then, expeditions had concentrated on the large sites, the Romes, Rheims, and Yorks of the Maya area, paying no attention to the Stow-in-the-Wold and Shrimp-in-the-Mud type of Maya center.

For three solid weeks my small gang worked without finding anything except small potsherds, apparently without any chronological significance. As a primary objective of the expedition was to obtain exhibitable material for Field Museum, I felt somewhat discouraged. One morning one of my Maya laborers suggested that we could hardly expect rich finds unless we made an offering to the Yuumil Kaxob, the Lords of the Forest, in whose domain we were working. This seemed fair enough, so I asked one of my Maya men, who was going home for the weekend, to bring back some copal.

On Monday morning we burnt the copal on a leaf in honor of the Yuumil Kaxob, hoping to persuade them to be a little more friendly. My Maya boys stood around as the blue-black smoke spiraled upwards into the bluer morning sky. Less than ten minutes later we found an incense burner almost immediately under the spot where we had burned the copal. It was not a very good one and it was in many pieces, but it broke the three weeks' run of bad luck, and for the rest of the season we had good finds. This, of course, pleased us very much.

Then Jacinto Cunil made a spectacular find. This was a votive cache a short way below the top of one of the three large pyramids. There were no traces of any building upon the summit, but about a foot below the surface Jacinto found a large pocket of very black fine soil, which probably was once an offering of vegetal produce, perhaps maize. In the middle of this were the broken fragments

Fig. 16.—Pottery. Left to right: incense burner, Chulutan, on trail to Coba; cylindrical stamp, Lubaantun; jaguar from doorway, Caracol, Chichen Itza, which resented my low opinion of his home; container of cache with fine jades, Camp 6, British Honduras.

of a large pottery urn, the front of which was decorated with a crude face in low relief (Fig. 16). An inverted shallow dish served as a lid for the urn and this, in turn, had been covered with the two halves of a huge oyster shell.

Among the scattered fragments of pottery and shell were three large pieces of carved jade which without doubt had originally been inside the urn. One was a round ear-plug of a beautiful apple green, almost three inches in diameter. The second was carved in very low relief to represent a full-length figure with hands placed immediately below the chin and with legs bent at the knees. This had an early feel to it, but in actual fact the cache was middle to late Classic. On its back was a yellowish stain to which adhered a very small quantity of a sticky black material. I thought that this might have been partially charred copal incense, which by a freak chance had survived, but, on burning, it gave out a smell very like the unmistakable odor of burned rubber. The Maya burned rubber as an offering to the gods, not because of the smell for one can't imagine anyone, human or divine, enjoying that, but, I think, because the black smoke evoked the black rain clouds under the old magical formula that like attracts like. Accordingly, it is reasonable to suppose that this little jade figure was placed on burning rubber in some sacrificial rite before being placed below the floor in the dedicatory ceremony.

The third piece, three inches high and almost as wide, was a little gem of an ornament of a soft green color in the form of a human head, and was without much doubt a breast ornament (Plate ixa). The piece is now in the British Museum, an item in their incomparable collection of Maya jades, and I often pause before the case in which it is exhibited to contemplate its serene beauty and to recall that day, now thirty-three years ago, when I had my first glimpse of it partly hidden in the black soil of the cache. Some archaeologists are very lucky in their finds. I am not among them, but there are three or four great finds in my career and that was one of them. I must confess to sharing with the Maya their love of jade. My wedding gift to my wife was a jade necklace, Chinese, alas! not Maya.

Small holes had been bored in the eyes of the face on this pectoral to mark the pupils, and these almost certainly had been inlaid with tiny pieces of obsidian or iron pyrites. There were also two holes bored under the nose, presumably for the attachment of a noseplug.

Possibly these attachments were of some substance long turned to dust, but had the material been indestructible, the chances of finding them were small. As the cache rested directly on the large boulders which formed the core of the pyramid, much of the soil had slipped through cracks, and the minute inlays might have fallen ten or fifteen feet into the center of the pyramid, and probably would not have been found even if tons of material had been passed through a sieve.

The back of the ornament was an excellent demonstration of how the Maya worked jade. A large piece had been removed, and in the base of this hollow are ten circular marks clearly made by tubular drills. Apparently first each hole had been drilled. Then the spaces between the drills had been broken away, and finally the whole surface of the hollow thus formed had been smoothed by rubbing. The circular parts enclosed within the drills might have been used as beads, if it had been possible to remove them without breaking. Jade was so valuable to the Maya that it seems most likely that the back was hollowed out in this way so as to produce a few extra beads.

An offering was placed in every Maya structure when it was dedicated or enlarged. These offerings vary considerably in richness, but one must remember that many of the finest offerings—feather ornaments, beautiful textiles, exquisitely carved pieces of wood—have turned to dust. Yet it is poor consolation when one finds some dust in a miserable pottery jar to remember that it may once have been objects of unexampled splendor. When, on another occasion I found in a cache the decapitated skull of some sacrificial victim between two pottery bowls, my disappointment, I am afraid, was too selfish to allow room for pity for the victim of long ago.

Fine jade is rare in the Peten and adjacent parts. Twelve season's work at Uaxactun produced with one exception no jade pieces approaching the Camp 6 pectoral. It struck me recently that as minor excavations at several quite unimportant sites to the east and west of the nearby Maya Mountains had yielded rich hauls of jade, there might be jade in that range, but I could find nothing in geological reports. Friends in Belize have now come upon a very rare report of C. H. Wilson, a geologist in that area in 1886. He noted along an upper tributary of Monkey River, which rises in that range, what he thought was serpentine (jade is usually found in association with serpentine) and, nearby, "flinty green rock resembling nephrite [jade]." The case is not proved, but it now looks as though there may have been a local source of jade (it has been found in the not distant mountain range north of the middle Motagua Valley, in Guatemala).

The Camp 6 site yielded little of interest except this cache. Accordingly, I moved camp to Mountain Cow, about fourteen miles south. This was an abandoned camp of the Mengel Company and takes its name from a local term for the tapir. It lies behind the Maya Mountains and, at about 2,200 feet above sea level, is, with Copan, one of the highest sites in the Maya lowlands.

We started work at a scattering of small groups about two miles south of camp. Our first discovery was a partially caved-in *chultun* which held a burial. *Chultuns* are artifically constructed underground chambers shaped roughly like a Chianti flask. A narrow well-like entrance, sealed with a stone disk like a manhole lid, expands below into a roughly spherical chamber about five feet in diameter, although there is considerable variation in the size and shape of the chamber. The purpose of *chultuns* is not known, although several not completely satisfactory explanations have been offered. Often, as in this case, they were reused as burial chambers.

In the chamber were some human bones in very bad condition and six human teeth. Bones decay in the damp climate of Central America, but teeth are much more durable. The finds, therefore, suggested a secondary burial; that is, the body had been redeposited here long enough after death to have lost most of its teeth.

The furniture comprised three pottery vessels. One was a bowl supported by four hollow breast-shaped feet. The exterior carried a pattern of *grecques* and dots in red and black on an orange ground. The second was an hourglass-shaped pot-stand; the third a globular jar with a T pattern in red and black on orange.

The first two vessels excited me, for they were typical products of what was then thought to be the oldest Maya horizon, and which until then had been found only in two or three other sites. Now we know of much earlier Maya levels, and this type of pottery is assigned to the false dawn of the Classic period. Mountain Cow was to prove a stronghold of this proto-Classic horizon, which even today is not much better understood.

One day Jacinto noticed beside the trail to the dig a hole in the side of a small mound quite close to the *chultun* we had excavated. In a few minutes the hole was large enough to squeeze through. I was so interested in what might be inside that I hastily wriggled through on my stomach, oblivious of snakes or scorpions which might have been lurking inside. The light of matches showed a narrow passage with three steps which led down into the north end of a large burial vault, about seven feet long and five feet wide, with a roof of Maya corbeled vaulting. The chamber was in excellent condition except that the plaster on the walls had long since peeled off. Scores of vampire bats, whose home I had disturbed, wheeled round my head and with the beatings of their wings blew out the matches as fast as I lit them. Exploration was impossible until a storm lantern could be fetched from camp.

Although we were the first men for a thousand years inside this imposing chamber, it had long served as a home for various small animals. Most of the pottery vessels were smashed; dampness and acids from the soil or animal droppings had destroyed the painted designs on several of the vessels. Outside the tomb we found pieces of pottery which fitted vessels in the chamber, and many pieces of vessels never were found. Conceivably rodents might have been responsible for that, but it is very much more probable that the tomb was looted in ancient times, the looters discarding bits of pots outside the tomb. We recovered twenty-five pottery vessels, complete or incomplete, of early in the late Classic Period, but the only pieces of jade were a small ear-plug, a button, and two very small beads, and there was no good shellwork. In a tomb of this size and with so many pottery vessels one might expect a nice haul of jade. Pillaging best explains the absence of good jade, for the four small pieces recovered could easily have been overlooked by looters working only with the light of pine torches. At Mayapan we found constant evidence of looting.

Excavation of the tomb kept us busy for several days. Jacinto and I sorted the soil and shoveled it into five-gallon gasoline tins. Another man carried them out of the tomb, when it was sifted again in the bright sunlight. The lack of room to work, cramped positions, the heat of the lamps, the bat dung, and the dampness did not make the work pleasant. The bones were in very poor shape and badly mixed up, but teeth showed that three persons had been buried there. From other tombs in this same mound, I think it very probable that the occupants had been buried at different times, for the Maya certainly reopened burial chambers to insert a new body as the occasion required.

A somewhat simpler vaulted tomb at the base of the mound also yielded much pottery. This was nearly seven feet long by three feet wide and less than three feet from floor to top of vault. At some time or other two of the capstones of the vault had caved in, and a jaguar or, just possibly, a puma had taken up residence in the tomb for we found its bones close to the surface. Its residence had not done the pottery or the skeletons any good. We recovered twenty-five vessels, whole or fragmentary, in this chamber also, as well as the remains of six persons, but not a piece of jade. The tomb was so small that it would scarcely hold two bodies, and there can be little doubt that the tomb was reoponed from time to time to put in a fresh body after decay had made room for it. The pottery vessels substantiate this conclusion. One vessel was a typical product of the early Classic (Tzakol) period, others were from early in the late Classic period, and still others of the full late Classic period.

Some time later, trenching across the top of a mound, we came upon a vaulted chamber concealed within it. The top of the vault was not closed with the usual line of capstones, but instead came to a point, the sides of the vault being continued upward with a row of large flat stones which leaned against each other just as cards lean against each other in a children's house of cards. A blow with the pick dislodged one of the tilted stones of the apex, revealing a large room below, but it was too dark to see what it contained. It seemed certain that this must be a large vaulted burial chamber in mint condition. No looter had broken in nor jaguar used it as his lair. I started to count my unhatched chickens of jade, shell, and painted pottery.

After ten endless minutes we had removed three more apex stones with great care so that they did not fall and smash the treasure below. I let myself down into the chamber. Inside, my eyes adjusted to the light from the opening we had made. The chamber was completely empty except for two coarse pottery bowls one inverted over the other, rim to rim. The lack of other furnishings was a great disappointment, but I decided that the two bowls concealed the treasure, for votive caches were usually in a pottery vessel with a second inverted over it as a lid.

It took some time to pry the bowls loose, as they had been sealed together with a coating of lime which had dripped from the roof in solution. At last the contents were exposed to view. Inside the lower bowl was a small quantity of ash and on top of it an extremely crude representation in unbaked clay of a seated man with outstretched legs. A child of five could have done better. I was sick with disappointment.

Analysis found the ash to contain a very high percentage of phosphate, indicating that it was in all probability calcined bone. My burial was a cremation. The Maya had gone to the trouble of building a beautiful vaulted chamber eight feet long, eight feet high, and nearly five feet wide to house an ounce of ashes and a

Fig. 17.—Archaeological Finds. Top row, shell "flowers," Mountain Cow; Veracruz spindlewhorl, San Jose; jade head, Camp 6; shell disks, Mountain Cow; center row, sherd with incised doodling, Uaxactun; jade amulet, San Jose; shell *oyoualli* snake, San Jose; bottom row, filed teeth with jade and obsidian inlays, San Jose.

lump of clay! Frequently Maya rooms were converted into burial chambers when a structure was enlarged, but this chamber had never been used for any other purpose, as the absence of a doorway demonstrated. Five stones, projecting at different heights, had been set in each end wall of the room when the tomb was under construction to serve as ladders for entering or leaving. I am usually oversentimental towards the Maya, but I hoped that the priest who had the nerve to place only two miserable bowls and a crude figurine with the cremation fell off one of the steppingstones as he climbed out of the tomb and broke his neck!

That is probably a bit unfair. Doubtless the chamber was constructed for the use of some family or lineage and it was planned to use it over and over again, but something went wrong and it was only used the once.

In compensation for that disappointment we found a rich votive cache in a pyramid which contained several pieces of jade, shell, slate and coral, a material which frequently appears in votive offerings (Fig. 17). The outstanding piece was a magnificent celt of highly polished diorite eleven inches long. This had been broken into three pieces, so that it could be placed in the pottery container. Eleven hieroglyphs had been lightly incised in two columns down one side (Plate ix*c*). None of the glyphs are of known meaning, but two or three were of recognizable early types, such as were being carved in nearby Peten sites quite early in the Classic period. I know of only one other polished celt with hieroglyphs. That, also of early date, is of jade and comes from the other side of the Maya Mountains, only some forty miles away.

We also found part of a fine sculptured altar. This was round to oval. The right half of the design was gone, but the left half remained, and on that were glyphs which gave the date of the altar's dedication and below a well-executed representation of a captive seated with one knee raised and with his arms bound behind his back (Plate viii*c*). Beside him was a small glyph which perhaps refers to him. The first pair of glyphs are the day 13 Ahau and the month position 13 Uo. This has the long-count position 10.0.5.0.0., and corresponds to February 15, A.D. 835 in our calendar, a somewhat late date near the close of the Classic period. The finds show that this rambling Mountain Cow site had been occupied from the threshold of the Classic period to near its close.

I wanted to take out this fragmentary altar, but its removal presented quite a problem. It was three feet wide by nearly two feet broad and must have weighed five hundred pounds. Man-power or mule were the only methods by which it could be moved, as the trail to Mountain Cow was too overgrown and narrow for a tractor to get through. Anyhow, no tractor was available; in the race to get the logs out before the rains came, every tractor of the Mengel Company was working twenty-four hours a day. Mule tranportation could also be eliminated as the usual load of a mule is not over two hundred pounds.

Obviously I would have to reduce the weight of the altar. I obtained some stone-cutting saws, but as there was no sand in the vicinity, they were of little use. Luckily, the stone was partly lami-nated, and with an old axe and a maul we chipped away much of the stone until we got the weight down to something under three hundred pounds, but it was a tedious business.

Two of my Maya boys agreed to carry the altar nearly five miles to the nearest truck pass. They carried it Maya fashion on the back, supporting the weight by a tumpline across the top of the forehead, the strain falling on the muscles of the neck. It is a common sight in the highlands of Guatemala to see Maya men carrying tremendous weights in that way; a man single-handed—single-foreheaded perhaps one should say—will, it is asserted, carry a grand piano in that way without too much trouble.

From where the altar was left, it continued on tractor, train, and pitpan (flat-bottomed boat) to Belize, and thence to Chicago, where it is now on exhibition, with much other material, in the Chicago Natural History Museum.

We had trouble with our water supply. Our water hole, when full, was twenty-five to thirty feet across and a foot or eighteen inches deep, but much of its cubic capacity was taken up by rotting tree trunks and other vegetation which gave the water the color of strong tea and a most peculiar taste. As the dry season advanced, the pool dried up until we were dependent on water that oozed through the mud into pits dug in the bottom. It was an uncertain and slow business, for a day passed while the mud settled, the water was poured off, strained, and boiled, and then allowed to cool; and at the end it tasted of mud crossed with herb tea. Things got to such a pitch that a small pan of water crawling with larvae had to last me over a week for washing. My Maya boys, belonging to one of the cleanest races in the world, disliked the lack of washing facilities as much or more than I did.

Finally, when it looked as though the water would last hardly another day, I threw coins into the mud in four directions, emulating Maya sacrifices to the Chacs, their rain gods. Less than two hours later it began to rain in torrents; in a short time our camp was almost under water, and it poured all the next day. As there now was plenty of water, I told the Chacs that we had had enough and to stop sending more rain. This they did, but I must have offended them, for not another drop fell at Mountain Cow during the rest of the dry season, forcing us eventually to close operations through lack of water.

A few days after the rains I spent a Sunday at Camp 6. Mr. Williams called me over as soon as I arrived to learn if it were true that I had brought the rain, for stories of the sacrifice had spread to the mahogany workers. On my telling him of our rain-making, he replied that had he known what success I was going to have, he would have sent water to me on the Mengel Company's mules, for that would have cost the company far less than the stoppage of several days in all the mahogany operations caused by my fooling around with the old Maya deities!

What with the archaeological finds after burning copal and the rainstorm after the offering to the rain gods, a good missionary for the Maya religion could have made mass conversions among the Negro laborers on the Mengel concession.

Because of its remoteness from any settlement, howler monkeys were as common at Mountain Cow as alley cats in a small town, and equally noisy, and we saw a lot of spider monkeys. Peccary were fairly abundant; once my Maya boys shot five in one afternoon and then barbecued all five together on a large wooden frame. Deer and brocket were scarce, but we frequently saw the spoor of jaguars and tapirs, and ocelots occasionally entered our camp at night in search of food. Larger game birds, such as the greeny-bronze ocellated turkeys and curassow were scarce, but parrots, literally in hundreds, flew around our camp every evening; toucans were common, and we saw an occasional macaw or king vulture.

Ticks and the minute but very irritating red bugs swarmed at Mountain Cow. One hears of the supposed torture inflicted by ticks, but I have never found them extremely troublesome. A tick is large and is pulled out of the body easily, provided you are quick and catch him off guard. On the other hand, it is useless to make a second attempt right away if the first attempt fails, for then he is on guard and resists the pull with, so to speak, every muscle tensed, with the result that the body comes away but the head remains imbedded in the flesh, perhaps to fester. Red bugs are much more unpleasant, for they are too small to remove and will continue to itch for several days, particularly at night, but they are real torture only for the first two or three weeks. At the end of that period one builds up an immunity, perhaps from the poison absorbed, or he gets used to them, and the itching is not so agonizing, despite perhaps fifty to one hundred bites, most of them around the waist.

Perhaps to compensate for the few mosquitoes, there were plenty of jiggers at Mountain Cow. The Central American jigger is a small insect that bores a hole in one's foot, usually between the toes or under the nail of the great toe, and in it deposits a bag of eggs, like the egg bag of the spider, but smaller. To avoid trouble, one has carefully to work around the edge with a needle so as to remove the bag without breaking it. If not treated, the eggs hatch into small larvae, and very serious infections can develop.

There were also beef worms to trouble one's life. The larva, hatched from an egg deposited in the body by a species of yellow and green fly, lets you know it is there by little sharp spasms of pain every time it moves. The natives remove the worm by spreading tobacco leaf or juice over the opening; after a few minutes it can be easily squeezed out.

Lack of water brought our work at Mountain Cow to a close prematurely, but at the opening of the dry season of 1929, I returned there to work. As the labor situation at Socotz had not been good, I first went to San Antonio, my old stamping ground in the south, to recruit laborers. A week later my force of fifteen reached Belize. That evening I took them to the movies, something they had never seen, but I could have saved my money; they were much more impressed by the many shop windows, for none of them had ever been in any town except Punta Gorda with its one general store. They were far more interested in the display of shotguns and the varieties of cotton goods. An airplane, inaugurating the Belize run of Pan American Airways, circled Belize shortly after their arrival, but, although it was the first plane they had ever seen, it seemed to leave them unimpressed.

The following evening we embarked on the *Tenny Fly*, which I had chartered for the journey up the Belize River to El Cayo. The *Tenny Fly* (it is the local name for the dog flea), a typical flat-bottomed motorboat of the Belize River, was about thirty-five feet long, but half of this was devoted to the engine, cooking range, crew's quarters, and odds and ends. There remained a space about seventeen feet long, five feet wide, and five feet high to accommodate our supplies, which included food for twenty persons for two months, my fifteen Maya laborers, Jorge Acosta, a young Mexican archaeologist who was to spend a month at Mountain Cow, and myself. Acosta and I slung our hammocks as best we could in the confined space amidships, sung to sleep by the phut-phuting of the engine immediately behind us and the occasional clicks of the glottalized speech of my Maya laborers ahead.

173

The voyage was uneventful except for one minor disaster. Muddy (Amadeo) Esquivel, Gann's faithful factotum, who was to spend the season with me, had persuaded me against my better judgment that salted fish was just the thing to feed our laborers. These immense specimens, cut open for salting, had been stacked on the flat roof of the *Tenny Fly*. Unfortunately, the boat's engine conked out, and we were carried by the current under a wild fig tree. The branches raked the launch's roof, our pile of fish was swept into the water, and we were soon surrounded by a fleet of toy rafts. Some were fished back on board, but others bobbed along on the bosom of the Belize River headed for their home, the ocean deep. Those we rescued were never quite the same. The smell had been very noticeable when the consignment was first embarked; the bath washed much of the preservative salt out of the survivors, and by the time we reached Mountain Cow, five days later, even the mule that carried them as a sort of supercargo gave a series of self-pitying brays. Two or three days later—but I'd better draw a veil over that.

On the third morning we reached El Cayo where a train of eighteen mules, procured by Muddy, awaited us. Stores were distributed for loading—the arrangement of pack loads is an art known only to muleteers—and a journey of three hours took us to Benque Viejo (Fig. 18).

The San Antonio laborers were billeted in an empty house on the plaza, while Acosta, Muddy, and I made for the *cabildo*. To our distress we found that the interior had been remodeled since our visit of the previous year, and all the hammock hooks had been removed by order of a district commissioner who obviously was accustomed only to a camp cot. Muddy and I had only hammocks, so we moved over to the verandah of the house which the San Antonio boys were occupying. The verandah was delightful, and swinging in our hammocks there, we had a charming view of the grass-covered plaza of Benque Viejo bathed in the light of a full moon, but, as later events showed, we were seriously mistaken in anticipating a peaceful night.

Early in the evening the San Antonio boys had gone to Socotz, where they were at home among fellow Maya. Recollecting that this was the feast day of the Christ of Esquipulas and sad at miss-

Fig. 18.—Loading Mules, Benque Viejo.

ing the fiesta then in progress in their native San Antonio, they had drowned their homesickness in anise rum.

Muddy and I were almost asleep when the first of a series of dolefully drunk San Antonieros coming out on the verandah to relieve himself proceeded to pour out his grief to me, dwelling on the wonderful dance then being held at San Antonio and his sadness at missing such a glorious time and the opportunity of dancing with so many pretty girls. Having witnessed frequently the absolute lack of interest shown by Maya men in their dancing partners, I took this statement with a grain of salt, and bidding the homesick one be of good cheer and go to sleep, I turned over in my hammock and tried to do the same. Fifteen minutes later a second Maya appeared to tell of his rum-inspired homesickness, and at short intervals for the next hour or so I had a constant succession of tearful recitals of the miseries of leaving home. In the face of such dejection, rum-stimulated though it undoubtedly was, I felt that any display of wrath might lead to a sudden desertion of the whole gang, so I held my peace.

Next morning our cavalcade of eighteen mules and their mule-teers, the fifteen San Antonio Maya, once more of good cheer, my *compadre* Jacinto Cunil and another Socotz Maya, Acosta, Muddy, a one-eyed negress, whom I had engaged as cook, and myself started for Mountain Cow. The cook had at first refused a mule, saying that as she didn't know how to ride, it would be better to walk and thereby get only knee deep in mud rather than risk a fall from the mule and a consequent mud bath from head to foot. However, after wading through several deep swamps and after having had an ocular demonstration of the slow-moving Central American mule, she decided to risk the mud bath and hoisted her two hundred pounds on the back of one of the smallest mules in the outfit.

The hiring of a negress cook was a serious error, for she was used to preparing the flour scones which the creole population eats and did not have the art of making the thin maize tortillas my Maya men demanded. However, I had not been able to get a Maya woman as cook, and needs must when the devil drives.

It took us three days to reach Mountain Cow. The journey was depressing, for everywhere were the signs of the defeat inflicted on the Mengel Company by the forest. Mountain Cow camp looked unkempt. Several huts had collapsed since our departure the previous summer, but the water hole was full, a blessing.

In a burst of optimism I had bought two mules in Benque, in the belief that using them to fetch mail and needed supplies from there once a week and then selling them at the end of the season, when the start of the chicle work meant a good demand for mules, I was being smart; to hire two mules for the whole time would have come much more expensive, I thought. Moreover, I fondly hoped that my mules, which had been very thin when I bought them, would put on weight. I was sadly deceived. Night after night vampire bats attacked them, and every morning we found streaks of coagulated blood on their necks or their rumps where the bats had gorged. Apparently the blood-sucking did not disturb the animals; I have seen three bats at a time busily sucking blood from one of my mules which took not the slightest notice. Hurricane lamps in the mules' shed helped, but as soon as one of them moved into a position where its shoulders or rump was in shadow, the bats attacked.

I gave my muleteer money to buy maize for the mules when he took them to Benque Viejo, but the wretch spent the money on drink, I subsequently learned. What with the vampire bats and the lack of food on the weekly trips to Benque, the mules got even thinner. When I came to sell them, I was in a hurry to be on my way and didn't relish spending several days in Benque or El Cayo on the chance of getting a bid raised a few dollars. The buyers, of course, knew of my hurry to be gone, and by an extraordinary coincidence mules were a glut on the market, although the chicle season was about to start. In the end, practically as a favor to me, I was given to understand, they were bought at a price I'm still ashamed to tell. A fool and his money are soon parted—the trouble was that in this case the money was not his own, but the museum's.

Our season's work was very much like that of the year before. I had brought two cheap shotguns, which I used to lend to my workers on Sundays. It kept them happy, provided the men with fresh meat, and I was always given a bit of anything shot. One Sunday, Jacinto had one of the guns. That evening he reported that while hunting he had come upon a new group of ruins that lay only some six hundred yards from camp and that the pyramid at the south end of the main court was scarcely fifteen yards from the much trafficked trail to Camp 6 and thence to Benque Viejo. The rain forest was so thick that the whole of this site (it comprised nineteen pyramids and mounds, the largest over forty feet high and occupying an area of over fifteen thousand square feet) had been invisible from the main trail and had not previously been seen by any of my laborers in their hunting trips.

The forest is deceptive: in places the vegetation overhead is so thick that there is little undergrowth or one can get lost, as I did once at Mountain Cow, in a series of abandoned truck passes. On that occasion I sat down to await rescue, which in the form of Jacinto and some of my men reached me just as I was contemplating a night in the forest.

A far more serious case of losing oneself in the forest happened some years later when I was at El Palmar in Quintana Roo. On the day after our arrival I had sent my men out to look for stelae in the main court, which was, of course, under forest. They started off in a line anxious to find stelae, for which I had offered a reward, while I went about some other business. In the evening shortly after the men had quit work, my foreman reported that Maurilio, a young Maya of eighteen, was missing. Now Maurilio, unlike the rest of the men, was not accustomed to the forest; he had spent his life in a Campeche village where there was only secondary growth. The foreman fired shots and blew a cowhorn from the highest pyramid, but by then the short tropical dusk had fled and no search was possible. Next day and for the following two days the whole gang searched. Unfortunately, Maurilio in his ignorance had followed neither of the two rules for anyone lost in the forest: sit down and wait to be rescued or blaze a trail that can't be missed if you keep moving. The undergrowth where he had disappeared was not heavy; he had kept on without leaving any trail that could be followed.

I knew that if he traveled west, he would come to the main trail for the mule trains bringing chicle northward from the borders of the Peten; if he made his way eastward, he would eventually come to the Hondo River, and there were settlements on its banks. If he headed north or south, he could travel for days and days without finding any settlement. Had he, I wondered, enough knowledge to go west or make the more hazardous trip to the Hondo? Naturally, I felt extremely worried and, as the boy's employer, largely responsible for him. I notified the authorities in Campeche and awaited a summons to report there—a twelve-day round trip by mule, lorry, and light railway.

One morning, crossing the main court in which Maurilio had disappeared, I disturbed a flock of vultures, which rose in their clumsy flight from some bushes a few yards away. As I hurried forward, my heart sank, for I knew what I would find—only a dead body would attract such a flock of vultures. So Maurilio was dead, probably murdered, for it seemed impossible that he could have died a natural death there without his comrades knowing anything. I felt pity for the boy, and, selfishly, I worried about myself as a gringo fly entangled in the red tape of Mexican judicial proceedings. I came to the spot. There lay, not Maurilio, but a poor spider monkey one of my men had wantonly shot the previous day.

Exactly twenty days after his disappearance and the day before we were to leave El Palmar, Maurilio returned to camp. He was a walking skeleton, with deep-sunken eyes and the look of an old man; his tattered clothes failed to hide his emaciation. After losing himself, he had wandered around with no idea of which way to go. By great good luck, on the second day he stumbled across an old trail which led him to the abandoned village of Icaiche. This, an old stronghold of Maya who had revolted against the Mexicans and had kept their independence for many years, had been abandoned three years before when the Mexican authorities had persuaded the inhabitants, reduced to seventy, to move to a more accessible spot on the Hondo River. It had been the only village in the whole of that area from the Hondo to the opposite side of the peninsula of Yucatan. There were still fruit trees in Icaiche and, more important, water.

Luckily, at that time of year there is fruit in the forest: the fruit of the sapodilla, which yields the chicle sap, ripens in April as does the cherry-size fruit of the breadnut tree, which also produces the foliage which serves as a substitute for grass as mule fodder, and there are other edible fruits. Maurilio from Icaiche cast about until he found another water hole, and in that way he spent those twenty days, camping where there was water and searching each day for other sources of water or evidence of man. Finally he had come across some of our outlying lines of sight cut through the forest in mapping of the ruins.

Seeing Maurilio in that condition, I repeated to myself the comment of an old-timer in Belize on some incautious remarks by a pith-helmeted "explorer": "Anyone who says he likes the bush [forest] is either a bloody fool or a bloody liar."

The new site which Jacinto had found in his hunting trip we named Cahal Pichic, "town of the emerald green toucanets," because of the numbers of that beautiful bird a visiting ornithologist had seen there. There were a number of stelae, but all, alas! were plain. We did, however, find one more inscription that season, a small stone with a worn Initial Series 9.19.0.0.0. 9 Ahau 18 Mol, corresponding to June 26, A.D. 810.

The stone was round, small (just under two feet in diameter), and had been set in the ground with its carved face flush with the floor. All these features suggested that it had served as a ball-court marker. The trouble was that ball-court markers are usually arranged in threes down the center of the playing alley of a court, but there was only this one possible marker at Mountain Cow, and it was at the extreme north end of the playing alley, if such it was. I wondered whether perhaps the good people of Mountain Cow, hard pressed for labor, had constructed a makeshift ball court.

As a rule, the ball court with its two flanking mounds stands alone, but here at Mountain Cow one side of the ball court had been formed by building a small addition to one side of the principal pyramid to obtain the desired length of the court, and then constructing a small building parallel to this to form the other side of the court.

Subsequently Ruppert found a ball court at Chichen Itza one side of which was built against the platform of the Casa Colorada, a building of considerably earlier date. That showed that the Maya did at times build ball courts against the sides of standing structures to save time, labor, or space, and I think authenticates the dated stone of Mountain Cow as a ball-court marker.

Another puzzling find came from a spacious vaulted tomb of the Proto-Classic period. The floor was covered to a depth of about one foot with soil, and in this were a few pieces of bone so fragmentary that it was impossible to say whether they were human, two magnificent tubular rods of gray-green jade, each over six inches long, a pair of jade ear-plugs of the same color (the rods were probably attached to the ear-plugs), an obsidian knife blade, and seven pottery vessels. One of these last, a flat-based bowl on four solid feet, was a most remarkable piece, for attached to the bottom was a squatting toad most naturally treated so that even the animal's warts were carefully delineated. The whole vessel, including the toad, had once had a red slip, but time had removed most of that. It was strangely like those table centers with bird or frog in them so popular a few years ago in our own culture.

The bowl was useless for domestic purposes, and the Maya are hardly likely to have anticipated the twentieth-century habit of table decoration, if for no other reason than that they did not use regular tables. One must therefore fall back on the archaeologist's handy explanation of anything he does not understand—a ceremonial object. In this case there is some justification for the term. Frogs and toads are closely connected with the Chacs, the rain gods, for their croaking announces the rains and in Maya legend the frogs are the musicians of the Chacs, and among the Zapotec Indians the frogs of the rainy season are called sons of the rain gods. Accordingly, it is likely that this vessel was used in some rite in honor of the Chacs.

We might take our reasoning a step farther. As it was a Maya custom to bury with the deceased the tools of his trade—Bishop Landa mentions books being buried with priests—the occupant of this tomb may have been a priest of the Chac cult, and, as the four fine pieces of jade indicated the owner to have been a person of position, we may assume that he was a high priest.

The workers from San Antonio were a great improvement on our laborers of the previous year, but they were homesick and could not adjust themselves to the lack of good tortillas, so I closed down work early in April.

On the last morning, after the men had left, I went to the new ruins of Cahal Pichic. From the top of the highest pyramid one could see the feathery tops of the slender *botan* (tall *guano*) palm left standing in our camp when the rest of the trees were cut down. The air was fragrant with the smoke of a cedar tree, which had been smoldering for several days. Below, the main court, which we had cleared of vegetation, was again putting on its mantle of green. Fresh shoots were springing from the stumps of felled trees, and young shrubs with leaves not fully grown had started to obliterate scars of excavations; the reconquest of the cleared land by the forest had begun.

I felt sad at leaving. The finds had not been thrilling, but some were of archaeological importance. The friendly cheerfulness of the Maya laborers had kept us happy when the archaeological luck was out, and except for a few cases of malaria there had been little unhealth. So, like Robinson Crusoe, I could tot up the ledger and find a credit balance for the mercies.

7

Cities of the Peten

TWO DAYS AFTER LEAVING MOUNTAIN COW we were back in Benque Viejo, ready to partake of the joys of civilization. My Maya boys soon found them, for going to Socotz, they promptly filled themselves with *aguardiente*. This complicated matters, as their passage had been arranged on a motorboat leaving El Cayo at daybreak. From Belize they would take the *Maggie B.* to Punta Gorda and thence proceed on foot to San Antonio. Luckily the motorboat's departure was delayed long enough for me to shepherd them, *gomas* (hangovers) and all, to El Cayo.

With them safely aboard, I turned to arranging for a trip to Uaxactun, in the heart of the Peten district of Guatemala, where my old friends Oliver and Edith Ricketson, to whom I owed my first job at Chichen Itza, were excavating for Carnegie Institution of Washington. With them was Ledyard Smith, with whom I was to work many years later at Mayapan.

Agustín Hob, one of the San Antonio Maya, had offered to go with me. He was a sturdily built, about twenty-five, and one of the best hunters I have ever seen (Plate VId). He rarely missed a shot, and had the faculty of hearing game when no one else had the vaguest idea that there was any wildlife in the vicinity. As soon as he heard or, as I am half inclined to believe, scented the game, his features, usually placid, betrayed intense excitement. He crept forward with the agility and silence of a cat until he could get a good shot. Most remarkable feat of all was his ability to identify the species of game before he sighted it. With Agustín on the trip, I knew we would not starve.

I learned that there were two other white men in El Cayo also planning to go to Uaxactun. As there were only three pure European residents of the town, it was a simple matter to locate the strangers. They proved to be a Californian schoolmaster and a young graduate of Yale, surely the first people not connected with archaeology or chicle to visit those inaccessible ruins. We agreed to share expenses. Mules were hired and arrangements made for an early start next morning. As invariably happens on the first day of a trip, there were delays, and it was not until 9:30 that our mules reluctantly nosed their way out of El Cayo.

That evening we camped at Yalloch, picturesquely situated on the east shore of a largish lake of the same name. The forest encircles the lake, but to the west one can see the low hills of central Peten. The settlement comprised two thatched-roof buildings, one of which was a huge warehouse, which had been the Shuffeldt chicle station at the time that he held the chicle concession for the whole of northeastern Peten, but which now served as the customs, for during the afternoon we had crossed from British Honduras into Guatemalan territory. At Yalloch we were on the eastern edge of the great wilderness inhabited only by scattered bands of chicle gatherers, and then only during the rainy season, which covered an area of about twenty thousand square miles comprising the Peten district of Guatemala north of Flores and the southern parts of the Mexican state of Campeche and Territory of Quintana Roo. Now there are air fields and settlements in that area, and the exploitation of oil, in the words of the Maya prayer addressed to the earth god, is "about to dirty thy face" in the sacred name of progress.

Yalloch had been a chicle station for so long that there was no fodder for our mules within two miles of camp. Everywhere in the Peten on high ground the breadnut tree grows, the leaves of which are the mainstay of mules in the grassless forest. Unfortunately, the Central American muleteer, with no thought for the morrow, frequently cuts down a whole tree for his mules, with the result that in a few years the forest within a radius of a mile or more of any water hole is denuded of breadnut trees. If he would cut off a few branches as needed, there would never be a shortage, but such foresight is alien to the makeshift attitude of the average muleteer; it is easier to chop down a tree than to climb it. I have seen muleteers lay their axes to a wild cherry tree as the quickest way of getting a handful of cherries. Consequently, next morning we again made a late start as Gregorio, our muleteer, had had to tether his mules so far from camp.

Five hours' riding through forest and swampland, luckily dry at this time of year, brought us to a water hole known as Dos Arroyos, "Two Streams," but the one muddy water hole we saw scarcely justified the name; I was told that in the rainy season the streams are in full flood. I wanted to push on to the next water hole, but was outvoted by Cook and Barney, who were weary, and by Gregorio, who claimed that there would be no time to seek breadnut for the mules if we rode farther.

We slung our hammocks in a flea-ridden tumbled-down hut, where even Cook and Barney lost a little of their enthusiasm for the romance of the jungle when attacked by the plebeian flea. Professional "Explorers" write at length of jiggers and ticks, which fit into a tropical background of full moon, waving palms, and sensuous romance, but they never mention the ubiquitous flea, which, alas, conjures up visions of crowded buses, dirty boarding-houses, and unwashed clothes. I have ridden through abandoned *chicleros'* camps where—and I am not exaggerating—one could hear the rustle of tens of thousands of hungry fleas as, smelling blood, they made their eager anticipatory hops through the dry vegetation in the sun-scorched forest opening. Then the rider disengaged his feet from the stirrups and rode through the camp with ankles clasping the mule's withers and a prayer that no flea could jump quite that high.

We started from Dos Arroyos at 7:00 A.M. for San Clemente, where, rumor had it, there was no water. I hoped the rumor was

FIG. 19.—On the Trail in the Forest.

true as I wanted to push on to the next water hole, La Juventud. Technically, there was water at the San Clemente water hole, but it was a slimy liquid of the consistency of a can of condensed vegetable soup. We agreed to continue to La Juventud, but there the water hole was completely dry. As we were then a scant six miles from Uaxactun, my suggestion that we continue was agreed upon after a bottle of whisky had circulated and Gregorio had had enough out of it to forget that we would be on the trail after dark. Luckily, a good muleteer can adjust his mules' loads and tighten their girths drunk or sober.

After twelve hours in the saddle, we reached Uaxactun. Those monotonous, unending mule journeys belong to an age now as extinct as that of the Pickwick Club and Sam Weller, but they loomed so large in Maya archaeological life thirty years ago that my hand still itches to write of them, although my brain warns that they are as monotonous in the black and white of print as in the dull-hued greens, browns, and grays of remembered reality (Fig. 19). The plane covers in less than thirty minutes the distance from near El Cayo to the airstrip of Uaxactun, which took us three days' hard riding. For all that the plane passenger has a wide field of vision from his window seat, it is not a Maya field of vision; he is looking at the forest from above, whereas the Maya saw it from below; his life was compassed about by the forest— his crops, his meat, the materials of his hut and all its contents, except for objects of pottery and stone, came from the forest, his constant friend and antagonist.

Uaxactun (Plate x) was discovered by Morley in 1916 on a trip that nearly cost him his life. His party, mistaken for Guatemalan revolutionaries, was ambushed only about three miles from Benque Viejo and two of the party were shot dead; Morley owed his life to the fact that, a few minutes before, he had dropped his glasses and, in retrieving them, he lost his customary position at the head of the mule train. It was a sad ending to a season of exploration which had included the discovery of this remote site and what was until only two years ago the earliest-dated stela in the Maya area and the first stela to be discovered bearing a date in the Maya eighth baktun (400-year period). This woefully weathered shaft of stone carried the date 8.14.10.13.15. 8 Men 8 Kayab —that is 8 baktuns, 14 katuns (of 20 years), 10 tuns (360-day years), 13 uinals (20-day months) and 15 days after the usual starting point of the calendar. Morley has written of his discovery: ". . . that dreary and overcast afternoon when, coming through the dense bush, hot, tired and thirsty, [I] saw for the first time this now famous monument leaning like another Tower of Pisa, the numeral 8 of its baktun coefficient standing out clear and distinct." It was almost the only distinct feature, for the details of the glyphs were dreadfully eroded. It corresponds to April 9, A.D. 328. The earlier monument found at Tikal two years ago bears the date 8.12.14.8.15. 13 Men 3 Zip, corresponding to July 6 A.D. 292, also an Initial Series. This had been buried and so was much better preserved, but only the top part was recovered.

I speak with some certainty on the equivalent in our calendar, since that was a problem that had preoccupied me from my earliest days in Maya research, for I had thought—almost certainly wrongly—that if we could convert dates recorded on Maya monuments into the exact equivalents in our own calendar, we could then isolate dates of astronomical importance and thereby identify glyphs for the planets, important stars, and for such things as equinoxes, solstices, and heliacal risings and settings of planets. The idea was wrong; we now know that the Maya did not record such matters on their stelae with the exception of a notation of the age of the moon on the opening date of a text inscribed as the so-called Initial Series.

Our old friend Bishop Landa had given information which boiled down to this: the Maya New Year's Day for 1553 was the day 12 Kan (ripe maize) falling on the first day of the month Pop (mat), and this was July 16 Old Style (July 26 Gregorian). But there was a snag: could we be sure there had not been a break in the Maya Calendar in the centuries following the Classic period when the great ceremonial centers flourished? Four years before my visit to Uaxactun, Blom and La Farge had found the Maya of Jacaltenango in northwestern Guatemala were still using the old 260-day sacred almanac of the Maya and celebrating New Year in the old Maya patterns.

In following years, Maya calendars were found to be functioning in many Maya villages in the Guatemala highlands as the ritualistic focus of a whole order of shaman-priests and with the luck of the days guiding life just as in pagan times. Those newly discovered calendars in the highlands of Guatemala and one among the Mixe, a non-Maya group living in Oaxaca, solved the problem of a possible break; for all, including that of the Aztec, projected back to the arrival of the Spaniards agree to the very day except Landa's calendar, which was one day out (he probably collected it in 1551, but forgot to allow for the leap-year of 1552).

Despite every effort of the Spaniards for four centuries to stamp them out as flagrant foci of pagan infection (which, indeed, they were), they have survived without a loss of a day. How much more certain, therefore, that there was no break in the calendar between the end of the Classic period and the arrival of the white man. Had there been a break, it could hardly have affected the Mixe in their mountain fastness and presumably not the Aztec in distant Mexico City. Let us be more specific.

According to the log of the *Santa Maria*, Columbus discovered America on October 12, 1492, but from one end of Middle America to the other, in Mexico City or the steaming jungles of the Peten, that day was 13 Jaguar. So far as the Maya lowlanders, the heirs of the Maya classic tradition, were concerned, it was called 13 Ix and was the sixteenth day of the month Zotz' (Vampire Bat). That combination of day and month would not recur for fifty-two years [nearly 19,000 days). As the evidence is overwhelmingly against any break in the Maya calendar, we have that first check. Any alignment of the two calendars which fails to make the discovery of America fall on 13 Jaguar 16 Vampire Bat is wrong; chances of being right are 1 in 18,980. That is perhaps a little too restricted. It is fair to allow one day each side for possible shift of time when the Maya day started—sunrise or sunset or midday.

We can do better pin-pointing: the discovery of America fell in the katun (Maya period of 20 years) called 4 Ahau, and that only recurs after 260 years. Accordingly, only every fifth repe-

tition of 13 Jaguar 16 Vampire Bat (13 Ix 16 Zotz') can coincide
with the discovery of America. The problem is somewhat the
same as if in our calendar we had the event recorded only as October 12, '92 and we had to decide whether it was 1292, 1392, 1492,
or even 1792; in the case of the Maya reconstruction, the missing
part of the statement refers not to centuries but to periods of 260
years. As a result, four different correlations at intervals of 260
years were proposed. For instance, the date which the Maya wrote
(with our transliteration) 9.15.10.0.0. 3 Ahau 3 Mol and which
fell at the very height of the Classic period was October 29, A.D.
221 according to the Bowditch (A) correlation; was August 29,
A.D. 481 according to the Spinden (B) correlation; was June 28,
A.D. 741 according to the Goodman-Martínez-Thompson (C) correlation; and April 28, A.D. 1001 according to the Lehmann (D)
correlation. You paid your money and you took your choice.
Correlation B was once the favorite, but John Teeple, a New York
chemical engineer, caused a shift in the odds one-third of a century ago.

Teeple's business required him to take long train journeys, and,
not finding the conversation in the men's washroom of the Pull-
man car inspiring, he took up the study of Maya glyphs to occupy
himself on his trips. Soon he had solved the very difficult glyphs
which recorded the age of the moon on many important dates
carved on the monuments. Among his many incontrovertible decipherments was one giving the age of the moon at the date mentioned above (9.15.10.0.0. 3 Ahau 3 Mol) as nine days. According
to Correlation B, the moon was about nineteen days old on the
equivalent date in our calendar; according to C about nine days;
according to A and D about twenty-eight days (*about* because
it is not certain whether the Maya counted from disappearance
of old moon, conjunction, or appearance of new moon). This
knocked out Correlations A, B, and D, and supplied excellent
corroboration for Correlation C. Material on the planet Venus

was equally helpful. At dates which the Maya gave as those of heliacal rising of Venus after inferior conjunction, Correlation C was in agreement or only a few days off, whereas B and D were about 290 days off, about as far out as was possible. Archaeological evidence (architecture and ceramic sequences) favored Correlations C or D, but disagreed with A and B. The fight was over; Correlation C was the obvious winner. Practically everyone accepted it, and I, as its leading proponent, relaxed with a smug I-told-you-so attitude.

There was a rude awakening when the Carbon–14 process was discovered. Carbon 14 is an element in plant and animal life which starts to be given off when death occurs. At the end of rather over five thousand years half of the C–14 content of a dead organism has been given off, so that by measuring the loss of C–14 one can tell when a piece of wood or of charcoal or a bone died. Soon, samples of Maya wooden beams from temples at Tikal dated 9.15.10.0.0. 3 Ahau 3 Mol (the date already discussed) were tested for C–14 content. The first reading reached A.D. 481 (plus or minus 110 years), right on the nail so far as Correlation B was concerned, and a second independent test produced a reading even thirty years earlier. Persons with no knowledge of the problem excitedly proclaimed that Correlation B had been proved by C–14.

All the Carbon 14 in creation couldn't dissolve the disagreement of Correlation B with the Maya data on the moon and on the planet Venus, nor could it readily reconcile the correlation with the historical and archaeological evidence. The uncritical acceptance of the new process savored too much of dancing round the golden calf for my liking. Few new techniques are perfect when launched; time is needed to spot and eliminate the weaknesses. At least, that was the massage I applied to my damaged ego, as I refused to concede defeat.

The ten years elapsed since the first readings have brought many improvements, as was to be expected. A new gas process increases reliability. Also, results are now based, not on a single reading, but on several runs of samples to reduce errors from contamination or other causes. New C–14 readings of Tikal lintels and beams—thirty-three from one temple, thirteen from another—overwhelmingly support Correlation C. It was well worth waiting for. At one time it looked as though I was cast for the role of "The boy stood on the burning deck whence all but he had fled," but now that the flames are quenched, the passengers are rowing back to the old ship as fast as they can.

The correlation problem is at last solved beyond doubt, and it is remarkable how many lines of research have converged to reach that result. The writings of the Spaniards—notably Landa—were carefully studied (a manuscript on the calendar used in the early seventeenth century by the Chol Maya a scant fifty miles from San Antonio was found only a few years ago); the colonial writings of the Maya had to be checked for every calendric statement; hieroglyphic texts on the moon and the planet Venus were deciphered and brought in as controls; evidence of the calendars of the present-day Maya of colonial Guatemala, and of the Aztec was collated; pottery and architecture and historical sources were studied, and finally physics supplied the C–14 technique—a very pleasant example of co-operation in research.

The most spectacular find at Uaxactun was a low stucco-covered pyramid with stairways flanked with huge jaguar masks on all sides. The general effect was un-Maya. In the floor which formed the summit the Ricketsons had found post holes, evidence that a small hut with roof presumably of palm thatch had once crowned the pyramid. This structure with the singularly un-romantic designation of E–VII sub was in such remarkably fine condition because, as they so often did, the Maya had covered it with a larger pyramid, which was largely destroyed.

We visited this group after dinner on the evening following our arrival. From where we stood on the summit of a pyramid at the edge of the group, the plaza below, crisscrossed with trenches dug to trace floor levels and in search of potsherds of stratigraphical significance, looked like a miniature battlefield, but the stucco-covered pyramid beyond, softened by the light of a full moon, was indescribably beautiful. Behind it the forest, spared at the time the ruins were cleared of vegetation, supplied a curtain of velvet black, enhancing the cream-white of the stucco (Plate x). Even the grotesque features of the huge stucco masks were converted into reposeful beauty by the magic touch of moonlight.

At the foot of the pyramid stood a weathered stela, the carved surface of which, gray with age, recorded its erection over four-teen centuries ago. It bore the date 9.3.0.0.0. 2 Ahau 18 Muan, January 28, A.D. 495, and almost certainly had been placed in po-sition when the later E–VII pyramid was erected (the hole for the butt cut through earlier floors). Providing the stela had not been moved from some other position—and that is quite an assump-tion, since the Maya moved stelae around—the later building is dated by the stela, and the earlier pyramid was earlier still. Sty-listically it appears to be a lot earlier.

Burials at Uaxactun produced amazingly beautiful pottery with painted scenes of ceremonies, mythological creatures and so on, but technically it is not first-class work, being soft and porous. The reason, apparently, is that the lowland potters normally tem-pered their pots with calcite which cannot be fired at high tem-peratures (the calcite disintegrates). Much of the finely painted pottery is, however, tempered with volcanic tuff which could have been fired at much higher temperatures to produce a harder and less porous ware, but the lowland Maya did not realize this and continued to fire in low-temperature open-air kilns.

In recent years, thanks largely to the research of Miss Anna Shepard of the Carnegie Institution of Washington, the petro-graphic analysis of ancient pottery has made great strides, yielding vital information on the trade in pottery. For example, certain pottery vessels found at a site in New Mexico were tempered with tiny bits of old pots, the constituents of which showed that they had come from vessels not made locally. Potters might go a long way to get suitable clay, but they certainly would not go to a distant village to collect old sherds as tempering material, when there were plenty of broken pots in their own backyards. Obviously, then, those pots tempered with sherds from another region had been imported. Petrographic analysis has shown that more than one type of pottery found over vast areas of Central America was distributed from a single center. Such data yield very important information on trade and help to make a chronological framework into which to fit deposits in widely separated centers.

Most interesting, but disappointing, finds at Uaxactun were the remains in two burials of what may have been Maya hieroglyphic books. Had they been books in good condition, they would have been priceless, for only three such books have survived and all date from after the abandonment of Uaxactun. Pages of Maya books were of paper made from the bark of the wild fig coated with thin stucco to make a good writing surface. In the humid climate of the Peten the bark paper would disappear, leaving only the thin stucco. In the tombs were very thin layers of stucco with traces of green and red paint on them. It is uncertain that these were the remains of books—one would expect different colors— but that is a reasonable explanation. Uaxactun also produced some unusual offerings. A hollow in a platform or altar contained huge quantities of shrew bones mixed with burned sherds, and a dedicatory cache of another altar included innumerable skeletons of bats, rats, and other small rodents. Bats were important in Maya mythology, but it is hard to imagine why the Maya should have made these offerings of rats and shrews on such a solemn occasion. The skull of a puma painted red contained in another votive cache or the skeleton of an ocelot in yet another are understandable, but on the whole my friends of Camp 6 and Mountain Cow with their offerings of jade pectoral and glyph-inscribed celt were more generous.

Common objects in votive caches under buildings or stelae, often nine in each offering, are flints and pieces of obsidian which we call eccentric flints or obsidians. Some are shaped as snakes, scorpions, or even dogs or men (Fig. 24) but for the most part they are oddly shaped crescents, tridents, or what look like sausage rolls with bites out of each side. No satisfactory explanation of their purpose has ever been made; and it doesn't get us much further to say they might be religious symbols.

South of Uaxactun, a few miles as the crow flies but a good six hours by mule, is Tikal, the largest of all Maya cities. This, Barney, Cook, and I decided to visit. We managed to lose our way, following the wrong trail, and slept in an abandoned chicle camp. Next day our mules had strayed, and we had an enforced stay in that tick and flea-infested waterless camp. We never learned its name, but that was perhaps just as well, for as likely as not it was called, in the best *chiclero* tradition, *El Triumfo*, "Triumph," *El Paraiso*, "Paradise," or *La Gloria*, "Glory." I have sometimes wondered whether *chicleros* frequently give high-flown names to their camps in moments of optimism or of disillusion.

In a second attempt we reached Tikal, Edith Ricketson coming with us. Of that journey I have written in *The Rise and Fall of Maya Civilization*. Then Tikal slept in all its grandeur beneath the forest. There was a troop of spider monkeys, and some agoutis, so important in Maya religion, were the living past. Now all is changed. Now Tikal has an air field and hotel accommodation (at twelve dollars a day) for tourists. The University Museum of the University of Pennsylvania has now been working there for several years on a very large scale, and has made dramatic discoveries.

I revisited the site in 1962, the comfortable hour's ride by plane contrasting strangely with that trip of thirty-four years earlier.

It also supplied me with a superb example of one-upmanship which would turn Stephen Potter green with envy. A lady sitting across the aisle from me, having decided that the detective story I was reading was not correct preparation for the other kind of mystery awaiting us in Tikal, leaned over and said to me, "You ought to be reading this, not a who-done-it." The book she showed was one I had written. "Madam," I replied," I don't really need to read it; I wrote it."

I had started on the trip with misgivings about what had happened to the tranquil beauty of Tikal, for it is not always kind to arouse sleeping beauties to our troubled world. I had visions of Tikal awakened, not by the brush of Prince Charming's lips, but by the biting caress of a bulldozer. My alarm was needless; Ed Shook, as director of the project, has done a wonderful job of fitting archaeological needs to the preservation of what was. Some needed restoration has been done, but a parklike atmosphere has been created which is altogether charming. The spider monkeys are still there; we saw some, not from a mule's back, but from the seat of a Land Rover!

Tikal is the premier Maya city not only for its extent, but for the height of its principal pyramids (Plate xiia). There are at least ten pyramids of outstanding size, of which the five huge ones in the main group are the most spectacular because they are within a reasonably small area. The labor that went into their construction staggers the imagination when one realizes that in addition to these giants, even more work and of a kind calling for proportionately more skilled labor went into erecting the many, many smaller structures. That work absorbed a higher proportion of skilled artisans because the ratio of standing building to substructure was higher than in the case of the great pyramidal constructions. It was the piling up of material for the massive cores of rock and rubble which kept the unskilled labor busy. From the top of the greatest of these temple-capped pyramids to the court below is about 190 feet, but the court itself was artificial, and, besides, part of the roof crest above the building had collapsed, so that the total height was once not far off 220 feet.

One large pyramid, with its temple, which because it stands in an outlying group was discovered only a few years ago, has a unique feature. The back and sides of the roof crest as well as the top molding of the temple are decorated with enormous glyphs, at least 186 of them. The roof crest (also called roof-comb) is a sort of huge wall which was placed on the roof of a temple to add to the height and consequent grandeur of the whole structure and to supply a space on which masks and figures of gods modeled in stucco could be displayed. At Tikal roof crests are of imposing dimensions, and this particular one on Temple VI has a height of forty feet. The weight of the mass on the temple below would have been too great had not the Maya made them hollow.

This roof crest, then, instead of carrying masks of gods and similar religious symbols, had a hieroglyphic inscription, but each glyph block is three feet wide and two feet high. The outline of the glyph was carved in stone, but the detail characterizing each was worked in the stucco with which the stone outline was covered, and finally the stucco was painted red. Unfortunately, the passing years, although they were the subject of the text, have dealt unkindly with it; much of the stuccoed detail has gone and the stone below is weathered. Also, standing there like small-print advertising on a hoarding around the cross of St. Paul's, it is hard to photograph; even now, a decade after its discovery, it has not been adequately photographed, and each year a little more stucco falls.

Tikal is enormous and solid, but in its heavy art and its architecture it has a kind of Teutonic–Pennsylvania Dutch atmosphere, and one feels that the rooms ought to be furnished Victorian style with antimacassars and fringed velvet table cloths. Yet in Palenque one would not dream of such furniture—those rooms call for Adam or Hepplewhite. At its height Tikal must have been a political power to reckon with, but why there should have been such a concentration in the middle of the Peten, where the soil is not too good and where there were few natural resources, it is hard to say.

The Maya in the highlands controlled the much prized jade, they had plentiful supplies of obsidian which as the raw material for knives was of great value, they had the very valuable trade in quetzal feathers in their northern fringes, and they also had the plentiful supplies of volcanic rock which made the best metates for grinding corn. Tikal could offer only worked flint, lime used for shelling maize and for mixing with tobacco, and the fauna and flora of her forests. I doubt that she was a large producer of cacao, the currency of Central America, for that grows best in the deep black soil of the river valleys. The city is not even located on any obvious trade route. Yet there must be some reason for its greatness which has escaped modern students.

Evidence is accumulating that at Tikal, as at other Maya ceremonial centers, the expulsion or massacre of the ruling class was not followed by a general exodus from the region. The University of Pennsylvania expeditions have found outlying mounds containing effigy pottery of the so-called plumbate type which was not made until after the close of the Classic period, clear evidence that people continued to live in the vicinity after rulers disappeared, and that they were wealthy enough to acquire this unusual pottery manufactured on the Pacific Coast on the Guatemala-Chiapas border, over three hundred miles away across mountain and swamp.

This peasant community made feeble efforts to keep up the stela cult, although one may suppose that no member could read the hieroglyphic texts. Broken fragments of stelae were reset. In most cases it is impossible to say when that happened, but in the case of one newly discovered monument, Stela 23, there is evidence that the top part was set up in its present location at some time not earlier than the very close of the occupation. It is a pathetic witness to past grandeur, for the figures on three sides lack legs and the hieroglyphic text on the fourth side breaks off in the middle.

The faces are mutilated, although whether that was their condition when the fragment was set up cannot, of course, be proved. The damage may have been done less than a century ago, when there was a small settlement of Yucatec and Lacandon Maya there. The Maya believe that the stelae, as well as other ancient things, notably incense burners, come to life at night, and they deliberately smash them in the belief that they harm the living.

Pennsylvania archaeologists also found evidence of a much later intrusion at Tikal. A pit six feet deep had been made in the floor of Temple 1 (Plate xiia), which with its pyramid forms one of the most spectacular buildings in the main court at Tikal. The bottom four feet were filled with burned human bones, and fragments of incense burners and other pottery vessels of types which were probably made around five hundred years after the end of the Classic period. It is tempting to attribute this deposit to the Itza, a Maya group which maintained its independence until 1697.

This attraction for the old sites continues to the present day. The Lacandon still made pilgrimages to the ruins of Yaxchilan and Bonampak a few years ago, leaving their incense burners in the temples. The Chorti Maya do the same at Copan, and in this present year of Grace, Maya farmers still sacrifice turkeys at one of the cenotes within the walls of the great city of Mayapan as their ancestors did before the coming of the white man.

It is interesting to compare the Maya reaction to the decline and final expulsion of the friars and the later overthrow of the landowning class with what almost certainly happened at the end of the Classic period.

Large-scale building of churches and religious buildings marked the domination of the friars from the sixteenth to the end of the eighteenth century, and the Maya peasant must have been kept almost as busy working for them on religious constructions and for the Spanish landlords on their haciendas as his ancestors had been in building pyramids and cultivating the land of the priest-ruler group. What happened after the disappearance of the friars and the expropriation of the haciendas is worth noting. Everywhere today in Yucatan and especially in Campeche one comes upon ruined hacienda buildings and cracked and roofless churches, the modern equivalents of the ruined Maya ceremonial center.

Just as the Maya of a thousand years ago crept back to the old centers for his religious rites, so today in villages which seldom see a priest and which are no longer under the shadow of the *hacendado* the recitation of a novena is one of the commonest features of village life and there are few houses without a domestic altar supporting crucifix or picture of the Virgin of Guadalupe; religion has passed to village control. Finally, in the courts of many once stately hacienda buildings are to be seen the thatched huts of the former peons, an exact parallel to the situation at Uxmal which I described in Chapter 2.

Our stay at Tikal had to be short for there was no water. We could have kept going for several days, but the mules could not. After dinner the others slung their hammocks from trees in the great court once crowded with spectators of some long-forgotten ceremony. I chose a room in one of the big buildings overlooking a deep canyon which bisects the city. On its far side towered one of the largest pyramids, and I looked forward to seeing it bathed in moonlight. Believing my room to be above the range of the many sandflies, I did not use my mosquito net. With Agustín's help I tied the hammock ropes to sapodilla poles the Maya had used to strengthen the vault, one at one end of the room, the other in a small L-passage at the other end. Agustín departed with the lantern, and in the dark I climbed into my hammock only to hear an eerie noise as though someone were slowly coming down the passage bearing some bulky object which brushed against the walls. Remembering stories of Indians and *chicleros* that Tikal was haunted, I wondered whether the irate ghost of some Maya priest had come to throw me into the canyon for desecrating by my presence his ancient haunts. Then I realized that the noise was made by the rope of the swinging hammock rubbing against the passage corner.

Later the rising moon silvered the sky, against which the vast bulk of Temple V was silhouetted. I saw more than I had anticipated of that stupendous sight; I was wrong about the sandflies. All night they stung me, creeping under the blanket which like Caesar's toga I wrapped around me.

Next morning Edith Ricketson and I looked wrecks. After warning Cook and Barney to overlook no openings in their mosquito nets, she, who had probably more experience in camping in the Peten forest than any other gringa, had forgotten to tie up the "sleeves" of her own net, through which the ropes of the hammock pass. The tenderfeet were as fresh as paint; the old-timers much the worse for wear.

We left next afternoon. On the way we passed directly beneath a troop of spider monkeys. One large one, perhaps the leader of the troop, resented our presence. With his legs against the tree trunk and leaning down with his weight borne by his tail wrapped around a branch, he shook another branch as hard as he could while he chattered at us in irate tones and then started tearing off small branches to throw at us.

The Maya say that monkeys descend from the young brother of the sun god, who climbed a tree in search of fruit. As he climbed, he gradually turned into a monkey; the blanket around him became the monkey's hair, and his loincloth its tail. When his brother on the ground asked him if he had reached the fruit, he chattered back at them *"wac-wac-wac,"* like a spider monkey. Clearly the Maya recognized that man and monkey shared a common ancestry perhaps a thousand years before Darwin reached the same conclusion.

They liked the spider monkey as a decoration on pottery (Fig. 20).

FIG. 20.—Animal Designs on Pottery. Left to right: monkey and cockroach, Uaxactun; heron, Labna; monkey, Mountain Cow.

A final night in Uaxactun and we started back for El Cayo. The trip had not been unprofitable for Agustín. The child of the caretaker had been ill, and his father, sharing the faith of all mestizos in the witch-doctoring power of Indians, had called Agustín in to effect a cure. Agustín's incantations and prayers to drive out the evil winds which had caused the sickness were, he thought, more efficacious than Ricketson's treatment, although Ricketson had had advanced medical training and would undoubtedly have cured the trouble in short time without cost.

There was an unwonted air of festivity in El Cayo, due, we discovered, to the arrival of a score of bicycle racers, the first ever to ride from Belize to El Cayo. "Ride" is hardly the right word, for in the absence of roads the bicyclists had had to carry their bikes on their shoulders along many miles of the trail. Everything else being equal, the man with the lightest bike stood the best chance of winning. That night there was a dance on the tennis court at El Cayo. Amid eulogistic speeches the riders were feted, and copies were circulated of a "poem" in which their feat was compared to Lindbergh's recent crossing of the Atlantic. A suggestion of Barney's that the race should continue to Uaxactun was not well received. Two days later the three of us and Agustín embarked on a motorboat for Belize.

In a few days I was back in San Antonio to get more ethnological information, and I decided to revisit Pusilha, where the British Museum was working.

Agustín Hob, his younger brother, Modesto, who came along for the fun of the trip, and I started on foot at 5:00 A.M. We made the journey, stopping only for a bathe in the Moho River and five minutes to eat some tortillas, in eleven and one-half hours, a distance of at least thirty-three miles. We could never have done it in that time on horse or mule, for their walking pace is slower than a man's and much of the trail would have had to be opened up to let a mule through. I took a weak whisky followed by four cups of tea and promptly vomited, for we had eaten only three tortillas apiece since our breakfast before dawn.

Next morning Joyce took me to see the most important find. This was an old cave or natural shaft in the limestone formation crammed with pieces of broken pottery, all late Classic. Many were painted, and enough pieces of some were recovered to allow complete restoration. A few designs showed human figures or gods exquisitely painted; others were clearly derived from plants. These were unusual, for plant motifs, aside from the water-lily design, are uncommon in Maya art. It is strange that the Maya, whose life was passed amid exuberant vegetation, should have made so little use of it in their art. This was obviously a city dump.

In the main court stelae were being prepared for shipment. They were too heavy to be shipped as they were, but large areas of uncarved or completely weathered stone could be cut away to reduce them to manageable weight. Later they were hauled by tractor to Punta Gorda along a road opened for the purpose.

It was a pleasant visit, and I was sorry when the time came to start for "home." We stopped the night again at the Kekchi village of Aguacate, lodging in the hut of the second alcalde.

At one hut an all-night vigil was taking place, for the owner was to sow his milpa the following day. The interior was crisscrossed with the hammocks of the ten or twelve men who were to help. They had joined the owner to insure the continence of all who were to take part in the sacred duty of sowing *la gracia*, "the grace." The men were lounging in the hammocks, talking and listening to the music of violin, guitar, and harmonica. At midnight copal and prayers were to be offered to Xulab, the god of the planet Venus and a protector of hunters and agriculturists, but I felt too weary to stay for the ceremony.

Mosquitoes and sandflies were plentiful and a tree bark spread on the ground made a hard couch, so I might just as well have stayed up to see the Xulab ceremony. Just as I was falling into a good sleep, the noise of maize being ground on stone metates for the men's breakfast of tortillas banished all hope of sleep, although it still lacked about two hours to dawn.

As a farewell I decided to give a dance for my Maya workers at Mountain Cow. I had first to obtain permission from the alcalde, a fine old Maya whose grandson had worked with me. I was summoned to the *cabildo,* where the alcalde was in session with the village elders. My request was speedily granted. At the close of the session the drum was beaten, but on asking the reason for this, I was told that no one knew; it had always been the custom. The Maya would have considered the Tzar of all the Russias a dangerous enemy of the established order.

As a dance at San Antonio would hardly have been a success without liquid refreshment, I sent to Punta Gorda for a gallon of *aguardiente,* and I bought locally a hog, maize to make tortillas, and a good supply af cacao. On the afternoon before the fiesta, while the hog was cooking, Agustín came to me to say that I had forgotten to purchase rockets, for, he informed me, it was a custom to fire them off when the giver of a dance took the floor. A firm believer in Maya tradition, I hastily procured some.

The dance was to have started about 9:00 P.M., but at that time not a woman had arrived, although all my Mountain Cow laborers were on hand. As the dance could not very well proceed on a unisexual basis, two of the boys and I went round the village from hut to hut, persuading the girls to hurry to the dance. Soon a number of them in their best *huipils* (long white blouses) put in an appearance.

After the dance had been in full swing for some time, I plucked up courage to invite a girl to dance, employing the San Antonio method of waving a handkerchief in front of her. As soon as we started to dance a *zapateado*, there was a tremendous crash and roar outside the hut. The rockets, which I had clean forgotten, had been fired.

Everything went splendidly. Soon after 4:00 A.M. I slipped off to my hammock in the *cabildo*, as I was leaving early next morning. At 5:00 A.M. I was awakened by a deputation, all of whom clearly had had one over the proverbial eight. They produced a bottle of *aguardiente* and invited me to join them. So far as I was concerned, it was no time for a drink of even the best Scotch, let alone a shot of raw anise-flavored *aguardiente*. I politely refused, whereupon the leader of the deputation renewed his urgings, giving them greater force by switching from Spanish into his idea of how to say in English that it would make me feel fine. "It will make you so pretty," he said. The argument was irresistible.

Soon after 8:00 A.M. I was on my way to Punta Gorda, mounted on a white horse so decrepit that it might once have carried old Uncle Tom Cobbley and all. Ten minutes' ride brought me to a slight rise, from which one catches a last glimpse of the village. San Antonio looked peacefully beautiful in the morning sun, the palm-thatched huts reflected a strange purple in the morning light. Beyond the slight hollow in which the village lay the forest swept up to the hills; in the foreground a group of women washing clothes in the small creek at the village edge was just discernible.

I have never returned.

8

Copan, Eastern Outpost

Two weeks after my farewell to San Antonio I left Belize for Puerto Barrios on a small Norwegian fruit boat with accommodation for two passengers. The passenger list consisted of the Ricketsons, a ventriloquist and his wife, a honeymoon couple, several Guatemalan girls from a convent school in Belize, myself, and, if memory is not trying to improve the story, a couple of other passengers. The convent girls spent the night on the starboard deck holding a novena; the honeymooners admired the moonlight in a single deck chair on the port side; Ricketson and I slept on diningroom settees, while the others fitted into cabins vacated by the ship's officers.

Puerto Barrios is a typical O Henry banana port. There can be recognized all the characters in his Central American stories—tropical tramps, pompous Latin-American officials, revolutionary leaders resting between bouts, diminutive shoeless soldiers, banana workers of every race and color, and the flotsam and jetsam of a port. The town, hot, dirty, and roadless, has none of the charm of the old towns of the highlands. It has been my fate, one time and another, to lose about ten days out of my life waiting there with scant patience for coastal boats. Knowing no one in the United Fruit Company's quarters, I could while away time counting the triangular fins of sharks patrolling the harbor as they waited for their daily ration of offal, or take the only walk inland, past innumerable *cantinas* and houses of ill-fame where sluts sat on dilapidated verandahs, sharks of a more tainted breed.

The train carried us from the humid heat of Puerto Barrios (it has an annual rainfall of a little over ten feet!) to the cool mountain climate of Guatemala City. For the first three hours the track cuts through an almost continuous series of banana plantations, an endless green tunnel with walls broken by occasional clearings in which stood the houses of farm managers and laborers, painted a uniform yellow. We were in the empire of the United Fruit Company, with its center at Quirigua, the great Maya city with its slender, beautifully carved stelae which rise to an amazing height. All empires end, and that had been the fate of that of the United Company on the Atlantic plain. A few years later Sikatoca disease swept it away and the area was abandoned; all that activity is no more, a strange repetition of the fate that overtook this same region one thousand years earlier. I understand that it is once more under cultivation.

The train left the banana lands, and suddenly we were traversing a semidesert of grassless fields strewn with pipe-organ cactus and stunted thorny trees. Verdant patches contrasting with the dun-colored landscape marked the course of the Motagua River and tributary streams.

After five hours the train stopped at Zacapa for a lunch, which even retrospection cannot endow with nobility. Zacapa must have been a great center in the old days, for the railroad bed is laid on a vast deposit of obsidian and everywhere are the rejects of Maya knappers. From here probably was exported much of the enormous quantity of obsidian blades, spear points, and cores which occur at every Maya site.

The train slowly snaked its way around hills with sparse semidesert scrub, but as the afternoon wore on, the vegetation increased and the temperature dropped with rising altitude. At stations close to Guatemala City were Indian vendors of fruits, tamales, and *tacos,* just as in Yucatan. At sunset the train pulled into Guatemala City, a small island of whites and mestizos in an Indian sea that stretched northwestward into Mexico.

Among the ultraconservative Maya of the highlands the fires of native inspiration still burn brightly. Arts and crafts, social organization, and religious observances of pagan times are tenaciously preserved. In large towns and remote villages alike the ancient 260-day sacred calendar of the Maya still flourishes, functioning in practically the same manner as in pre-Columbian times. Sorcerers still dice the days in search of favorable formulae, and the Maya farmer of the highlands continues to govern his life by its arrangement, planting and reaping his crops on propitious days, and consulting the calendar experts for days favorable to every activity he contemplates. The tally of the days has been kept unbroken despite every effort by church and civil authorities to stamp out this relic of heathenism.

The empty towns to which the Maya flock for their religious and civic functions are relics of the ceremonial centers of ancient times. To understand Maya archaeology, one must immerse oneself in these survivals, but for the moment my interests lay elsewhere.

Two weeks later I was back in Zacapa, that time in the company of Dr. and Mrs. Spinden. Our destination was the great Maya site of Copan, in the Republic of Honduras, best reached in those days by mule from Zacapa.

The trail stretches eastward across the cactus-strewn plain for a few miles, and then starts its climb into the hills. Mud huts are grouped in scattered settlements along the watercourses, but the farther from Zacapa the fewer there are. The rough road narrows to a boulder-strewn footpath which zigzags up the hills, descending into rugged valleys to cross dried watercourses, to rise more steeply on the far side. Progress was slow, for with halts to adjust cargoes and other delays the pace was under three miles an hour.

Riding in single file made conversation difficult; the silence was broken only by the shouted curses of the muleteer at a laggard mule and the metallic clang of iron-shod hoof against rock. The higher country was uninhabited, and life seemed to be confined to innumerable lizards, that resentfully abandoned their sun baths at our approach, and myriads of crickets vibrating a hidden chorus.

Late in the afternoon we filed into the little town of Jocotan, halfway between Zacapa and Copan, and high enough to insure a cool night. Jocotan, like every Latin-American town, sprawls around a large plaza, flanked on one side by the long, low municipal courthouse, on another by the church. In the seventeenth century the Spaniards were few; the surrounding Indians many and not friendly. The architecture of the church clearly reflects the dual purpose of worship and defense for which it was built: an outside staircase leads to the roof, which is surrounded by a brick battlement. Thither the little settlement could retire in times of danger—the women and children to safety; the men to line the defenses. Now the staircase slowly crumbles, its neglected appearance adding to a scene already pregnant with beauty.

In the cool of the early evening the plaza was very restful, with the whitewashed walls of the houses, topped by weathered red tiles, against the background of mountains with their earth colors broken by the dark pine forest on their upper slopes. A cerulean blue in the direction of Zacapa faded into the pale lemon of a cloudless sunset. There was no hotel; we slung our hammocks on the verandah of the little straw-thatched *posada*. Close at hand the mules seemed content with their vitaminless diet of dried corn-stalks—the best fodder in this grassless land. A guitar was half-heartedly strummed, but the sparse oil lamps in the houses were dimmed early, and Jocotan relapsed into silence broken only by the barking of dogs and the steady munching by our mules of the diminishing pile of cornstalks.

Next morning we were on our way as soon as coffee had been

drunk and the inevitably broken girth had been mended with string. A mile or so beyond Jocotan lay Camotan, a small town with a striking eighteenth-century church decorated in a local plateresque style. Camotan means place of the sweet potatoes; Jocotan, place of the plums. The country became wilder and more mountainous. In places the narrow trail clung to the mountainside, while, hundreds of feet below, the torrential Copan River roared its protests at the boulders impeding its hurried rush to the sea. High up the mountain slopes were little scattered settlements of the Chorti Maya. The Chorti we saw appeared a timorous lot, either passing with downcast faces, or, in the few places where that was possible, slipping off the trail to let us pass. All traditions of their great past lost, they lived in apparent contentment in little settlements of four or five huts, tending their maize and sugar-cane fields. These were high up the mountain sides and frequently so steep that one wondered why they did not slide into the valleys below.

Probably the ancestors of the Chorti built Copan, for the Chorti occupied the area between Copan and Quirigua at the time of the Spanish conquest, while their cousins the Chol occupied a strip across the base of the Yucatan peninsula covering the south of British Honduras, the great cities of the Usumacinta, and parts of Chiapas, including the great ruins of Palenque. The Chorti language differs from Cholti, spoken by the Chol, only in the substitution of an r for the l of the latter, and both are as close to Yucatec Maya as Spanish is to Portuguese. I was struck by the strong resemblance of some of the Chorti to Maya portraits on stelae of the Classic period.

Chol and Chorti are dying peoples. The former are reduced to an island around Palenque; the culture of the latter is being rapidly infused with Latin-American elements and survives only in the smaller settlements. A century and a half ago Jocotan was Chorti-speaking, but today culturally, linguistically, and racially it is predominantly Spanish. This disintegration of native culture before the advance of "civilization" is sad, for material advances do not bring greater happiness or compensate for lost spiritual values.

The mountain home of the Chorti is reminiscent of the remoter parts of the Scottish highlands. Soon we were in sweet-smelling pine forests. At the top of the pass there was a small pile of stones, surmounted with a cross and decorated with little bunches of flowers and bundles of pine needles, a Chorti offering to the old Maya mountain god with a touch of Christianity imparted by the cross. Similar offerings, except for the presence of the cross, have been made by the Maya since time immemorial on mountain tops, at springs, and at the forks of trails or streams.

For several hours we rode around or over mountains until, just before sunset, we topped yet one more rise and found ourselves looking down into the Copan Valley. Three miles away the mass of the main group of ruins could be distinguished beyond the modern town of Copan. A few feet from where we stood a solitary stela appeared to welcome us to the city.

We found quarters in the house of a German, owner of a store on the town plaza. The Spindens were given the guest room; I swung my hammock in the verandah of the patio. Our hosts invited us to dinner, a cosmopolitan meal, for we comprised the German, his French wife, the Spindens, who were Americans, a Hondurenian maid, and myself, an Englishman.

The Copan authorities charged us the outrageous amount of five dollars apiece to visit and photograph the ruins. They knew that visitors, having spent two days on muleback to get there, would hardly refuse. Spinden vociferously maintained that it was disgraceful that he who had done so much to make Copan known to the world should have to pay, but his protests went unheeded. The ruins, a little over a mile from the town, stand on one bank of the Copan River. In assemblage and general orientation, they resemble the cities of Peten rather than those of Yucatan or the Usumacinta-Chiapas region.

Passing through the great court with its numerous stelae and altars and the ball court, excavated by the Carnegie Institution (Plate xv), we made straight for the ruins of the great hieroglyphic stairway, which I was most anxious to see. This, thirty feet wide and comprising sixty-three steps, led to the summit of a pyramid. Each step had been carved with hieroglyphs, and at every tenth step was set a stone statue, almost in the round, of an individual or god of heroic size with elaborate headdress surmounted by the mask of a deity or mythological creature. Unfortunately, the greater part of this magnificent construction had collapsed. Excavations, made about sixty years ago, revealed a few steps *in situ* at the base of the pyramid. A few others were still in their original sequence, but not in their original position, for they had slid down the side of the pyramid en masse after the facing, of which they had formed part, had become detached from the core of the pyramid.

Much of the text is lost or irrevocably out of sequence—a sad end for what had been perhaps the longest Maya text ever carved. In 1940, Gustav Stromsvik, whom I had first known at Chichen Itza, completed the rebuilding of the stairway. The intact steps are back in position and the disarranged remainder have been reincorporated. Of the temple on the summit nothing remains, but the hard lime floor, although badly smashed by tree roots, was carefully fitted together, and indicates the plan of the original single-room temple, a fine piece of careful reconstruction.

The Copan River, which flows past the base of the great acropolis dominating the city, had been carrying off a little of the great structure every rainy season. A sixteenth-century account tells of a great stairway leading down to the river, but that has been entirely swept away, and it looked as though in time there would be no Copan left. When the Spindens and I were there, erosion had left a nearly perpendicular cliff one hundred feet high, like a gigantic cake with a slice off it. In the face one could pick out drains, floors, and construction levels. In a brilliant piece of en-

Fig. 21.—Hieroglyphs. Left, entwined figure glyphs for 9 baktuns and 15 katuns. Gods of numbers are white; birds, representing the periods, are shaded. Glyph of a god of the night. Right, jade from sacred cenote, Chichen Itza. The glyphs and the figure show it was incised at Palenque, over three hundred miles away, about A.D. 700.

gineering Stromsvik built a diversionary canal, and, damming the river, sent it flowing down its new course away from the ruins, so that when next I was in Copan, the great acropolis—it is calculated still to contain over two million tons of man-laid material—was safe, but it will require constant vigilance to see that the river does not resume its wicked course.

Copan stone is not the limestone used in most Maya cities, but a volcanic stone, andesitic tuff. This has two very pleasant features about it—it is colored a pistachio green which gives it a most attractive appearance, and it is so hard that the hieroglyphic texts exposed to the elements for so many centuries are much better preserved than those in limestone country (very many texts in the northern Peten are totally eroded). Copan has a large number of hieroglyphic texts—a quick reckoning shows 101, counting the hieroglyphic stairway as a single text—but some are very fragmentary. As a matter of fact, I supplied one of these on the 1929 trip. Climbing the steps flanking the north stairway of the great court, I noticed what looked like numerical bars on one step. We pulled the stone out, and found that it was part of a stela which probably had been discarded and then cut up to make steps. The few glyphs were not enough to give the dedicatory date, but they are of early style and probably date the stela about A.D. 550.

Most Maya monuments were erected to mark the end of a katun (20-year period) or a half- or quarter-katun. Both Morley and I found it very useful to know by heart the day and month positions on which each katun and half-katun ended for the 350 years during which most Maya monuments were erected (Morley, I believe, could also recite all the quarter-katun endings). A knowledge of those endings often made it possible to identify immediately badly damaged glyphs. Once as I was lying on a hospital trolley waiting to be wheeled into the operating room, I began to recite those endings to keep my thoughts off a serious operation. Partly doped as I was, I forgot two or three and began to calculate them on my fingers. The nurse, seeing my lips moving and my fingers working, thought I was praying desperately for my life and kindly told me not to be frightened as all would go well.

When our son was quite small, I tried to teach him the rudiments of the Maya calendar, bouncing him on my knee to the rhythm of the twenty Maya day names (he loved the big bounce for Ahau, the greatest of Maya days), but something went wrong with the incantation; he has chosen Peru as his field of archaeology.

There are no very early texts at Copan. The earliest which is beyond doubt carries the date 9.2.10.0.0 3 Ahau 8 Cumku (A.D. 485) and the latest is 9.18.10.0.0 10 Ahau 8 Zac (A.D. 800). Right up to the end, Copan was carving hieroglyphic texts, although not of the magnificence of some years earlier. Then a complete break.

Copan ceased to function ninety years before some of the latest Maya sites. The city is set in a most fertile valley (now a great zone for tobacco raising), small comfort to the advocates of the theory that exhaustion of the soil was the cause of the end of the Classic period. Quirigua, thirty miles to the north, which ceased to erect monuments ten years after Copan, is situated in the even richer Motagua Valley, as the United Fruit Company recognized when they placed their banana plantations there.

The stelae and altars are scattered through the various courts: the great court, that of the hieroglyphic stairway, and the western and eastern courts (Plate XVI). The great court, with the annexed court of the hieroglyphic stairway, is no less than 780 feet from north to south, and from its south end a steep stairway eighty feet high rises to Temple 11, which separates it from the two remaining courts. The temple now is badly ruined, but it must have been spectacular viewed from the main court, and no less inspiring must have been the vista from the acropolis of the river below when the great stairway, now washed away, was in being.

At the southern base of the mound of Temple 11 are four steps popularly known as the Reviewing Stand. The uppermost is inscribed with glyphs which give the date 9.17.0.0.0. (A.D. 771), and at each end kneels on one knee a human figure with strangely grotesque and un-Maya features (Plate xv*b*). Each has a snake knotted around the waist and another snake emerges from the mouth. Somewhat similar sculptures occur elsewhere in Middle America, and I have sometimes thought that they might be meant as caricatures of the Pipil, a non-Maya Mexican-speaking group who dominated parts of the area during the Classic period.

At the north end of the great court is the grave of John Owens, director of the second expedition of the Peabody Museum, Harvard University, who died of fever at Copan in 1893. Vay Morley also nearly died there. Earl Morris has left an extraordinarily vivid account of how Vay was taken ill when the two of them were at Copan in 1912. Morris had been asked to set a stone over Owens' grave. He tells how he was inscribing the last word of the epitaph when Vay, who had been ill since the previous day, came up to say that he had almost finished copying an inscription he wanted for his great book, *The Inscriptions at Copan.* "He came closer," wrote Morris, "laid a hand on my shoulder and looked down at the grave stone. Suddenly the hand became heavy with most of the weight of the body behind it. 'My God, Earl,' he sobbed, 'I don't want to go like Owens did. Let's get out of here.' "

They got out that afternoon, slept the night at Jocotan, but descending to the plain, Vay grew worse and Morris lashed his feet tightly together beneath the mule's belly lest in his delirium he should fall off. Early in the afternoon they reached Zacapa, surely a record time for the long trip. Morris continues:

When the rope was untied, Morley slid into my arms like a bag of salt. I carried him through the doorway to a cot that showed invitingly inside. In those days the bar at the far end of the barracks offered the most refreshing drink it has been my lot to quaff—fresh lime juice squeezed into simple syrup, served in a huge tall glass with ice and carbonated water. A lump of ice rubbed over Morley's cheeks and forehead brought him to full consciousness. He tugged at the straws with the avidity of a nursing lamb and when the glass was drained, closed his eyes in what I hoped would be a long and restful sleep. I went round to the bar for a drink on my own account.

The story has a sequel. In 1926, Joseph Lindon Smith, the artist, was with Morley in Copan for a few days. In his book *Tombs, Temples and Ancient Art*, he recounts this story, moving it to 1926 with himself an eyewitness. He tells how Morley was lashed *under the belly* of the mule and from that position carried on a lively conversation on the long journey back to Zacapa. Anyone who has ever seen a mule perform when a cargo slips under his belly would know that poor Vay in that position would have been in for a ride that would put all the broncho-busting in creation in the shade. Even were that not so, picture him strapped there when the mule stopped to make water. Vay—rest his soul—would have loved that embroidery of his journey.

When I returned to Copan in 1938, my arrival coincided with the festival of San Jose patron of the town. All work, including that of the Carnegie Institution, had ceased, and the whole population was enjoying itself with dances, horse races, and especially cock-fighting, a sport I had not previously witnessed. Gus Stromsvik, in charge of the Carnegie Institution's project, was loved by every man, woman, and child in Copan, and he, entering into the fiesta spirit, made Carnegie headquarters on the town plaza open house. Outside a public bar, I've never in all my life seen so many bottles. Full, half-full, and empty, of American, Scotch, Dutch, and Hondurenian manufacture, they, and as many glasses with the dregs of past conviviality in their bottoms, occupied every table, shelf, and closet in our office.

When the fiesta was at its height, an American missionary of an ultra-Protestant sect arrived at our office requesting permission to stay there until he could arrange transportation for himself and one of his flock to Zacapa and thence to Guatemala. He sat very upright near the door, visibly registering his disapproval of the intemperate display of bottles. One of those with the fiesta spirit was George Roosevelt, a young man at a loose end who had attached himself to the staff of the Copan project as supernumerary and chief bottle-washer, and who had distinguished himself already by persuading a group of German tourists that the Copan pyramids were faced with a concrete made from baked beans by a secret formula now lost to science (the *ah so*'s of joy at learning such a surprising fact from such an unimpeachable source echoed round the eastern court and were carried by the wind beyond the Copan river).

George, a friendly bloke, seeing the minister taking no part in the festivities, came up to him, whisky bottle in hand, and cheerily remarked "How about a snorter, padre?" I don't know whether "snorter" was in the minister's vocabulary, though the action made the meaning pretty evident, but "padre" implies to ultra-Protestants of the Middle West and South a disciple of "The Scarlet Woman," against which our visitor had long striven with might and main but indifferent success. "Snorter" and "padre" were just too much for him. Shaking the dust of Carnegie Institution off his shoes, he wandered out into the plaza, out of the frying pan into the fire, so to speak, for there the festival of San Jose was in full swing.

San Jose is a popular saint in Central America, but his festival falls on March 19, in full Lent. Socotz, the Maya village in British Honduras where my *compadre*, Jacinto Cunil, lives, also has San Jose as its patron and celebrates his day with dances in which the girls, dressed in their best *huipils*, and the young men dance *jaranas* and *zapateados*. Booths are set up as at St. Bartholomew's Fair, and there is an unholy consumption of liquor. My old friend Father Versavel, the Belgian Jesuit at Benque Viejo, viewed with Latin tolerance such goings-on, but the day came when he was replaced by American Jesuits, straight from the seminary in St. Louis, with stricter ideas. Socotz was told it must stop those infractions of Lent or no priest would sing the festal mass. The village fathers countered with an ultimatum: the festival would continue as always or they would become Protestants. The poor dears hadn't the vaguest notion of Protestantism, nor that, as *evangelistas*, there would be neither mass nor festival in or out of Lent. Nevertheless, the threat was successful, and Socotz still celebrates the festival of Saint Joseph in the good (?) old way.

For the Copan festival a marimba band had come from Chiquimula, south of Zacapa. We had met the musicians on their long way, their ungainly marimba carried by each in turn on his back supported by a tumpline. I hired the band to serenade a honeymoon couple on the Carnegie staff who, with a complete indifference to everyone's feelings, had gone to bed at the ridiculous hour of 4:00 A.M. Unfortunately, the *marimbistas* had refreshed themselves too frequently through their long hours of playing, and we had our hands full propping up the marimba one moment, the players the next. Finally they were shunted into position beneath the window; I counted three and gave the signal. The night was rent with an incredible cacophonous roar, which would have made even Beethoven—for all his deafness—start.

A most perplexing find at Copan comprised two small fragments of the legs of a Panamanian gold figurine in the vault beneath a stela dedicated in A.D. 731. These, except for a gold bell said to have been found at Palenque a century ago, an attribution which rests on very shaky evidence, are the only pieces of gold ever found in a ceremonial center of the Classic period. There is good evidence that the Maya had no metals at that time. How, then, did this piece find its way into the vault of a stela dedicated over 150 years before the end of the Classic period?

The cache also contained over one hundred jade and stone beads, mostly broken, fragments of jade plaques, and two marine shells, an assemblage quite untypical of votive deposits at Copan, and also part of a copper bullet and a piece of brass wire. The last two, of modern manufacture, might have slipped into the cache in recent years through a crack in the masonry, as did bits of plaster of Paris from a cast of the stela made years ago. However, it would be a strange coincidence that the only brass and copper ever found in a Maya site should be in the same cache as the only pieces of gold.

The queer contents of this cache can perhaps best be explained by supposing that all was deposited in fairly recent years by Chorti Maya returning to the old ceremonial center to make an offering. The Chorti still collect and cherish polished stone axes used by their pagan ancestors; the Lacandon use ancient Maya jades in their ceremonies; and a beautiful jade head of Classic period was found on the breast of a Tzotzil Maya slain in the uprising of 1869. These are examples of ancient artifacts cherished by the present-day Maya. It is, therefore, plausible that these beads and broken amulets and the four fragments of metal were collected and later offered to "the ancient ones." The Chorti were interested in the ruins, for while Carnegie Institution was working there, copal and candles were repeatedly offered on a small altar in the eastern court.

The area around Copan was not depopulated at the end of the Classic period. One large tomb with corbeled vaulting held a burial, the pottery of which was of post-Classic types. Abandoned rooms falling into ruin were also used as burial places or tombs were constructed of sculptured and plain stone taken from neighboring mounds.

With one post-Classic burial was a vessel of Nicoya ware imported from Nicaragua. This and sherds from the Uloa Valley and the Lake Yohoa region of central Honduras are reminders that Copan was on the eastern boundary of the Maya area, for although the Uloa-Yohoa pottery often carries bands of broken-down Maya glyphs, there is no reason to believe that the makers were Maya any more than that we who use willowware china are Chinese. Nevertheless, the Maya certainly extended to the southeast of Copan, for Cerquin, the area around the modern city of Gracias a Dios was very probably Maya, and Lempira, the Indian chief who fought so intrepidly against the Spaniards, may have been of the same group.

Despite its peripheral position, Copan appears to have been a progressive intellectual leader among the Maya. It seems that Copan was the first Maya city to adopt (in A.D. 692) a system of counting moons in continuous groups of six, a style which spread rapidly to almost every city, replacing with uniformity the chaotic systems previously used. Then, fifty-four years later, she seems to have adapted the recording of moons to an eclipse table, a fine intellectual achievement which has survived in the eclipse table of the Maya hieroglyphic book called the Dresden codex. What seem to be computations to show the gain of the Maya year of 365 days over the solar year of 365.242 days are extremely accurate at Copan, but there I am treading on shaky ground, for some of my colleagues do not accept those calculations as such.

In her sculpture, closer to the round than in other Maya cities, Copan was pre-eminent. The beautiful figures of the maize god in the British, Peabody, and Copan museums are worthy of a very high place in the history of world art (Plate xiv), and the charming lines of seated priest-rulers on steps and altars have the quality of portraiture (Plate xvic). There is a vitality in Copan art which contrasts with the serene postures found in the cities of the Usumacinta Valley, but it was not always so, for in the first half of the Classic period the human figure at Copan is stiff and gawky.

Copan also produced a very fine carved pottery of a chocolate-brown ware which was traded west far into Guatemala and south to El Salvador. In addition to finely carved personages, these vessels, usually tall and cylindrical, carry glyphs which seem to mean something, whereas glyphs painted on Maya vessels were copied haphazard by one artist from another. Among those glyphs are some typical of Copan, showing that the vessels must have been made there or within Copan territory.

The traveler J. L. Stephens had tried in 1840 to purchase the ruins of Palenque with the idea of transporting them bodily to New York. The idea was typical of the period. Asia Minor and Iraq were alive with archaeologists shipping their loot to western Europe; Rawlinson was digging at Nineveh, Layard at Nimrod, Bolta at Khorsabad, and so on. Why should not the sculpture of Copan be shipped to the British Museum? A year before my first visit to Copan I came upon a copy of a letter from Lord Palmerston, then foreign secretary, to Frederick Chatfield, British representative to the five Central American republics. This instructed him to inquire about the practicability of obtaining sculpture for the British Museum from Copan, "at the bottom of the Bay of Honduras, and to the south of the British settlement of Belize." The letter continued:

> It appears . . . that these ruins . . . are held in little or no estimation by the natives of the country, and it seems possible, therefore, that the chief difficulty to be encountered in removing specimens of the sculpture would consist in providing means of transporting them to some place of embarcation. You will be careful, therefore, that in making any enquiries in pursuance of this instruction, you do not lead the people of the country to attach any imaginary value to things which they consider at present as having no value at all.

A German, Karl Scherzer, was commissioned to carry out the mission, but never reached Copan, having heard that a landslide had badly damaged them and so the site was not dismembered.

Imaginary value, forsooth! The five dollars admission I paid was more than imaginary.

9

San Jose and La Honradez

ON MY NEXT VISIT to British Honduras, in 1931, Charles Wisdom, student of anthropology at the University of Chicago, came as my assistant.

As usual, I stopped at the International Hotel, a ramshackle wooden two-story building with a barroom which was never empty from 7:00 A.M. to 6:00 P.M., at which hour the frequenters moved to the Polo and Golf clubs. An ancient billiard table stood at one end, the green baize entirely worn away by dicing for drinks, but the slate below served the same purpose as well or better. Tradition has it that Belize, which lies on the edge of a swamp, was built on rum bottles and mahogany chips, and I can well believe it. The consumption of liquor was extremely high and would have been even higher had it not been that the ancient Negro bartender shuffled along so slowly with each round of drinks that he markedly slowed down consumption. You were sure to find C.O., for long Belize agent of the Uaxactun project, there. He used to claim that he was American by birth, but Scotch by absorption. Alas! he fell on bad times and had to substitute Belize rum for the product of Scotland, thereby becoming Beliceño by rite of immersion. Scots, English, Americans, Bay Islanders, and an assortment of beachcombers were all there eternally rolling for drinks. Looking back with such wisdom as the years have given me, I feel pity for the inanity of those shipwrecked lives; it was such a stupid way to fight the boredom of the "romantic" tropics.

Upstairs, bedrooms gave off the three sides of a corridor. To take advantage of the breeze, partitions between rooms did not reach the ceiling, with the consequence that sound traveled all over the second floor. On one occasion a mahogany man in Belize from the Vaca concession came to his room very much the worse for his celebrations. He kept calling out, "I'm going to die," and the words traveling over the shortened partitions were more than audible in every room. Repetitions of "I'm going to die" echoed down the corridor, waking every sleeper. Peace came when Edith Ricketson, also a guest of the hotel, answered in a very exasperated voice "I wish you were."

The food was bad, especially on Friday, when the New Orleans boat arrived, for it brought the proprietor a consignment of oysters which he sold at a good price to his customers. The refrigerator dated from the close of the Maya Classic period so the simplest way of disposing of the whole consignment before it went bad was to serve such an intolerable meal that the guests were forced to buy the surplus oysters. Once or twice there were some still unsold on Saturday. After all those years, I can't bring myself to write of what was set before us. The International Hotel was wrecked in the hurricane of 1931, a few months after this season's work. Belize has never been quite the same again.

British Honduras is somewhat egocentric. The handbook has a historical table in which several sequent entries for 1914 (I quote the dates incorrectly from memory) run as follows: "July 31. Austria declared war on Serbia. August 1st. Russia declared war on Germany. August 2nd. Germany invaded Belgium. August 4th. Great Britain declared war on Germany. August 10. Belize dog pound opened."

I had a concession to dig on lands of the Belize Estate and Produce Company, which owned and worked vast mahogany forests in the northwest part of the country. Our plan was to excavate at Kaxil Uinic, "forest man," close to the Guatemala border, the only way to reach it being via Hill Bank, logging headquarters of the company at the bottom of New River Lagoon. Hill Bank is only forty miles west and a little north of Belize, but, unless traveling light, it was a three days' journey which entailed sailing to the northern tip of British Honduras and then south down New River, paralleling the first leg of the journey.

We left on the *Afrikola*, a small boat, flat-bottomed (to navigate the New River) but with top-heavy superstructure. The boat got its name in a strange way. The owners were the proprietors of a soft-drink bottling works in Belize. Things went well until Coca-Cola cut heavily into sales. To meet this competition, they launched a new drink which they named Afrikola, presumably in honor of the original home of the dominant race in Belize. This new concoction was highly successful (it was so sweet you had to buy several bottles to quench your thirst), and with the profits the proprietors bought the boat, naming it in gratitude after the drink which had paid for it.

The *Afrikola* threaded its way northward along the island-girt coast, keeping to the smooth and shallow waters within the coral reef. As the sun sank, a red ball, behind the mangrove-fringed shore, we sat down to a dinner of rice and red beans, the national dish of British Honduras. Early next morning we reached Corozal, a pretty little town set amid coconut groves, lying only a few miles from Chetumal (then called Payo Obispo), capital of the Mexican Territory of Quintana Roo. Corozal, "stand of cohune palms," was settled by Yucatecan refugees from the atrocities of the "War of the Castes" between whites and Maya which for nearly half a century devastated much of Yucatan. Except for the presence of blue-uniformed Negro policemen, the town was typically Yucatecan.

On the outskirts of Corozal lies the sugar plantation of Santa

Rita, where some sixty years ago most interesting Maya frescoes were found on the walls of a building which had been protected by a superimposed mound. Gann set to work to copy them, but before he could finish, they were destroyed by Maya. The Indians are said to have wanted them to make medicine, but I suspect the Maya destroyed them because they were afraid the painted figures would come to life and harm the living, the reason they smash most survivals of *los antiguos* they come upon.

The style of the fresco painting is distinctly Mexican, although the hieroglyphs and the subject matter are Maya. The scenes show the gods ruling the tuns (360-day years) that made up a certain Katun (20-tun period). The gods are roped together, while the glyph for the day on which each tun ended is given in correct sequence. Without question the paintings were made not long before the Spanish conquest. At that time northern British Honduras was part of the Maya province of Chetumal, and pottery of types closely allied to those of Mayapan as well as copper bells and tweezers show the area to have been heavily populated then. The loss of the long hieroglyphic section of the fresco was a disaster since no other good text of that period has survived.

Crossing the bay, the *Afrikola* entered New River. For many miles we steamed past mangrove swamps, the monotony occasionally relieved by sandy patches of bank dotted with clumps of palmetto palms. On areas of high land were rare villages or plantations, where the *Afrikola* stopped for a few minutes to land passengers or supplies. About 4:00 P.M. we reached Orange Walk, the destination of the *Afrikola*, a small, attractive town of Yucatecans and hispanicized Maya. In British Honduras "walk" is synonymous with "plantation."

Next morning we loaded our supplies on a flat-bottomed barge owned by the Belize Estate Company and made ourselves as comfortable as possible on top of the load. With a high-powered motorboat hauling our barge, we continued along New River. The upper reaches were more beautiful than the mangrove-lined banks we had passed the previous day. In places the sluggish river broadened into small lagoons, carpeted with water-lily leaves over which egrets flitted; turtles sunned themselves on tree trunks partially submerged in the black waters. Sometimes we caught a glimpse of a small alligator slipping into the water at the chugging approach of the motorboat.

Late in the afternoon we entered New River Lagoon, a narrow stretch of water nearly fifteen miles long. Against the setting sun the forest-clad pyramids of the ruins called Indian Church were silhouetted, deep shadows delineating the depressions of the plazas. The forest swept to the shore, the upper branches of the outer fringe of trees leaning over the water as though they had lost their balance in trying to halt. Between the shore and our barge the little waves made by the passage of the motorboat were tipped with pink, reflected from the sky. Overhead a flock of waterfowl winged their way to the Caribbean.

More than three centuries earlier Franciscan friars from Yucatan, on their occasional visits to Tayasal, stronghold of the pagan Itza in Lake Peten, passed, as we did, up New River and the length of New River Lagoon. Indian Church (there are the ruins of an early church there) was then the Maya village of Lamayna. Things have not changed much. This is from the account of a journey across the lagoon by Friars Fuensalida and Orbita in 1623:

> Lamayna is on the shores of a great lagoon formed of rivers and streams which flow into it, and with abundant catches of turtles and fish, all very good tasting as they come from fresh water. Were it not for the mosquitoes which cause so much distress, the navigation of those rivers would be delightful. The vistas are charming, and the Indians continually harpoon fish without stopping [their canoes]. They crossed the lake, leaving the canoes on the shore, for from there one travels up to about twelve leagues overland to reach the River Tipu [now Belize River]. There is along that road a huge pine forest three leagues across.

Five years later, Fray Diego Delgado probably followed that same route on his way to Tayasal and martyrdom, and this may have been almost the last scene of peace and beauty on which he gazed. On landing at Tayasal, the whole party of fifteen—for he had been joined by soldiers and Maya of Tipu—were slain by the Itza and their heads set on stakes.

A little before midnight we reached Hill Bank, just across the south end of the lagoon from where the fathers had landed, where we transferred our supplies to a flatcar, which was waiting by the pier. With everything loaded, we started for Sierra de Agua, thirteen miles away and then the terminus of the lumber railroad. Cots awaited us in the headquarters hut when we arrived about 2:00 A.M. Here the logs hauled from the woods by tractors were loaded on the train for Hill Bank, and here were the commissary and repair shops.

Next morning mules arrived from San Jose to carry us and the greater part of our supplies to Kaxil Uinic, but in the meantime we had learned that this village had been abandoned and all its inhabitants had been moved to San Jose. This was a serious blow, for, counting on getting our workers from the village, we had not brought food supplies for laborers. As much time would be wasted in recruiting labor and sending to Belize for their food, I decided to see if there were suitable ruins in the neighborhood of the Maya village of San Jose, where we could count on local labor.

Two hours' ride from Sierra de Agua, "water sawmill," brought us to San Jose. In response to my inquiries, a villager offered to show us some ruins about three miles to the east. After riding for an hour along abandoned mahogany truck passes and through alternate sections of virgin forest and abandoned milpa, we climbed a short, steep trail which was badly overgrown. Rounding a bend in the trail, we caught a glimpse of two pyramids rising abruptly in front of us. The trail, passing between these, debouched on a small court overgrown with breadnut trees except for one dense patch of cohune palms. Stumbling and hacking our way through the undergrowth, we found that the court was flanked by seven substructures, two of which were about forty feet high, while others were also of considerable size. As there was a small spring with good water close by and as probably there were other mounds in the vicinity and a plentiful labor supply at San Jose, this little site seemed to fill all our requirements, for I wanted a small site to see how life there contrasted with that in large cities. We slept that night in the village *cabildo* conjecturing what this little site might hold in store for us.

San Jose was a peaceful little village (it is no more; the whole population was moved to Orange Walk in 1935), but it had a war-like past. Between 1848 and 1879, Maya of the independent groups in Mexico raided British Honduras, particularly the area stretching west from Orange Walk and Hill Bank to the frontier. The Chichanha Maya, who about 1860, after the destruction of their town, moved to Icaiche (where Maurilio, as recounted in Chapter 6, had taken refuge when lost in the forest), were particularly aggressive. In 1866 their chief, Canul, captured Quam Hill, north-west of San Jose, carying off seventy-nine women and children, whom he successfully held for ransom, and then occupied San Pedro, about ten miles south of San Jose, where the Maya were friendly to him. A small force of the British West India Regiment sent to attack him there was decisively routed. Next, he captured Indian Church, which we had seen as we sailed down New River Lagoon, as noted. This had once been the Maya village of La-mayna, an outpost of the old Maya province of Chetumal, but at the time of the raid was a mahogany camp.

Retribution was on the way. A stronger British force captured San Pedro and then San Jose. The San Jose Maya put up a resistance, and the British force had three wounded. In the town were found equipment belonging to the West India Regiment and guns, ammunition, and mules looted from Indian Church, clear evidence that San Jose had fought on Canul's side. The village was burned in reprisal; since then it has been pacific. It is a strange quirk of history that the Maya once took on the British Empire.

By evening of the next day we were established at the ruins and had a roof over our heads. Our Maya laborers under Jacinto's supervision had felled trees for corner posts and roof supports, collected and split cohune palm leaves for thatch, stripped vines and inner bark for tying material, and assembled the whole. There wasn't a nail in the whole construction (Plate xı).

Our cook was Hazzard Bonner, a mulatto of about fifty, of a peculiar appearance. Bushy tufts of hair protruded from his ears like exaggerated jaguar whiskers. Like many "creoles" from remote villages, he spoke an English which was extremely difficult to understand. Finally we talked in Spanish, mutually more intelligible than our mother tongue.

Soon we had the ruins cleared of growth, leaving only large trees for shade. We had labor difficulties. The best men in San Jose were working for the Belize Estate or on their milpas; the residue were hookwormy or malarial.

We started on a large mound in front of which a plain stela had stood. A short way below the summit a dedicatory cache rested on a dome-shaped layer of mortar which traversed the mound. It consisted of flints, obsidian blades, a jade bead, and the remains of an iron pyrite mirror, all within a bowl with hemispherical cover, which was in almost sixty pieces. This, in turn, had rested on a large pottery dish. The whole surface was set with small clay spikes, and in relief on top of the cover was a crude head between two projecting upraised hands. Vent holes in the head and the "hands" communicated with the interior of the bowl. It had been a censer for burning copal, as smoke stains on the interior confirmed. With the lid in position, the copal smoke would have poured through the eyes, mouth, and supposed hands of the relief figure on the top.

Seven of the flints were leaf-shaped blades exquisitely fashioned in the pressure-flaking technique, and made with such care that, although averaging over four inches in length, they were scarcely more than one-tenth of an inch thick. Three other flint implements were more coarsely made, while the remaining fourteen were eccentric shapes of types described in Chapter 7 with the addition of a jaguar or other member of the cat family, an impressionistic portrait in flint (Fig. 24).

A little below the mortar layer on which the cache rested were three pairs of bowls, placed lip to lip to form containers. Each pair held a skull. Presumably three persons had been decapitated for this sacrificial offering when the period of construction was concluded by laying the mortar cap.

At a still lower level and beneath a well-made floor we came upon a skeleton laid full length, but in poor shape. The four upper incisors were inlaid with little jade plugs, a common Maya custom (Fig. 17). Around the skeleton were four pottery vessels of types earlier than those in the cache. In addition, there were crushed fragments of jade and, almost touching the bones of the right forearm, two round pieces cut from conch shells placed lip to lip. This container held the carapace of a crab, probably marine, and an orbital bone very probably of a dogfish.

One wonders why these last had been placed with the dead; they can hardly have been a food offering, for part of the head of a dogfish is no dainty dish to set before a king, or, at least, an important person such as the jade-inlaid teeth and jade ornament indicated. The careful placement in a special container also argues against a food offering to nourish the deceased on his journey to the next world. The crab was of religious importance in some parts of Central America, but the orbital bone of a dogfish is baffling. The Maya used the eye of the dogfish as a remedy for coughs and a crab shell as an ingredient in the cure of another disease, an obscure seizure called spotted parrot spasm. The idea is perhaps far-fetched, but could our friend have died of some coughing spasm, and the crab and dogfish eye, complete with bone, have been buried with him as medicine on his last journey?

Still lower there was yet another votive cache. Inside a barrel-shaped pottery jar were eight pieces of pumice, fragments of coral, a marine shell with a hole for suspension, and pieces of charred wood. The pieces of pumice had probably been washed ashore. The cache has a marine flavor.

In the course of the work at San Jose we found a large number of burials. For the most part the skeletons were flexed and lay on their sides with knees drawn up; rarely they lay full length on their backs. Methods of burial of the Maya are infinite, and as yet no clear pattern has emerged; but chiefs were often seated in early Classic times and at a much later date (there were no seated burials at San Jose), and persons of little consequence were often flexed. On the other hand, an early Classic chief at Tikal was flexed in a bundle and lacked his head, perhaps kept as a memento. Late Classic persons of rank were often in an extended position. Burial in large pottery jars was practiced in some parts; cremation was common shortly before the Spanish conquest. Burial practices are so closely tied to religion that we can reasonably suppose that in years to come a regular pattern based on position in the society, but modified by regional and time differences, will become apparent. For instance, the decay of formal religion at Mayapan is accompanied by casual burial in ossuaries with little or no grave furniture.

The arrival of Easter week put a stop to work, and Jacinto and I decided to visit La Honradez and Chochkitam, little-known sites in northeastern Guatemala, leaving Charles Wisdom in charge at San Jose. Our guide, Julio Torres, was part Kekchi and had been born in Guatemala, but following a cold-blooded murder in Mexico, he had skipped across into British Honduras. He went with us on the strict understanding we would not enter Mexican territory, which lay only about sixteen miles north of Chochkitam. He was a mild-looking individual marred only by having the tops of his ears eaten away by *chiclero's* ulcer. That is a virulent infection, caused by the bite of a fly, and is common among those who work in the forests. The fly attacks animals also, and the Maya frequently depicted dogs with both ear-tips eaten away.

Fig. 22.—Part of Abandoned Kaxil Uinic Water hole in foreground, frequented by hogs and mules for wallowing, was only source of drinking water for villagers.

Late in the afternoon of the first day we reached Kaxil Uinic, near which we had originally intended to work. The score of huts scattered around a dirty water hole presented a melancholy appearance (Fig. 22). Although the village was supposed to have been entirely abandoned, we found two residents. One was a Spaniard, who was there to receive chicle shipments. These, I suspected, were contraband, for the Spaniard displayed a nervous curiosity about our movements. Kaxil Uinic, near a remote corner of Guatemala, was well situated for getting chicle out of Guatemala without paying export tax, and, in fact, had for many years been a smugglers' hangout. Also, practically all the chicle legitimately exported from Guatemala had by Easter crossed the frontier, and the excise men had been removed from outlying posts including Chochkitam, nearest chicle station to Kaxil Uinic, so that the coast was clear for getting out contraband. I did not learn whether my suspicions were correct, for it was no business of mine, and in remote parts of Central America it pays even less than elsewhere to poke your nose into the affairs of others.

The second resident was a Maya of perhaps seventy, a considerable age for an Indian. Seeing him seated at the door of his hut, I asked him why he had remained behind after all the other villagers had gone. It transpired that he was too old and infirm to walk with the others to San Jose, the nearest village. He had refused the offer of a horse, saying that he had never ridden in his life, and was not going to start at his age. Furthermore, he had no wish to leave Kaxil Uinic, where he had spent most of his life. Relatives had arranged for him to travel to San Jose with the last consignment of hogs, which would be driven, Irish style, with a string around the hind leg of each. In this manner, they would take three or four days, allowing the old man to travel a few miles each day without overtiring himself. He strenuously denied any intention of leaving, but his objections must have been overcome, for on our return to Kaxil Uinic a week later he was no longer there. We learned later that he and the hogs had reached San Jose without mishap.

Unlike the old man, I did not find Kaxil Uinic attractive. There were too many fleas, and the hogs wallowed in our drinking water. We were on our way by sunrise. A few miles brought us to the British Honduras-Guatemala frontier, marked by a straight swathe cut through the forest, and about an hour later we were at Chochkitam, "peccary entrails," a plant. Despite its name, this chicle camp was prettily situated beside a small reed-encircled lake. It had been an important chicle station of the P. W. Shuffeldt concession, but, when the concession was canceled, it had fallen into ruin. Luckily, the stoutly built commissary, in which we slept, still stood.

The large ruins lie about two miles from the camp. Two or three archaeologists had examined them, and I had, therefore, no expectation of discovering anything new on our short visit, but I hoped to find architectural resemblances to San Jose. In this I was disappointed, for the standing buildings were in poor shape. The site, set on top of a hill, is of considerable size, comprising no less than eight courts with buildings set around them. Of the six stelae reported only one is known to be carved, but the figure and text on its front were in deplorable condition (the limestone in this part of the Peten weathers very badly). The personage had his feet planted on a design probably representing two captives who crouched back to back, as on a Coba stela (Fig. 9), but details were hard to make out. Tatiana Proskourikoff, by the very accurate trait chart she developed, places the monument within forty years of 9.17.0.0.0. (A.D. 771), quite a lot later than the Coba stela.

Beside the stela were a rotted mahogany tree and a felled breadnut tree which had thrown up fresh growth. In my notes I wrote that the mahogany must have been cut many years ago and that the fresh growth of the breadnut must have been at least ten years old. I had badly underestimated the rate of decay and growth in tropical rain forest; these trees had been felled three years previously when Blom's party discovered the stela.

There were a great number of *chultuns* in the area, three of which we examined. Two had an interesting second chamber leading off the main one, and I had hoped for burials in them, but one contained nothing, the other only a large number of leaf-nosed vampire bats. The third, at the edge of the main group, had an accumulation of white powdery soil containing many large sherds of storage jars. It has been claimed that *chultuns* were used for storing water, and one's first thought was that these were large pieces of jars accidentally dropped in drawing water; but were that so, they would have been under the soil, not scattered through it. Moreover, the highest part of the *chultun* floor was immediately below the mouth; for storage of water that would have been the lowest point.

Game was very plentiful in the region and we were well provided with curassow. The male and female of this large species of bird are extremely handsome. The male is black with a bright yellow wattle; the female has a rich brown plumage speckled black, black tail feathers with a bar shading from white to brown, and a speckled black and white crest. The muleteer shot a *coba*, a sort of partridge with short black crest; Julio, a *quam*, a black pheasant-like bird called *cox* in Maya (*Dactylortix thoracicus*); and we came across a covey of about nine ocellated turkeys, a magnificent bird with eyes in its tail rather like those of a peacock and a bronze-green plumage. I was glad that the men did not have guns with them then, for we had more than enough to eat. In the ruins of La Honradez we came upon a band of about twenty spider monkeys, including one young one which seemed able to leap and swing just as well as the adults. Monkeys are often seen near ruins, and the reason may be that breadnut trees are always abundant near Maya sites and the fruit ripens during the dry season when archaeologists bestir themselves.

Leaving the luxury of the large commissary hut at Chochkitam, we moved to La Honradez, "Honor," about twelve miles away. On the journey we crossed a wide bed of flint, a source of wealth to the two cities in time passed, as scattered rejects on the surface showed. There was a small water hole there, but our shelters were very sorry affairs—cohune leaves leaning against a crosspiece supported by two forked posts, just wide and long enough to swing a hammock and capable of keeping out only the lightest of showers (Plate XI).

The site had changed its name to Corozal. The place had been unoccupied and forgotten for many years until rediscovered and used again by a new lot of *chicleros,* who renamed it. Similarly the camp at Rio Bec, "oak stream," was later rediscovered and given the grandiloquent name of Aurora. The original name of the Uaxactun water hole was Bambunal, "stand of bamboo"; Morley rechristened it Uaxactun, "8 stone," because of the Baktun 8 stela there. Blom tells that two *chicleros* were discussing the new name. The more traveled one explained to his comrade: "A gringo came here and renamed the place Uaxactun [pronounced Washactoon] in honor of the great gringo revolutionary Uaxactun [Washington]."

The interesting feature at La Honradez is the only standing building. This has one long room with a room projecting at right angles at each end to enclose a shallow court. A kind of cross between a tower and a roof crest stands above all three rooms, and stone masks are set in the façades. It stands to the impressive height of eighty feet above the main plaza. This building is not in Peten style, but has affiliations with the great site of Calakmul, about sixty miles northwest in the Mexican state of Campeche, where similar flanking rooms form a narrow patio, and these were also crowned with short roof crests. Resemblances to the Rio Bec style about the same distance to the north can also be seen.

I had mislaid my tape and so I measured the building with my machete, handspan and finger breadths, but I have never drawn the plan. I lost the machete before I had recorded its length and then I lost the notes which are probably moldering in the basement of a museum! All archaeologists are reputed to be absent minded. *Noblesse oblige.*

The oblong main court, enclosed by structures on all four sides and with the great length of close on six hundred feet, holds ten sculptured stelae, before five of which altars stand. This is a small number for such a large site, but no excavation has ever been carried out there, and there may be more buried under fallen debris. Morley believed that there is probably another undiscovered court with more stelae. The forest is so impenetrable that that may well be the case; unfortunately most of the stelae are badly weathered. Six of them have an unusual feature: the personage stands on a mask, perhaps a representation of the sky monster. Only one definite date is known—9.17.0.0.0. 13 Ahau 18 Cumku (January 22, A.D. 771). This was a popular katun ending represented by at least eighteen monuments in cities from all parts of the lowland area. Although at that time the stela cult was very active, I think the reason for this number is that katun 17 fell on a day 13 Ahau and 13 was for the Maya a very lucky number (the previous katun ending 9.16.0.0.0. 2 Ahau 13 Zec is marked by only 8 monuments perhaps because 2 was of ill omen).

At the foot of one stela scattered in the surface soil we came upon the broken pieces of an incense burner of a type ancestral to those of the present day Lacandon-Maya. It was probably deposited there several centuries after La Honradez ceased to function.

After another day in Chochkitam we started home. We got off at 6: 15 A.M., passed through Kaxil Uinic, completely deserted, and rested by the Rio Bravo. The water was only two feet deep, but the stream had a bed of rock, a welcome change from water holes or the lake at Chochkitam where one sinks deep in mud and a bathe is not too pleasant. I had found I had an incredible rash of tick and redbug bites. There was a pleasant group of ruins near the river which I briefly examined, one of the hundreds of small unrecorded sites scattered over the whole Maya area. It was placed on top of a low hill with a court surrounded by mounds, the tallest thirty feet high.

We had planned to continue by moonlight, but we decided not to wait for the moon, which would not rise till about 9: 30. Jacinto and I took it in turns to carry the oil hurricane lamp; Julio led the way, and Juan Tzul, the muleteer, brought up the rear. We reached

San Jose at 1:15 A.M. By then all Maya villages are normally fast asleep, but it was *sábado de gloria*, Easter Saturday, a great festival in Central America, and everyone was awake. We got coffee at Juan Tzul's hut, and I learned that Charles Wisdom was seriously ill with fever. The moment was not one for celebration, but Jacinto and I had been on the go for twenty hours except for a short rest at the Rio Bravo and we felt we needed a stimulant. We shared a half-bottle of *aguardiente*, and started on the last lap to the ruins. There had been much sickness at San Jose, and now Charles was the victim. Slightly exhilarated by our drink and, perhaps, by the beauty of cohune palms silhouetted against the moon, Jacinto and I agreed that we were tough. We could take it. We didn't fold up. I had to eat my words in just two weeks.

We got to our camp just before dawn. The moon was lost behind a cloud and the twilight had a strange effect. Our hut, standing on a little raised court, took on the form of an English barn and Charles' mosquito net inside the wall-less room swayed gently in the dawn breeze, white and ghostly like some fearsome specter. A shadowy form detached itself from the background, and Bonner's creole speech brought back reality.

Charles had a really bad attack of malaria. Unfortunately he had little confidence in my medical knowledge, for instead of the fifty grains of quinine a day which I urged, he would take only ten, hardly more than a prophylactic dose. He got worse, so the following evening he went to Sierra de Agua, where there were hospital facilities and where, by good luck, the district doctor chanced to be. Later the doctor told me that at one time he feared the malaria would develop into blackwater fever, recovery from which is always problematical.

Charles returned about ten days later. The doctor had advised him to get out of the rain forest as another attack in his weakened condition might be serious. Since he was most interested in ethnology, I suggested he should made a study of the Chorti Maya between Jocotan and Copan. No one had worked among them, and, strategically located in the heart of the lowland Maya area, they ought to have a lot of survivals of pre-Columbian practices. Charles was enthusiastic about the suggestion. Next day he left for Guatemala via Belize. His report, published some years later, on the Chorti is an extremely valuable source, and I take pride in having been, so to speak, its godfather.

Work had gone well in the meantime. We found several burials, some with very fine pottery (Fig. 23), more caches, and another

FIG. 23.—Pottery Vase, San Jose. Late Classic period. Perhaps made in a mold.

group of ruins. This group lay only two hundred yards from the one we were excavating, but the dense forest had kept it hidden. It comprised a plaza, several large mounds, and a ball court, but there was so much to do at the main group that I deferred excavation there to another season.

Soon after Wisdom left, I became ill. A beef worm had died a little above my ankle and could not be squeezed out. An infection spread up my leg, and I had to hobble down to the ruins each day on homemade crutches. Eventually, with my leg swollen to nearly twice natural size and swellings under my arm, I beat a retreat. Bonner and the muleteer lifted me on a mule, and I started on the most painful ride I have ever had. At Hill Bank, Prince, of the Belize Estate, took me in hand; with hot fomentations he softened the abcess and pressed out sacs of puss extending to the knee.

Three days later I began to feel myself again except for an unromantic crop of boils on a part of my anatomy which made riding an agony. I felt that I must get back to the ruins, and, as I could walk only a short distance, my behind had to take it in the neck.

Jacinto had a simple explanation for my trouble. The pregnant wife of one of the men had come to camp just before the start of the infection and everyone knows that if a pregnant woman looks at a sore (I was bathing it when she was in camp), it will turn septic. Still, I don't remember any pregnant women around when Job got his boils.

The day after my return we found an interesting burial. The skeleton lay on its side bundled with knees almost touching chin. The damaged skull, with a large bowl inverted over it, was far longer than average. It may have belonged to an unusually long-headed member of the community or perhaps to a stranger. The five pottery vessels with the burial were not of local manufacture, but that fact could hardly be used to argue that the owner was a foreigner. One was a drum, the shape of an hourglass, open at both ends and under one foot high, the only one found at San Jose. The slip showed it wasn't a local piece. Close to the skull lay an eccentric flint shaped as an alert dog, clearly in the middle of an interrogative bark (Fig. 24).

Things went along nicely for a few days. Then, like Charles and six or eight of my laborers, I went down with malaria. Coming before I had wholly recovered from my poisoned leg, it reduced me to a low ebb, but luckily it was the tertian variety which brings fever only every other day, so I was able to supervise the digging between bouts. After a week of fighting the fever with large doses of quinine which, in turn, produced splitting headaches, it became apparent that I must either let the dig continue with inadequate supervision or stop work. My decision to close down the camp was hastened by the drying up of the little spring on which we depended for our water supply. Furthermore, recent finds indicated that there was a good chance of obtaining a ceramic sequence with care; badly supervised work might destroy vital evidence.

It was three years before I could return to San Jose. Good old Jacinto met me in Belize, and soon we were again aboard the *Afrikola*, bound for Orange Walk on the first leg of the journey. There I took on as cook Nicolás Iglesias. As a boy in Spain he had enlisted to fight for his country in the Cuban War. Later he had moved to Yucatan, where, between revolutions and dubious adventures, he had followed the trade of baker. About twenty years before, he had joined the revolutionary force of Argumeda, but in the rout of that force (Argumeda fled, leaving his men to shift for themselves), he was taken prisoner by the federal force. Strangely, this happened at Dzitas, the station for Chichen Itza. Mexicans don't look kindly on Spaniards who meddle in their affairs; he was condemned to be *tronado*, "thundered," as the Mexicans picturesquely say of one shot by a firing squad. As he awaited execution, a friend serving in the federal army happened to see him, and, on his intercession, Nicolás was reprieved and allowed to join the federals. Later he had worked with Blom and Ricketson, so he was in the Maya tradition.

Our old hut had gone; there remained only a few very rotted posts beneath a tangled secondary growth, but by the following day a new hut stood on the same spot. There was plenty of water in the little spring, but no sign of the ruby-throated hummingbird which the previous season had had its nest nearby and used to dart past me as I bathed. In the summer these hummingbirds migrate to the States, and I sometimes wondered whether he or his son or grandson could be among those who so enjoyed the delphiniums in our garden in Harvard, Massachusetts, some years later.

We concentrated work first on outlying mounds of the main group and later on the new group we had found near the end of the 1931 season. The results were highly successful, for we got stratified deposits of five periods. The lowest levels produced sherds in large numbers of the late Formative period, none of which were polychrome. Above lay sherds of the early Classic, and above them two divisions of the late Classic. Finally, there were very late Classic deposits and some surface material which was of post-Classic period. On the surface were some sherds of what is called slate ware and in doorways or immediately outside doorways were three complete jars of this ware. All were decorated in "trickle-paint" technique, in which the potter apparently dribbled a jug of paint over the pot, allowing the liquid to trickle down the sides. Slate ware was made in enormous quantities and for centuries in Yucatan, and the storage jars I found are not sufficiently distinctive to be dated, but these at San Jose were certainly post-Classic and had come from Yucatan.

On the surface, too, were specially made pottery spindlewhorls, unknown during the Classic period and among them was one with a design in asphalt (Fig. 17), an import from Veracruz, probably not far south of Tampico. There were also a fragment of a marble vase from the Uloa Valley in Honduras and other tiny pieces which may have been of *tecali* (Mexican onyx) from Puebla in central Mexico. A very elaborate pottery figurine from a late burial came from the Campeche-Tabasco area on the west coast of the peninsula. These and other finds mentioned later showed how active was trade at the end of the Classic period and even afterwards.

The most exciting find was in a cache under the floor of a room in the new group of ruins. It wasn't much to look at, for it was merely a deposit about six inches long, rather more than three inches wide and one-fifth of an inch thick of verdigris and, above, five small deposits of verdigris mixed with soil, but these were the remains of the only copper until then reported from a Classic site (there have been subsequent finds of copper in Tabasco, but in sites which were still occupied or reoccupied centuries after the end of the Classic period). It was an epochal discovery and confirmed my conclusion that San Jose lived on after large sites had been abandoned. All the seasons' intensive work at Uaxactun produced no copper, but had that been known to its inhabitants before the site was abandoned, it surely would have been imported in view of Uaxactun's far greater prominence. The outlines of the small heaps suggested copper bells.

That wasn't all. Over the verdigris lay the blade and part of the haft of a splendid obsidian axe just under one foot long with a few specks of pink stucco still adhering to the haft. It is unique; nothing so fine in its class has ever been found. (Plate ix*d*). As I worked to clear the dirt from it, I thought first that I had a point or chipped obsidian blade, then an eccentric obsidian. The work of clearing with mason's trowel and whiskbroom seemed an eternity, but at last its whole length lay exposed, a sight to make an archaeologist's heart leap for joy.

With the cache were a small pearl with hole for suspension, five small pieces of cinnabar, two pieces of ore with a high percentage of lead, a highly polished disk of iron pyrite with a slate disk backing with two holes for suspension, a spondylus shell, three obsidian blades set upright with their points missing, and, scattered over an area about eight inches square, about 120 spines later identified as from the skin of a porcupine fish.

What the spines of the porcupine fish were doing there, I don't know, but in some islands of the Pacific the natives wear head-dresses of porcupine fish. The area over which the spines were scattered suggests that they were probably still attached to the skin when placed in the cache. Alternatively they could have been used for drawing blood from tongue, ears, and other parts of the body. For that the Maya used sting-ray spines, thorns, obsidian blades, and so on. The porcupine fish spines would have served admirably, but in that case why so many and why not in a small heap? The Maya seem to have been interested in the creature, for six teeth of one were with a burial at Kaminaljuyu, near Guatemala City. As far as is known, the Maya never used lead, so the two pieces of ore were probably kept as curiosities because of their unusual weight. The axe could have served only for ceremony; at one good blow with it, it would have shattered. I felt pretty happy that evening.

The adjacent building we excavated completely. It had been a two-storied structure, but had collapsed into a shapeless mound without any sign of a room. Six weeks' work revealed all eleven rooms. The center one of the ground floor, obviously the most important in the structure, was entered through a wide doorway, opposite which was a niche in the back wall. In this stood a large stone dais on stone legs with its front decorated with a band of stucco glyphs painted russet red. Most of these had been destroyed, but a few were in good condition.

The removal of the glyphs, each about five inches long, was difficult. They were thin and friable, but the backing was extremely hard. I painted the surface with a solution of ambroid, and then with a pen knife sawed away the hard backing. It took several evenings to remove them without serious damage.

An interesting feature of this structure was an interior staircase which led to a roof terrace above the front ground floor rooms. Behind were rooms of the second story. This staircase, which had three flights of stairs at right angles, was not at first apparent, for part had been blocked off in ancient times, and the first flight had been built over to form a raised passage.

I had hoped for rich caches in this building, the most important at the site, and I had confidently expected one under the dais with the stucco glyphs, but under it we found nothing more exciting than a common or garden red-ware bowl, badly smashed and of poor workmanship. In other likely places, beneath back walls and under doorways, we also drew blank; in the southeast room we had better luck.

This room had undergone various alterations such as the Maya loved to make. The floor level had been raised, and two stucco-covered benches built. Subsequently, these had been altered and extended and finally covered with yet another floor. It has been claimed that the Maya were slightly effeminate; in these constant alterations to rooms, perhaps they shared a trait with the majority of housewives.

Under one bench in this room were the skeletons of two children of, perhaps, nine. They lay one on top of the other, in the usual San Jose position, on one side with legs flexed so that the knees were in front of the chests, and with the skulls at the south end of the double burial. On the chest of one of the children had been placed a very nice jade carved in low relief to represent a human face in the jaws of a monster.

Since carved jade was scarce at San Jose, it was surprising that this fine piece was with a child. The presence of children under a bench of the most important building at San Jose raise another point. I think the answer is that the skeletons were those of children sacrificed, presumably in some rain-making ceremony. As sacrificial victims were regarded as messengers to the gods or, sometimes, as their impersonators, it was natural to deck them in costly raiment and precious jewelry and bury them in the temple where they were probably sacrificed.

Several other burials of children were found. Some were provided with pottery whistles shaped as men or birds, clearly toys. In other cases the playthings included tiny spearheads of flint and scrapers of the same material. The high percentage of child burials at San Jose argues for a high infant mortality rate. The rate is very high among the present-day Maya, and the archaeological evidence suggests that the same was true in ancient times.

About half of the adult burials lacked pottery or other funerary furniture, and presumably the remains were those of poor people, but of the remainder several yielded imported pottery of great interest. Two of the skulls had the incisors and canines of the upper jaw filed and inlaid with jade and iron pyrites respectively, while several others had the same teeth filed in various ways (Fig. 17). According to Bishop Landa, only the teeth of women were filed, but his statement refers to Yucatan; it may be that in earlier times the men of this region also filed their teeth. Unfortunately, skeletons with filed teeth were too rotted to give any indication of sex, and the associated artifacts might have belonged to men or women.

Our camp was set in a small court, surrounded by forest. I felt at times, not claustrophobia, but a desire for a good view. Jacinto came to my rescue by making an observation post on top of the high mound south of camp. He found two trees growing close together and made rungs of pieces of wood held in position by lianas which passed around grooves he had cut in the trunks. This nailless ladder led to the observation post fifteen feet above the mound, and from there, after he had felled the surrounding trees, I had a fine view. I felt like Peter Pan in his house in the tree, but there was no Wendy.

Close to the ruins a man from San Jose had cut his milpa. Late in the season he burned it, and then, as the rains had come early, he and his helpers sowed it. From my post I watched them sowing, making holes in the ground with a pointed stick and dropping in a few grains of maize. It was a scene Maya priests must have witnessed from this same pyramid many times (Fig. 12).

There was much breadnut around the ruins. Men of San Jose came to cut branches for the mules of the Belize Estate Company. One day a man fell and had to be carried to San Jose on a litter, where the poor fellow died, and not long afterwards another cutter suffered serious injuries from a fall close to the ruins. I was blamed for the tragedies, for it was said that my digging had released evil spirits which had caused the men to fall. I pointed out that any malignant spirits were more likely to turn on me who had disturbed their rest, but I did not succeed in changing their ideas. It was a variant on the curse of Tutankhamen.

The cutters earned eight dollars a month plus the ration of seven pounds of flour and four pounds of pork, which has been standard in the country since, I suppose, before the slaves were freed. One settlement on the Belize River is named "Four Pounds of Pork" with obvious reference to this allowance. I once published an index of archaeological sites in the country and tried desperately to find someone who had seen mounds there so that I could include the name as an archaeological site, but without success. In the end I could only work in that glorious name by noting that the small site of Platon lay below and on the opposite bank to Four Pounds of Pork.

About halfway through the season my old friend Agustín Hob joined us. His travels to Belize, Mountain Cow, and Uaxactun must have given him a taste for wandering as he had never settled down again in San Antonio. He had arrived at Socotz, and learning that Jacinto was working with me at San Jose, he had come over to ask for work. San Jose had seemed to be in an area without game, but Agustín soon brought in a peccary and curassow and later an agouti, most delicious of all game. The place was alive with parrots, and we occasionally had one. Parrot meat varies. A young bird makes a very tasty dish, but an old bird is as tough as old boots. One we ate must have been flying around when San Jose was a bustling settlement. For a joke I once tried a *zopilote*, the black vulture, but I only managed to swallow two or three mouthfuls; my Maya workers, with their love of tomfoolery, talked of it for days.

The men came upon a very large boa constrictor (but not as large as they grow in the Amazon), and we had one or two encounters with fer-de-lance, the most dangerous of Central American snakes, but by and large, snakes are of far less consequence in the forest than one would gather from the accounts of topee-clad explorers. It is queer that the Maya in their art should have paid so much attention to the rattlesnake; I have never seen or heard one in Central America, not even in Mayapan where dry rocks abound. They do occur, but they like sunny, dry places, and there are few of those in the forest. I think the rattlesnake as a religious symbol must have arisen on the plateau and spread to the rain forest later. It is strange that the god Quetzalcoatl, who was renowned for his gentleness, should have been represented by a feathered rattlesnake.

One day at Coba two of the men were walking down a trail ahead of me. As the second man passed under the bough of a tree, a snake struck at him, but missed. I was wearing shoes (my top boots were soaked). A few minutes later I felt the cold body of a snake writhing up my leg. I slapped my hand against where I felt his head to be, pinning him there between thumb and fore-finger. Cautiously I let down my trousers, and there was its evil head. I was at a loss what to do next for I thought that if I let go he would bite me. Then I realized the head was that of a lizard—the two are not dissimilar. My thoughts had been on snakes or I would have realized that no snake could run up the inside of a trouser leg.

Snake-charming formerly was practiced in Yucatan, and Maya in the Guatemalan highlands still summon snakes with a flute, but there is no detailed account of the ceremony. The Quiche Maya, also highlanders, have a snake dance somewhat like the famous snake dance of the Hopi Indians of Arizona. The snakes, both venomous and harmless, are made drunk with *chicha* and then are released in the middle of a court, and the men dance around them. Next they are hung around the neck of a man dressed as a woman.

Then they are pushed through the open shirts of the dancers, and emerge through sleeve and trouser openings somewhat in the style of my lizard. Later, as with the Hopi, the snakes are released.

There are certain erotic elements in this dance, and I suspect that it was, and perhaps may still be, a fertility rite. Among the Aztec there were three goddesses—Snake Woman, Seven Snake, and She with the Skirt of Snakes—connected with the fertility of the land or of the human race. Our knowledge of the hierarchic cults among the ancient Maya of the highlands is limited. There may well have been a corresponding snake goddess, for religious ideas were much of a sameness throughout Middle America.

To return to San Jose and less noxious animals, a kinkajou, which is called *mico de noche*, "night monkey," in British Honduras, lived in the tree immediately above us, undisturbed by our presence. Every night soon after dark he could be heard stirring overhead. Then he would climb down the tree and go about his business. He probably descended that way because we had cut down most of the big trees around the hut. I don't remember ever hearing him climb up to his home, and he seemed to live alone.

An unpleasant feature of camp—and one I've never had in any camp of my own making—was fleas. I had one end of the hut for my cot and the many pole-topped tables I used for spreading out sherds, and for my writing desk and dinner table (Plate xi*b*); Iglesias, Jacinto, and the kitchen shared the other end. I suppose some visitor had brought a female flea, and her progeny throve in the dusty floor. They increased with extraordinary rapidity.

In the last week of work I again came down with malaria. The ruins seemed a bad place for it, and there were many mosquitoes. Archaeologically, it had been a highly successful season. The long ceramic sequence was very important, and the architectural work had produced some interesting results. We had also spectacular finds such as the obsidian axe, the copper, and a fine assortment of unusual trade pieces. Perhaps most important was the evidence of an occupation continuing for a while after the close of the Classic period.

I shipped our finds on muleback and disposed of surplus equipment, persuading the alcalde of San Jose with an excellent sales talk that shallow graves dug with a machete weren't worthy of the village and that the authorities could do a far better job with a pick and shovel going cheap. Jacinto returned overland to Socotz, and I started for Sierra de Agua, railhead of the Belize Estate. That evening I rode down to Hill Bank on a flatcar ahead of the gasoline engine. Leaving the clearing of Sierra de Agua camp where negresses were gossiping or scolding their children in shrill creole dialect, the light train plunged into the secondary-growth jungle as the brief dusk gave way to darkness. The headlight cast a short beam in which gray moths danced. One by one the stars came out, shining with a brilliance suggestive of an approaching storm. I pleasantly anticipated exchanging my lonely uninteresting meals at the ruins, a bath in a gasoline can of water, and purely Spanish conversation for a comfortable bed, a hot bath, and the hospitality of Mr. and Mrs. Brown, the company's manager and his wife, which I was soon to enjoy. The flatcar swung round a bend, and the scattered lights of Hill Bank came into view.

Next evening I was in Orange Walk. The district doctor sent to invite me to dinner and bridge. He lived for bridge; I loathe it. When I arrived, he shook hands, said, "You've got fever," and sent me to bed—the only occasion I have found anything to be said in favor of malaria.

10

Across the Peninsula of Yucatan

In 1936, I was once more in Yucatan, as a permanent member of the staff of the Carnegie Institution of Washington, with which I was to remain until the liquidation of its Department of Archaeology in 1958. Ruppert, a fellow occupant of the bachelors' hut at Chichen in 1926, had had two very successful exploratory expeditions to southeastern Campeche, investigating a series of unknown Maya sites and adding enormously to our knowledge of the local Maya culture known as Rio Bec.

Reports had come in of new sites in that area and to the east of it. One was said to have over 100 stelae, which would put it at the top of the competition with nearby Calakmul, with 103 stelae (some plain), as runner-up. It was to investigate these that I was in Yucatan. We planned afterwards to visit San Jose to tie up a few matters before publishing the report on the work there. This would be, to the best of my knowledge, the first crossing of the peninsula from Champoton to British Honduras made by anyone except an odd *chiclero*. There was nothing remarkable about that; it was only in the past two or three years that exploration for chicle had opened up the region, and few people had any reason for making the journey.

We started from Chichen Itza, which was little changed from my visit of six years earlier except that there was a road from Merida and, as a natural corollary, a tourist hotel at Chichen. The

Carnegie program of excavation continued, but at a slower pace; Mexican archaeologists were active on a fine program of repair and restoration work. Vay Morley, my *compadre* for he was my son's godfather, was a bit stouter, less inclined to make trips in the forest, and, despite a long marriage, more uxorious. Scientists of various 'logies and guests filled the long Carnegie dinner table at the head of which Vay and his wife sat side by side. Between mouthfuls he would turn to kiss Mrs. Morley. Constant repetition was too much for one visitor, Dr. Proctor, who proceeded to kiss his wife each time Vay kissed his. Mrs. Proctor passed on the kiss to her neighbor, and a wave of osculation eddied gently round the table till Vay had received a kiss from the last in line, an almost complete stranger. After that Vay swallowed his mouthful and chased the next one round his plate without any amatory interlude.

A most interesting structure had been partially excavated by Karl Ruppert since my last visit. That was the so-called Mercado, "market," although there is considerable doubt that it ever functioned as such. This, a building of the first Mexican period, comprised a colonnade with corbeled vaulting of the same general type as the colonnades annexed to the Warriors. It was narrow but had the immense length of 247 feet. Behind lay a patio, about 50 feet square, around which was a colonnaded ambulatory, so the whole was roughly comparable to a garth with its surrounding cloisters, although its frequenters were probably horses of another color. There was a careful drainage system to carry off the water.

There were two interesting features: First, the almost complete absence of debris made it certain that the roof had been thatched (see the reconstruction, Plate XIII); Secondly, the columns had the exceptional height of fifteen and one-half feet, perhaps for coolness, as the sun beating into the patio would have converted a low-roofed ambulatory into a furnace. Several structures of this gallery-patio type occur at Chichen Itza, all of the Mexican period, and the idea seems to have been introduced from Tula, where there are similar patio and ambulatory buildings, but with the gallery detached or less imposing.

There was much evidence of burning, and it is likely that the thatched roof was fired by the conquerors of Chichen about A.D. 1250 (our work at Mayapan produced many data of deliberate burning of buildings, presumably when the city was conquered and looted about A.D. 1450).

I had as assistants J. C. ("Pinkie") Harrington and Conrad Kratz. The first, now archaeologist with the U. S. National Park Service, went as surveyor, to map and to get the latitude and longitude of any new site we might find—an important job in the forest where more than one site has been lost again after discovery because its exact position was not known. Conrad was a happy-go-lucky youngster who had previously helped in the mapping of Mayapan, but had no archaeological training. His main job was to make rubbings of hieroglyphic inscriptions by means of a pad dipped in Chinese ink on a tough spongy paper, a technique only recently tried in the Maya area. He is now a Benedictine monk in Blue Cloud Abbey, South Dakota, a destiny I would have given far greater than a hundred-to-one odds against when we were together in the forest of Quintana Roo. His Maya interest is not dead; recently he persuaded his abbot that he was the man to answer an emergency call to Central America. Benedictine affairs did not get all his time; he found his way to some Maya ruins and made a return visit to Chichen!

We had a busy time in Chichen compiling a rough map of chicle trails and known water holes from Ruppert's explorations and sundry other much less reliable sources. We lingered in Merida, where carnival was in full swing, long enough to recruit a cook, Feliciano ("Feliz") Chac, who had been busy cooking for the revelers and hankered for the peace and quiet of the forest. With all our equipment we moved to Campeche, the port on the

Gulf of Mexico south of Merida, the train leaving at the usual ghastly hour of 5:30 A.M.

Campeche is a charming town surrounded by a great fortified wall (then demolished in places) which had been erected at the close of the seventeenth century as a defense against the English, French, and Dutch buccaneers, who had sacked the place more than once. The name is a corruption of the Maya *canpech*, "snake tick." In ancient times an idol which had a snake and a tick on its head stood there. There is a delightful cathedral of colonial construction, but it was shut as the religious persecutions of President Cárdenas were then at their height and every church was closed and every priest in hiding or driven from the state. This persecution was highly unpopular among the people, who felt bitterly the absence of priests particularly because no child could be baptized—baptism by a layman was not regarded as valid by most parents.

Carnival was as lively in Campeche as in Merida. The place was bedlam, with thousands of firecrackers exploding in all directions. Youths, inside ingenious frameworks of mats to simulate bulls and with horns attached, charged the crowds, but the favorite sport was to throw blueing or a red powder, probably anatto, at any male from seven to seventy. The only way to avoid this was to stay off the streets or walk down them with a girl on each arm. As we knew no Campeche girls, we stayed close to the Cuauhtemoc Hotel after 4:00 P.M., when things got lively. I prefer the gentler custom in many towns of hitting you on the head with an eggshell filled with confetti. It was Shrove Tuesday, climax of the carnival, and the old town was really hopping.

Next morning we sailed on the *Gilda*, a small boat with sail and petrol engine, following the coast for about six hours to the little port of Champoton, another settlement of the Maya in ancient days. There, after discharging many passengers, the *Gilda* took us up the Champoton River to the little town of Kanasayab, where we and our supplies were landed. It was the terminus of a narrow-gauge tramline, originally built to transport logwood, which strikes inland in a southeasterly direction to La Gloria, a distance of about forty-five miles.

We had arrived about 10:30 P.M., and we were told that loading would start at 2:00 A.M. and we would be on our way by 3:00 A.M. We lay down on top of one of the flatcars. Feliz, who had much sleep to make up, and Conrad were soon asleep, but Pinkie and I were less lucky. We were kept awake by our hard beds, much talking, the wailing of babies, a continuous coming and going of carts, and the crowing of cocks, which in Central America, in complete contradiction to the prevailing *mañana* spirit, hail the morrow from any time after 11:00 P.M. and keep it up with brief interludes to rest larynges till rosy-fingered dawn arrives. The Indian or mestizo never seems to sleep the night through, but is continually getting up to tend the fire, stretch himself, or to saunter over to see if his great-aunt is awake and, if so, chat with her for a pleasant hour or two. In fact, we left at 5:45 A.M. just when the cocks were willing to call it a day or call it day.

The track was twenty inches wide and of very light rails. The train or, better, convoy consisted of seven separate flatcars, and the haulage mechanism was a pair of mules tandemwise to each flatcar. The engine driver manipulated a whip and turned on a brake on the downgrades. Keeping in convoy was important as we had four derailments in the first half of the journey, and the aid of other crewmen was needed to get the flatcar on the tracks again. At one place half an hour was needed to cut up a tree which had fallen across the track—with typical improvidence no member of the crew had that indispensable item of equipment, a machete. We should still be there had I not unpacked my own.

Most of the way was through forest, but in the first two hours we passed several haciendas abandoned after the expropriations; Maya families had moved in and were encamped in the ruins, a remarkable parallel to what had happened a millenium earlier, as I have already pointed out. We reached La Gloria, railhead, about an hour before sunset. La Gloria, "Glory," is synonymous with heaven, but if the real thing bears any resemblance to this earthly prototype, I would just as soon be in the other place; there, at least, the fleas of La Gloria would be fried to a frazzle. It was a miserable collection of five huts and a large storeroom, one corner of which we occupied.

There Liborio Mar, our foreman on the trip and the man who knew of the supposed 100-stela site, met us with the news that one of the sites we planned to visit had nothing of consequence, and that the man who was to have guided us to another had departed to enjoy such fleshpots as Campeche had to offer. There, too, I got the first symptoms of an attack of dysentery which was to make life miserable for several days. Neither opium pills nor kaolin, of which I took enough to convert my inside into a miniature pottery, did much good.

We started next morning for Rio Desempeño in a truck, but it had rained during the night and we got stuck in a logwood swamp. Almost as soon as we got out, rain came down with tropical intensity and made travel along the dirt road impossible, for there were sections of low land which quickly turned to swamp. We were marooned in an abandoned little settlement for the best part of two days, and what with one thing and another, it was a week after we sailed from Campeche that we left Rio Desempeño, "obligation-carried-out river," headquarters of the Buenfil chicle concession. If, as well may be, there is now an air strip there, the trip from Campeche should take about thirty minutes.

It was quite a mule train. We had rather over an English ton of supplies, largely food for ourselves and the men, thirteen of us all together, but with such awkward cargo as picks and shovels,

Pinkie's theodolite, a heavy lorry jack for raising fallen stelae, a wireless set for getting time signals for latitude, tins of kerosene for our hurricane lamps, maize for the mules, and two kerosene drums to carry water, a necessary provision in an area where widely spaced water holes dry up at that time of year. We had ten cargo and nine riding mules.

We had planned to leave at 1:00 A.M., but it was 3:00 A.M. before we got off. The cargo mules would follow; for with frequent halts to adjust the difficult loads, they would travel at a slower rate. The ten-day-old moon was low and hidden by the forest by the time we left, and we were dependent on Liborio's flashlight. However, mules see better in the dark than humans, and ours had no difficulty in following the narrow forest trail. It was a grueling trip to our destination, San Lorenzo—eleven hours in the saddle and forty-five minutes for meals and a quick examination of some ruins beside the trail. Pinkie, unused to riding, was in bad shape; I, although the dysentery was far better, was not in top form, but Conrad and Feliz took it in their—or the mules'—stride.

We had gone to San Lorenzo to examine a site reported to be near that abandoned chicle camp, and this we visited next morning. It was small, and the one standing building was of Rio Bec masonry typified by a veneer of large and most beautifully cut stone blocks. These blocks are fitted together with great care without mortar so that, as in Inca masonry, it is usually impossible to insert the blade of a penknife between two blocks.

The most interesting feature was a stela with six crudely carved hieroglyphs, the first recording the day 10 Ahau, which probably marks the end of a katun. The crude, decadent style and the presence of other late texts in the area make 10.5.0.0.0. 10 Ahau 8 Muan (October 5, A.D. 928) the probable date of erection, the latest known date of the Classic period. It seems that in this remote corner of southeastern Campeche the custom of erecting dated stelae hung on later than elsewhere in the lowland forests; perhaps here the old theocracy was able to maintain itself, whereas elsewhere it had crashed, because the isolated peasantry did not feel the winds of change until quite a while after they had had their effect in more exposed parts.

From there we passed to No te Metas, "Do not enter," near which there was a report of standing buildings. This was a large water hole in the middle of an extensive logwood swamp. Logwood, a small contorted tree with hard red center, yields a black dye once in enormous demand in Europe, but with the growth of synthetic dyes its exploitation has ceased. It was to obtain this wood that Belize was settled, and so much of it was exported from the state of Campeche that it was long known as Campeachy wood. The site of No te Metas we found to contain two standing buildings of the Rio Bec style and others completely gone. One building was interesting, but there was not enough to detain us long; we struck northeastward two days for Aurora, a large water hole which had a curious history of archaeological hide and seek.

In 1908 the French traveler Count Maurice de Perigny discovered a site which he named Rio Bec (*bec* in Maya is the evergreen oak) from a dry watercourse in the neighborhood. In 1912, this was visited by R. E. Merwin of the Peabody Museum, Harvard University, who found six other groups of ruins in the immediate vicinity. These he lettered B to G. Group B, containing a stunning building in Rio Bec style with high ornamental towers at each end, lay only a quarter of a mile south of Group A (Perigny's group), but Perigny had failed to find it. In 1933, Ruppert, heading the first Carnegie expedition in southeastern Campeche, came to Aurora and discovered a number of scattered groups. Later it was noted that three of the buildings of Ruppert's Group I were part of Merwin's Group F, but Merwin had failed to find the great part of this group lying some three hundred yards to the west; Ruppert had found the three buildings of Merwin's Group F because they lay beside an important trail. At the time Ruppert had no idea he was at Rio Bec, for *chicleros*, on rediscovering the water hole, had renamed it.

Ruppert returned to Aurora in 1934 to locate the remaining Merwin groups, but he failed to do so. The forest was so thick that he could not find one of them, although he knew from Merwin's notes their approximate position in relation to Group F, and all were close together.

We arrived at Aurora without any intention of searching again for the missing ruins, but to examine yet another group in the vicinity. This we found about three miles east-northeast of the Aurora water hole. We passed yet another group about halfway there, and on a subsequent visit to it we came across a pleasant four-room structure with a nice design of lines of short engaged columns. According to the maps we should have ridden bang through Group B, where the outstanding building was found by Merwin, and we should have passed close to his Groups C, D, and E, but we saw not a trace of them. It is said that one can easily cross the Pacific without sighting an island, and something similar applies to ruins in the sea of tropical forest. Our two new groups added to Merwin's and Ruppert's discoveries brought the total of thirteen, a good Maya number for this widespread Maya site.

Our buildings were of typical Rio Bec architecture and masonry. One had had a very ornate façade with masks of the rain god and serpents. We carried out some minor excavations under floors seeking sherds to date the building, but we had no luck. Nevertheless, it seems fairly certain that this Rio Bec style flourished not long before the close of the Classic period, and may have continued for a short while after. Ruppert had found stelae at two of his groups, but they were in miserable shape and no date could be read. Still, enough remained to show that four had carried Initial Series type of dating which did not continue after the close of the Classic period.

As happened in other Classic period sites, later occupants seem to have reverenced old stelae without apparently understanding the hieroglyphs or even recognizing the human figures. The lower half of Stela 5 was found upside down on top of a mound, but there was no sign of the top half, more than a hint that later unlettered folk had set it, upside down, on top of the mound. Stelae at another group seem to have been moved around, presumably after the departure of the theocracy.

From our little claims staked on the Rio Bec vein we moved south via Placeres, "Pleasures," which were singularly lacking, to the large archaeological site of El Palmar. I see in checking with my diary that the Pleasures were more than I had remembered. Placeres was a large chicle center and until shortly before we left 144 mules were carrying chicle to a bigger depot. The attraction was a *casa de asistencia,* or eating place, where three ladies dispensed meals, hardly up to Le Pavillion standards, to *chicleros*—beans, rice, eggs or game, chile, and perhaps plantain or sweet potatoes formed the standard meal served on a pole-topped table. The second evening there they sang, in very shrill voices, popular Mexican songs. A trio of men sang next to the accompaniment of a guitar, and, finally, I sang in English. My voice has never been anything to write home about since I sang treble in my preparatory school choir, but Mexicans are very polite and I was applauded as though I were Ezio Pinza, then a popular singer, in person. "We have heard the chimes at midnight, Master Shallow," but the good ladies of Placeres were no bona robas.

One of our muleteers was sick. I gave him two spoonfuls of castor oil, but he demanded a third, and later asked for a fourth, saying he had a tough stomach. I hesitated to give it to him, whereupon Liborio told me that my scruples were absurd and that he never took less than half a tumblerful of castor oil. I obliged the muleteer. Mexicans have asbestos-lined stomachs, otherwise they could hardly drink so much *aguardiente* and eat so much chile. There are perhaps fifty-seven varieties of chile peppers, each hotter than the last. On one occasion I collected some peppers from a bush growing in an abandoned chicle camp. I dumped them out of my hat and put it on. In a minute I felt a burning sensation where the hatband was in contact with my forehead. If an indirect contact could do that to my forehead, I shudder at what direct contact could do to one's intestinal tract. I've never heard of a Maya or a *chiclero* with stomach ulcers. Perhaps the chile keeps them from growing, or it may be that those carefree people have no worries. Most probably, as they seldom come in contact with doctors, their ulcers grow unseen.

While we were lotus-eating in Placeres, some of our men were opening the closed trail; and finally bidding farewell to the ladies of the *casa de asistencia*, we moved to El Palmar, "the place of palms," well named because of the large quantities of *escoba* and *guano* palm, the first used for making brooms, the second for thatching.

El Palmar proved to be a very large site of Peten, not Rio Bec, masonry with those typical Peten features, a grandiose ceremonial court, nearly 150 yards long by 80 yards wide, in which stelae were set, and a large "acropolis" or huge raised platform supporting a smaller court around which other buildings stood. There was also a ball court. It was here that Maurilio was lost in the forest for twenty days.

The big concentration of buildings were to the north and east of a large water hole. The low land around this may once have formed with the water hole a large reservoir. There was a big group of structures on high ground to the south, but nothing to the west.

In the center of the reservoir there was a small island which comprised a mound with a plain stela on its west edge. The whole thing seemed to be man-made. In front of the stela we found twenty-five flint chips and rejects, three leaf-shaped flint blades, a fourth notched down the sides, an obsidian core, and a few obsidian flakes, but they seemed to have had nothing to do with the stela. Probably sacrifices to the rain gods were made on this little island, and dredging the water hole might bring to light stuff thrown into it as offerings, but that was a lengthy operation for which we were not equipped nor had permission to undertake.

The water hole was the home of several crocodiles or alligators whose eyes would reflect the ray of a flashlight in a strange way. Alligators are far commoner in Central America than crocodiles, but they seek coastal waters and deep rivers, whereas the crocodile prefers inland water holes, and may be found in quite small ones—for many years there was a lone one in the small water hole at Uaxactun; the poor dear must have suffered dreadfully from claustrophobia by the end of the dry season when the pool had shrunk to a bath full of mud. A small daughter of Shuffeldt, who had had the chicle concession of northern Peten and was a friend of all archaeologists, was seized and dragged down by a crocodile. Her father attacked the beast and forced it to let go of the child, who, except for some bad cuts and scratches, was unharmed. The presence of the crocodiles made carefree bathing at El Palmar difficult, for I always felt unreasoningly apprehensive of those sharp teeth in water, but the water hole was really mud with a thickish film of water on top, and a bathe meant mosquito bites over most of the body and leeches on your legs.

We found forty-four stelae, about five were plain and sixteen so weathered one couldn't say whether they had once been carved. Even those definitely sculptured were dreadfully eroded. In that belt of southern Quintana Roo, southeastern Campeche, and northern Peten the limestone is of very poor quality. I found that I could scratch marks on the undersides of fallen stelae and that the stiff brushes we used to remove lichen and dirt could not be used on recently exposed stone; they rubbed off the surface. It was very disappointing. Nevertheless, we were able to get a few dates which showed the site was at its height during the late Classic period. Trenching for sherds brought to light many of types close to those of the Peten, but closer to British Honduras variants. Beneath them were early Classic sherds, earlier than any dated stela at the site, and a sprinkling of sherds of the late Formative period.

Stela 10 was leaning forward so that the greater part was buried. We dug it out, hoping to find the buried design in better shape. It was weathered but enough remained to yield the date (9.15.15. 0.0. 9 Ahau 18 Xul. [A.D. 746]) and to show that the personage had stood on a mask, as was the case at La Honradez, about forty miles south in a bee line, but the trackless forest was so impenetrable that La Honradez might have been Jericho so far as we were concerned.

The stela faced west. Just by the north corner we found a votive cache comprising seven eccentric flints, two leaf-shaped flint blades, nineteen obsidian cores and at least as many obsidian flakes. Note that the flints numbered nine, the favorite Maya number for these caches. The eccentric flints were of poorish quality except for one of those three-pronged rings which often appear in caches. I find that in my diary for that night I wrote that the asymetrical location of the cache suggested there should be something buried at the south corner of the stela. I continued, "In a way I am sorry the find was made, as it may encourage *chicleros* to dig under stelae when on their own." That was on a Saturday, and it was not until the following Friday that there was a chance to get back to Stelae 10. I sent Conrad to dig a little deeper round the south corner to see whether there was not a balancing cache.

He came back in triumph to report one of the finest eccentric flints ever found. I forgot my misgivings about *chicleros*. This was a queer-shaped affair with human profiles at all four corners (Fig. 24). It has been suggested that once a blade projected from the top of the left-hand head to convert the whole into a ceremonial sacrificial blade. That is a possibility, but one can hardly imagine

Fɪɢ. 24.—Eccentric Flints. Left and right, portraits of ocelot or jaguar and dog, San Jose; center, Conrad's find, El Palmar.

a more awkward affair to carry. There seems to have been a competition to see who could make the most elaborate design in flint. The hard part was not the making of the profiles, but the removal, without shattering the whole, of the central piece of flint and, to a lesser extent, the inverted shirt-shaped piece between two of the heads. The work, of course, was done by pressure flaking, not by percussion. I think the Maya were the only people in the world who went in for portraiture in flint, but, strangely, they never used flint as a form of decoration in architecture as did the builders of so many churches in East Anglia. Checkerboard designs of cut flint and small limestone are so attractive that one is surprised the idea never occurred to the Maya.

There was a ball court, down the center line of which were three undressed stones about equidistantly placed, but I could not make up my mind whether these were markers or had rolled there in the collapse of the structures flanking the court. Every building at El Palmer had collapsed. It was sad that such a large site should yield so little.

Pinkie was kept busy surveying the site. Occasionally we listened to the news, not too often, as the batteries had to be kept in good shape for picking up time signals. The B.B.C. came in very well. One night we heard the news of Cunninghame Graham's death. There was interference from a Havana station which not inappropriately was an Argentine tango. He had been a friend of my father's, and the news of his passing took my thoughts far from the surrounding forest to the treeless pampas over which all three of us had ridden so often.

Three weeks completed our work, and we headed north again to Placeres. Conrad, with the precious eccentric flint, Feliz, and most of the mules continued to Campeche; Pinkie, Liborio, and I started for British Honduras. There was nothing to detain us at Placeres; the *casa de asistencia* was shut and its ladies were in Glory (La Gloria).

Liborio had been very elusive about the site with over one hundred stelae. It was supposed to be near the abandoned town of Chichanha, but the problem was how to get there. There was a narrow band of unknown territory down the center of Quintana Roo. The western part was part of the Buenfil concession and was worked from Rio Desempeño and Placeres; the eastern part was worked by concessions operating from the Hondo River, the boundary between Quintana Roo and British Honduras. Chichanha lay in the eastern zone, and there was no trail from the one zone to the other. Liborio had had a large payment the previous winter to search for the site, but had returned saying that he could not get to Chichanha and therefore could not locate the site. He had asked for more money for a trip by sea to the Hondo to search again, but Vay had begun to suspect he was being led up the garden path and had refused. Now we hoped to get into that eastern zone.

We lost some time opening the overgrown trail (it had not been used for some months), but reached the old chicle camp of Maximiliano Baños in six hours. It was from here that cockcrows from an outpost of the eastern zone had been heard. We had made an early start and gone ahead of our cargo mules, so Liborio was able to search for the old camp. He had no luck, but we were not discouraged. It was not like looking for a ruin; there would be chicle trails radiating from it, and once one was found, it would be a simple matter to locate the camp. The men found it next morning and soon were at work cutting the four miles of trail so the mules could pass. In doing that they found a largish site with fifteen to twenty mounds scattered over a fairly wide area. One had walls with typical Rio Bec veneer masonry.

When the trail was open, we visited the frontier post beyond the evergreen curtain. It was as though one had passed from one culture to another. Instead of huts, there were lean-to shelters; the occupants had used pole beds instead of hammocks; fireplaces were three stones on the ground, not set on pole tables plastered with mud, as on the Campeche side; empty tins of baking powder showed the diet had been based on flour, not maize; discarded cases of soap, milk, and matches carried English names and had obviously originated in Belize, in contrast to the Mexican names on the Campeche side; finally, there had been no women in this camp in contrast to the family life of *chiclero* camps in the western zone. Had the camp been occupied, we would have noted minor linguistic differences: *akalche*, *kum*, *tuch*, for instance, replaced by *bajo*, *escoba* and *mico* (swamp, broom palm, and spider monkey).

We crossed the frontier into unknown territory and followed the more important looking trails leading in an easterly direction. After traveling for ten hours and passing two or three abandoned chicle camps, I noticed broken walls first on one side of the trail and then on the other. At first I supposed they were old cattle corrals, perhaps for oxen of some former mahogany operation, but then I realized we were riding down the street of an abandoned town, which I knew must be Chichanha, the only one in the whole area. Soon we came into what had once been the main plaza of the town, on the south side of which were the ruins of a large church. It was a weird experience, for the town stood in what to my untrained eyes was the same virgin forest we had been traversing all day. A botanist might have spotted the absence of some species which mark the climax forest, but I noticed no difference.

We dismounted and entered the roofless church. A narrow room held three niches in which were long bones and several very Maya-looking skulls. Liborio said they had been picked up in the former plaza and placed there. They were relics of the battle in which Santa Cruz de Bravo Indians had captured the town, driving out its inhabitants, who had taken refuge at Icaiche to the south, as I have related. That had been in 1852. The forest had come back, excellent evidence against the theory that often cleared forest becomes permanent grassland, an explanation offered for the supposed abandonment of the cities of the Classic period. The plaza must once have been grass grown as in any Yucatecan town.

We had come upon Chichanha quite by chance, and, according to Liborio's story, the site with most stelae in the whole Maya area was only two leagues away. When I suggested that we should make for them, he produced a whole lot of excuses, although he would have earned a very high reward for finding the stelae. It was obvious that there was no such site. Argument was useless. I held my peace, and we proceeded to the next water hole to the east, La Caoba, "mahogany tree," which we reached after twelve hours in the saddle. There was only a little mud and water in the water hole and it was raining. There was one hut, a second in a state of collapse, and a lean-to. Everything was wet and we had trouble coaxing a fire to cook supper. Pinkie was so tired he went to bed without undressing.

A stop next night at another abandoned camp with an incredibly large number of fleas, and we reached the Hondo river at Botes on the following day. We had planned to cross the river and head for Orange Walk, but the one Mexican official there stood on his dignity and insisted we must go to Payo Obispo, now Chetumal, some distance beyond the mouth of the Hondo, to get permission to leave Mexican soil. We did, however, make a quick journey across the river to buy maize for our mules. That night we put up our cots in the schoolhouse.

We had been asleep a short while when the Mexican official woke us to say that a boat from the mahogany works at San Francisco had stopped en route to Payo Obispo and would take us if we hurried. In record time we had dressed, paid off the men, and were aboard the *Nautilus,* where we made ourselves as comfortable as possible on wooden seats in the bows. With numerous halts we reached Payo Obispo in ten hours. It was not possible to cross to British Honduras that day, so we took rooms at the very fourth-rate Hotel de Mexico.

After lunch I retired to my room and lay down for a while until I found there were bedbugs in the bed, whereupon I sat down in the only chair and started to make up accounts. There was a knock at the door, and in walked the mayor of this capital city, the head of the port authorities, the chief municipal engineer, a representative of the governor of Quintana Roo, and two others. It was a welcome-to-Payo-Obispo deputation.

My experience of mayors, port commanders, and municipal authorities was limited, and I was in my underwear. As I shook hands with my right hand, I tried to don my sweaty old breeches with my left, while I was planning how to seat my distinguished guests. There was only one chair, and the bed, I knew, was full of bedbugs. Somehow I managed to get the mayor in the chair and the three visitors with the heaviest looking trousers on the bed, for I hoped that the thick material would foil the bedbugs. Between compliments and remarks on the trip I got my breeches on, although I was never able to lace them below the knee. A pleasant time was had by all, and my guests departed before the frustrated bedbugs had found how to circumvent the heavy clothing.

Next morning we crossed in a little sailing boat to Consejo on the British Honduras side, where I saw Gann at his coconut plantation ("walk," they call it in British Honduras). Not long after, we were aboard the *Afrikola* bound for Orange Walk and thence to San Jose. Since my last visit railhead had been moved forward to there. At San Jose, Jacinto was awaiting us. We quickly built yet another hut at our old camping site, and were soon at work tidying up points which had been left unsettled from the 1931 and 1934 seasons. The rainy season had started and conditions were not too good.

The once pleasant village of San Jose was no more. The inhabitants had been forced to move to Orange Walk. This was not an isolated phenomenon: Kaxil Uinic had been cleared because it was believed to be a center of chicle smuggling; the inhabitants of San Jose and nearby Yalbac had been uprooted because it was said that in making their milpas they might destroy valuable mahogany trees, whereas at Orange Walk they could enjoy all the amenities of civilization; lastly, Icaiche had been evacuated so that the Mexican authorities could more easily bring the supposed benefits of the revolution to its inhabitants if they were more accessible. It was history repeating itself, for the Spanish officials and friars had herded the Maya into new and accessible towns nearly four centuries before with a similar lack of consideration for their real happiness.

The old ways were in retreat. Two years later, when I worked at Benque Viejo, there was plane service from Belize to El Cayo, and when Jacinto and I passed through San Jose on our way to the site of La Milpa in the north of British Honduras, an emergency air strip was being constructed nearby. This has been a story of conditions as they had been in a more leisurely age. With their passing I must bring it to a close.

Epilogue

In 1959 I was once more in British Honduras. Jacinto, whom I had not seen for twenty-one years, was little changed. He had been working for other archaeologists, and my godson, Eufracio, had done the same. He served us a wonderful dinner in his hut at Socotz, but perhaps in deference to my wife the chile pepper only singed our tongues. It was a very happy reunion, but there was little opportunity for reminiscence. We visited the nearby ruins, now stupidly called Xunantunich, where we had dug together in 1938. We had crossed the Mopan River each day in a dugout and walked the three-quarters of a mile to the ruins; now there was a chain-guided ferry and we went by Land Rover. Where I had bathed peacefully each evening, the quiet was destroyed by heavily laden lorries carrying pipes for oil drilling in the Peten. Faustino Bol was dead, and Agustín Hob never returned to San Antonio. "He drew a good bow; and dead!" San Antonio is civilized; it now has shops, a policeman, a telephone, and three juke boxes. The old Maya gods must have fled.

Two weeks earlier I had seen Eugenio Mai. The years had dealt kindly with him, too. He had broadened out and looked, what he was, a prosperous Maya who had made a success of life. He was foreman of the excavations at the site of Dzibilchaltun, near Merida, but each week he returned to his home in Piste, near Chichen

Itza, and to the wife supposedly received with the canceled laundry bill.

In a way Eugenio had had a glorious resurrection, for I had seen his carcass for sale five years earlier on a butcher's booth in Telchaquillo. This little Maya village adjoins the ruins of Mayapan, and we had had our headquarters there during the Carnegie's five-year program of excavation of that very late Maya site. On the occasion of the annual fiesta in honor of the patron of the village, *la santísima Virgen de la Concepción*, there had been a bullfight—a very unsophisticated performance in which the bullfighters, from a nearby town, quickly discarded their shoes to recover their normal agility. Although many bulls were fought—and they were pathetically small and friendly—only those few were slain which had already been sold to the local butcher. Many bulls had their owners' names painted on them, "writ large," and one carried the name of the Virgin in whose honor he performed, but the owner, confusing the Spanish *v* and *b*, had painted *Birgen* on the bull's flank.

Mai is a fairly common Maya name, and there chanced to be a second Eugenio Mai in the village (my old friend of Coba days was foreman of the Carnegie excavations and so was a temporary resident there). The local Eugenio Mai had painted his name in large letters on his bull, and as it had been sold for meat, it was slain in the ring, but with a skill which would hardly have won Ernest Hemingway's approval. A little later its scraggy carcass was hung up for sale (you could hardly see it for the flies). I used to joke Eugenio about his inglorious end.

Of Carmen Chai I have no news. I like to think of him as enjoying the evening of his life in the peace of Chulutan which he refounded, but, I trust with an *arrimada*, "a drawn-near lady," as they say in Yucatan, to prepare his tortillas.

On that same visit to Central America in which I renewed my old friendships with Jacinto and Eugenio, I sat one afternoon in the *salón de actas* of the Merida building which had been opened in 1711 as the Jesuit college of San Pedro, but which now houses the University of Yucatan. A long table extended the length of the large room, down each side of which the university faculty sat in stately high-backed chairs. At the end were three similar chairs. The rector of the university occupied the center one; the governor of the state of Yucatan and I sat in the other two. The university was conferring on me the honor of an LL.D. degree. Had I had the choice, I would have chosen no other university, for none was more closely connected with my life and my work. It was just one-third of a century since I had first come to Yucatan and seen the Maya past and present, and to this land of Mexico I had given a large share of my heart. Then, and at the subsequent banquet in a restaurant set in a cenote, from which Maya women perhaps drew water a millenium ago, my thoughts recurred to those early days, to my first view of Chichen Itza, to Vay's voice heard long before I saw him (he should have been the recipient of the honorary degree, but he had been dead some years), to Coba, Quirigua, Bonampak, Palenque, Copan, Tikal, and all that long roll of cities I had known, to my colleagues and my workers, and to the glory and the boredom of the forest.

Next morning I slipped into the cathedral. There was the usual coming and going. Mass was being said at one altar; Maya families—the men in their white clothes, the women with shawls over their heads, children wide eyed and so well behaved—passed to and from their devotions. I knelt to pray for the land which had brought me so much happiness.

Index

Acosta, Jorge: 173, 176

Afrikola (ship): 225-26, 242, 270

Agoutis: xv, 43, 90, 248

Agriculture: 45, 80, 115-16, 122-23; rites, 138-41, 203-204; divination, 208; *Fig. 12; see also* milpas

Aguardiente: xv; *see also* rum

Alligators: 77, 227, 263

Altars: 27, 212, 215, 237-38; hieroglyphic, 169; offerings on, 220; *Plate VIII*

Archaeology: overspecialized, 4-5; techniques, 25-26, 32, 91, 146, 189-92, 193, 212, 237, 244f., 254, 257-58; dependence on folklore, 131; blamed for death, 247-48

Architecture: 18-70 *(passim)*, 196-98; Peten, 18, 48, 262; masonry, 20, 46, 48, 66, 83, 111, 147, 258, *Plate VIII;* Puuc, 21, 66; stone lintels, 21f., 69; colonnades, 25; columns, 25-34 *(passim)*, 69, 253; *Fig. 6, Plate II;* pyramids, 25-83 *(passim)*, 160, 178, 196, 212, 215; 228-29, *Plates I, X, XII;* corbelled vaulting, 25-26, 58, 69, 165-67, 253, *Plates IV, V, XIII;* façades, 25-26, 28, 51, 58, 67, 237, 259, *Plate III;* temples, 25-37 *(passim)*, 51, 66, 201, 212, 215, 237, *Plates I, III, IV;* wood lintels, 26, 36, 88; benches, 27, 246; serpent balustrades, 28; frieze, 29-30, *Fig. 2;* inner pyramids, 32f., 86, 192; floors, 46, 83, 137, 192, 231, 246; *sascab,* 46; assemblage, 48, 57-58, 83-87, 196-97, 212, 235-40 *(passim);* roof-combs, 48, 197, 237; dock, 50; acropolis, 52, 212-13, 262; platform, 52; stories, 58, 69, 245, *Plate III;* "palaces," 66-69, *Plates III, V, XII;* patios, 66, 253, *Plate XIII;* stairways and steps, 66, 69, 212, *Plates XV, XVI;* courts, 67, 83-84, 196-97, 200, 215, 237, 262, *Plate XV;* gateway, 70; thatched roofs, 82, 253; buildings absent, 83; construction, 83, 86-87, 97-98, 147, 192; retaining walls, 97; post-holes, 192; drains, 213, 253; dais, 245, *Fig. 8;* interior staircase, 245; Rio Bec, 252-61, 267; interior rooms, *Plate XIII*

Arson: 254

Art motifs: monkeys, *Fig. 20;* masks, 27, 28, 67ff., 237f., 260, 264, *Plate II;* jaguar-eagle, 30, 33, *Fig. 3;* personage on captive, 56, 235; lattice, 67; engaged columns, 67; grecques, 67; balusters, 68; axes, 126; plants, 203; portraits, 221, *Plate XIV;* vitality of, 221; roped gods, 226; charted, 235

Index

Astronomy: 37–38; 63, 89–90, 147, 190–91, 192
Atlantean figures: 21, 27, *Fig. 2, Plate II*

Bacardier: xv, 110
Balance scales, lack of: 46
Balche (drink): xv, 136
Ball courts: 19, 50, 84–86, 160, 180–81, 212, 240, 262, 265, *Plate XV;* markers, 85–86, 180, *Fig. 10, Plate IX;* players, 97
Bananas: 206–207
Bats: in metaphor, 126; vampire, 165, 177, 235; in cache, 194; month sign, 189–90
Belize, Br. Honduras: 71–72, 118–20, 150–173, 223–25; Estate & Produce Co., 225–26
Belize River: 71–72, 151–53, 156–58, 173–74
Benque Viejo, Br. Honduras: 153, 174, 182; ruins, 127, 156–57, 271
Birds: *chachalaca,* 13, 63; dove, 37; motmot, 37; heron, 77; parrot, 79, 89, 104, 172, 248; macaw, 104, 172; toucan, 104, 172, 180; trogon, 104; vulture, 142, 179; king, 142, 172; in legend, 143, *Fig. 14;* curassow, 172, 236, 248; egret, 227; *coba,* 236; cox, 236; hummingbird, 242; as food, 248; *Fig. 14*
Black Caribs: 74–75, 89, 92, 122, 124
Blom, F.: 50, 188, 235, 237, 242
Blow guns: 141
Bol, Faustino: 106–14 *(passim),* 117, 144–45, 271, *Plate VIII*
Bonampak, Chiapas: 50, 199, *Figs. 8, 11*
Books, hieroglyphic: 19, 194, 221, *Fig. 12*
Brazil wood: 88
Breadfruit: 158
Breadnut: xv, 105, 185, 228, 247; fruit, 180, 236
Bridge, stone: 110–12, 146
British Honduras: 71–182, 223–51, 264, 269–70; history of, 229–30; invaded by Maya, 119–20
British Museum: 71, 146, 162, 203, 222
Buccaneers: 71
Burials: 243–44, 246; of children, 97, 245–46; secondary, 164; vaulted, 164–67, 181–82; looted, 166; reopened, 166; books with, 182, 194; in abandoned room, 220; full-length, 231f.; in jar, 232; seated, 232; flexed, 232, 241; bowl over skull, 241

Cabildo: xv, 101, 122, 204, 229
Cacao: cultivated, 122; drink made from, 129; used as currency, 198; drying beans, *Plate VII*
Calakmul, Campeche: 237, 252
Calendar, Maya: 8, 19, 24, 56, 146, 169, 180, 226, 235, 238; correlated with the Gregorian calendar, 187–91; 260-day almanac, 190, 208
Camp cooks: Florence Thompson, 60–61; Alfredo, 89, 92; negress, 176; Hazzard Bonner, 230, 239; Nicolás Iglesias, 242, 250; Feliciano ("Feliz") Chac, 254, 258; *Plate VI*

Index

Maya Archaeologist has been set in Linotype Janson, which is a modern recutting of type cast from the original seventeenth-century matrices still preserved at the Stempel Foundry in Germany. Because today's revival of this design parallels the delighted discovery in our own time of the rich Mayan tradition, it has seemed only natural to complement Eric Thompson's account with Janson.

UNIVERSITY OF OKLAHOMA PRESS

Norman